Cassino

Cassino

Portrait of a Battle

Fred Majdalany

CASSELL&CO

Cassell Military Paperbacks

Cassell & Co
Wellington House, 125 Strand
London WC2R 0BB

British Library Cataloguing-in-Publication Data
A catalogue record for this book is available from the British Library

ISBN 0-304-35232-2

Printed by Guernsey Press, Guernsey, C.I.

AUTHOR'S NOTE

I WISH to record my particular debt to the late Maj.-Gen. Sir Howard Kippenberger, K.B.E., C.B., D.S.O., Editor-in-Chief of the War History Branch of the New Zealand Government, for the most generous and comprehensive assistance extended to me, including access to extracts from captured German documents.

For the benefit of their first-hand experiences and for the loan of personal papers, notebooks, and maps, I am grateful to Lt.-Col. J. B. A. Glennie, D.S.O., and Lt.-Col. G. S. Nangle, D.S.O., O.B.E., who commanded battalions at Cassino; and to Mr. Geoffrey Cox, M.B.E., M.A., and Mr. D. M. Davin, M.B.E., M.A., who served on the Staff of 2nd New Zealand Division as Intelligence officers.

I desire also to acknowledge the help and co-operation of Maj.-Gen. V. Evelegh, C.B., D.S.O., M.C.; Dom Peter Flood, OSB; Major Kevin Hill, M.C.; the Rt. Rev. Abbot Primate Bernard Kaelin, OSB; Col. Arthur Noble, D.S.O., T.D.; Sir D'Arcy Osborne, K.C.M.G., British Minister to the Vatican during the period covered by this book; Mr. B. W. Rycroft, O.B.E., M.D., D.O.M.S., F.R.C.S. (Eng.), late Lt.-Col. R.A.M.C., Adviser in Ophthalmology to Allied Force H.Q.; the Rt. Rev. Ildefonso Rea, OSB, Abbot of Monte Cassino; and the Rt. Rev. Abbot Aidan Williams, OSB.

My thanks are also due to Miss R. E. B. Coombs of the Imperial War Museum and Mr. W. G. Williams of the War Office Library.

I would like to record my gratitude to Lt.-Gen. Lord Freyberg, V.C., G.C.M.G., K.C.B., K.B.E., D.S.O., for his advice and sympathetic interest.

Finally, I am indebted to Mr. J. F. Trotter, who drew the maps.

For the account of events inside the Monastery during the battle I have consulted *Monte Cassino: La Vita L'Irradiazione* by Tommaso Leccisotti (Vallecchi: Florence), a report based on first-hand testimony.

I have referred to all military and political personalities by the titles and rank they held at the time of the battle.

Little Saling   F. M.
Essex
1957

ACKNOWLEDGMENTS

We are indebted to the following for permission to quote copyright material:

The Controller of H.M. Stationery Office for extracts from General Alexander's C.-in-C. Official Despatch "The Allied Armies in Italy from 3rd September, 1943 to 12th December, 1944" which appeared in *The London Gazette Supplement No. 38937* dated 12th June, 1950; Messrs. Cassell & Company Ltd. and *The Daily Telegraph* for extracts from *Closing the Ring* by Sir Winston Churchill; Messrs. E. P. Dutton & Co. Inc. for extracts from *Command Missions* by L. K. Truscott, copyright 1954 by L. K. Truscott; and Messrs. George G. Harrap & Company Ltd. and Messrs. Harper & Brothers for extracts from *Calculated Risk* by General Mark W. Clark.

CONTENTS

PHOTOGRAPHS

between pages 116 and 117

THE COMMANDERS IN CHIEF

General Alexander (*Imperial War Museum photograph*)
Field-Marshal Kesselring (*Camera Press photograph*)

THE ARMY COMMANDERS

General Mark Clark (*Imperial War Museum photograph*)
General Leese (*Imperial War Museum photograph*)
General von Mackensen (*Camera Press photograph*)
General von Vietinghoff (*Imperial War Museum photograph*)

SOME CORPS COMMANDERS

General Truscott (*Imperial War Museum photograph*)
General Freyberg (*Imperial War Museum photograph*)
General Anders (*Imperial War Museum photograph*)
General Juin (*Imperial War Museum photograph*)
General von Senger und Etterlin

TYPICAL FIGHTING GROUND

German emplacements on reverse slope of Point 569 (*Imperial War Museum photograph*)
Troops in action on Snakeshead ridge (*Imperial War Museum photograph*)

BATTLE CASUALTIES (*Imperial War Museum photographs*)

AFTER THE BOMBING (*Imperial War Museum photographs*)

BEFORE AND AFTER

Central courtyard of the Monastery (*photographs by E.N.A. and Imperial War Museum*) *between pages 116 and 117*

Clearing a house (*Imperial War Museum photograph*)

Point 593 (*Imperial War Museum photograph*)

View from the town ruins of Castle Hill (*Picture Post Library*)

THE THIRD BATTLE

New Zealand infantry and tanks attack Turreted House area (*Imperial War Museum photograph*)

View from Continental Hotel of Northern approach road by which New Zealanders entered town (*Imperial War Museum photograph*)

BATTLE CASUALTIES (*Imperial War Museum photographs*)

MONASTERY AND CASSINO TOWN TODAY (*photographs by Alterocca, Terni and Brunner & C., Como*)

MAPS

I

PRELUDE

'People must be of the profession to understand the disadvantages and difficulties we labour under, arising from the uncommon natural strength of the country.'
GENERAL WOLFE

I

ABOUT half-way between Naples and Rome there is a bend in the road which takes it round the shoulder of a long brown whale-shaped mountain named Trocchio. At this point the road emerges from the corridor of hills through which it has curved for many miles, and cuts across the three-mile width of the Rapido valley in a dead straight line. At the far side of the valley there is a great wall of mountains which, from this distance, especially if there is any mist, resembles a painted stage back-cloth. This barrier extends limitlessly to the right and to the rear into the main mountain mass of the Abruzzi, but it ends with an almost artificial abruptness at the point where the road disappears out of sight; and to the left of it there is an open space, indicating the entrance to another and wider valley, the valley of the River Liri which is a tributary of the Rapido. So sudden, so theatrical is the appearance of this mountain barrier three miles away across the valley, that one has the impression that it reaches out to the road for the sole purpose of menacing it.

As one draws nearer, the flatness of the mountains begins to dissolve into three-dimensional separateness. The long vertical shadows deepen into great ravines; grey and fawn shadings harden into rocky ledges, slopes, and fierce jagged crests; the mountains assume individual shapes within the tight mass. One in particular catches and holds the eye: the one directly ahead, on the extreme left of the mountain wall, at the point where the road disappears. It is starker, more sheer, more majestic than the others, and on its summit there is a splash of white which soon focuses into the outline of a large building.

Soon after you begin to cross the valley, this mountain,

detaching itself from the mass, transfixes your attention so completely that you are hardly aware of the olive groves through which you are passing: and by the time you cross the Rapido to enter the outskirts of Cassino you barely notice the river or the buildings but only the great mountain towering above the far end of the town half a mile ahead, like a gigantic flying buttress to the mountain mass stretching away to the right. And by this time the cream-coloured building on its crest is seen to be grotesquely huge, and there is a fine arrogance in the way it appears to be looking down over its shoulder on the town far below.

Before the Second World War Cassino was a typical Italian country town of 25,000 inhabitants: noisy, cheerful, busy, and, in summer, hot and dusty. About three-quarters of a mile long, stretched between the Rapido and the great mountain towering above its western end, it was a thriving, well-built town of strong stone buildings, and because of its situation it was more prosperous than most of its kind.

As a market town it was the centre to which the peasant farmers of seventy-two parishes brought their produce and also the seat of justice to which they brought their troubles. As a railway depot with extensive engine sheds and workshops it served the main north–south railway line which at that time passed through Cassino. Its position on the main road half-way between Naples and Rome made it an obvious stopping point for the stream of travellers between the two cities, so that it enjoyed a considerable hotel and restaurant trade. Finally it could point to strong links with antiquity.

Cassino existed as far back as the fourth century B.C. when it was known to the Romans as Casinum. In addition to the usual fragments of aqueducts and temples, and a fine amphitheatre, there survive to this day in good working order the thermal baths the Romans used: attractively buried in a wooded retreat where the streams are overlaid with weeping willows more thickly plangent than their English counterparts, as if to demonstrate that in a Mediterranean climate even the willows are more

emotional. There are references to Casinum in the works of
Cicero and Livy, and the town was evidently of some social
standing as it is known that Mark Antony had a villa there—
where he devoted himself to what the discreet Baedeker has
described as 'his nameless orgies'.

But Cassino's special claim to fame rests on the great mountain
which rears up behind the town and bears its name. For it was on
Monte Cassino, in the sixth century, that the monk Benedict
founded the Benedictine Order and set in motion one of the
great civilizing movements of history.

It was the massiveness of the Abbey of Monte Cassino that was
impressive, and the beauty of the setting as a whole. It was not
an especially beautiful building.

> And there, uplifted, like a passing cloud
> That pauses on a mountain summit high,
> Monte Cassino's convent rears its proud
> And venerable walls against the sky.

Longfellow's description is a little fanciful. No cloud, passing
or otherwise, was ever quite so substantial. It was the rectangular
hugeness that was overwhelming: the enormousness of such a
building in such a place.

It was built of cream-coloured Travertino stone in the form
of a trapezium, its longest side being 220 yards long—more than
twice the length of Buckingham Palace. It was a four-storeyed
building in the uniform design of a fortress, with a thick battlemented base and long even rows of small cell windows. Even the
corridors along which the cells were ranged were nearly two
hundred yards long. The Abbey was mostly built around five
cloistered courtyards, and the buildings included a cathedral,
a seminary, a fully equipped observatory, and a college for boys.
The great library ran nearly the full length of the building and
there were in addition workshops of various kinds, where many
different crafts were practised. There was a kitchen garden, and
a large building to house the animals required for food. And

yet, improbably, this vast self-contained citadel lay sprawled across the summit of a steep mountain.

Monte Cassino is 1,700 feet high and growing out of its base at the northern end of the town there is a miniature version of it, a rocky 300-foot knoll, the *Rocca Janicula*, crowned with the remains of a mediaeval castle. This knoll, which was to become better known as Castle Hill, seems to crouch at the foot of the larger mountain like a watchdog, and the saddle of rock which links them is the startpoint of the shortest, though the most strenuous, way of climbing the mountain. For the less active there is a switchback motor road which winds up the steep eastern slope through a series of hairpin bends, covering five miles on its twisting route to the summit.

In spring and early summer much of the mountainside is thickly wooded with olive, wild oak, fir, and the ubiquitous acacia. Elsewhere it is terraced and tiny patches of cultivation bear witness to the rugged diligence of a peasantry determined to grow a few square feet of corn or vine wherever it is possible to scratch up a little soil. The whole mountain at that time of year is lit with great splashes of *ginestra*, the beautiful and vicious yellow-flowering broom. In spring and summer the trees do something to soften the base of the Monastery, so that from certain angles it may seem to be reclining on a sumptuous green cushion rather than crouching on a hard mountain top. But in winter, when the slopes are bare, and the gales and the black thunderclouds sweep incessantly across from the wild hinterland of the Abruzzi, the Abbey of Monte Cassino hardens into a gaunt symbol of defiance, a great fortress in the sky.

On the summit the tranquillity is tangible, the silence almost audible. From here Cassino is an architect's model and Monte Trocchio, the long brown mountain at the bend in the road, looks quite insignificant although it is two miles long and 1,200 feet high. It is like a land-bound whale, anchoring the highway with its tail, nuzzling the railway with its lips, and it is difficult to realize that the distance between them is two miles. The main road is merely a taut grey line drawn across the dusty green

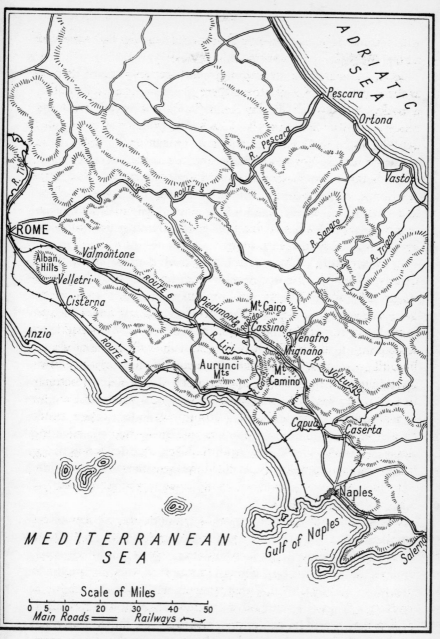

CENTRAL ITALIAN BATTLEFIELD

September 1943–June 1944

velvet of the Rapido valley. There are two roads between Naples and Rome: the *Via Appia*—now known more plainly as Highway Seven—which approaches Rome by way of the coast and the Pontine Marshes; and this inland road, the *Via Casilina* (Highway Six) which the Romans laid twenty-five centuries ago.

The *Via Casilina* is one of the great roads of history. It was down this road in the fourth century B.C. that the Roman legions marched to fight the Samnites in the mountains near Cassino. It was down this road a century later that the Roman general Fabius came to resist Hannibal. It was up this road in the sixth century A.D. that the Byzantine General Belisarius marched to recapture Rome from the Goths: and down this road a few years later that Totila led the Goths in successful counter-attack. Along this road in 1503 came Gonzalo Fernandez de Cordoba and the army of Isabella of Spain to fight the French.

Sometimes Monte Cassino had been able to look down passively on these events, but more often it had been involved in them. For standing as it did at the junction of the two valleys and commanding a perfect view of both, it was the strategic key to this lovely plain which was fated from the beginning of recorded history to become, at regular intervals, a battlefield. Monte Cassino has been likened to the Rock of Gibraltar, and there is a rough similarity in the way it commands the 'straits' at the entrance to the Liri Valley, forcing the road to Rome to make a wide detour around its base, and looming over that road like a sentinel.

The Abbey of Monte Cassino was founded by St. Benedict in A.D. 529. He had previously established a number of small communities of monks in Subiaco, and it was there that his ideas were conceived and tried out. It was at Monte Cassino, during the last eighteen years of his life, that they reached maturity and fulfilment, and the first large community of the Benedictine Order came into being. It was during this time that Benedict wrote his famous *Rule*—a comprehensive guide to the organization and government of a monastic community that became the practical blueprint for Western monachism generally.

His choice of location was not accidental. He was not the first to be struck by its exceptional qualifications both as a retreat for worship and a fastness reasonably secure against attack. When he arrived there a temple of Apollo occupied a part of the summit, while not many yards away there was a Roman tower. Benedict's first action was to demolish the temple and consecrate his own altar on the spot where the pagan shrine had been. His second was to start building his monastery in such a way as to incorporate the sturdy Roman tower in its walls. A part of this tower is the only fragment of Benedict's original building that survives to modern times.

The fame and influence of Monte Cassino spread rapidly, and among its earlier pilgrims was the Gothic king himself, Totila. Then, in 581, forty years after Benedict's death, the Monastery suffered the first of its four destructions. It was sacked by the Lombards who wanted to use it as a stronghold against the Romans. The Abbot and monks fled to Rome, and this flight proved to be a turning-point in the history of the Order. For when the fugitive Benedictines settled into the general current of ecclesiastical life in Rome, their qualities and ideas so impressed the Papal authorities—especially the great Pope Gregory—that they were given the apostolate of the Germanic countries. What had been conceived by Benedict as a purely self-contained local community became from then on an increasingly influential missionary movement.

The Abbey was not rebuilt until 717—an English monk, St. Willibald, taking a leading part in its restoration—and this time it survived for nearly two centuries. Then it was destroyed a second time—by the Saracens in 883—and seventy years passed before it was again rebuilt.

During its third lease of life, the Monastery entered a golden period of influence and prosperity. While the monks devoted themselves to the Benedictine ideal of sanctity through work, prayer, and study, the Abbey estates in the surrounding valleys managed to grow to the formidable total of 250,000 acres. The Abbots became powerful squire-landlords as well as spiritual leaders.

One of the Benedictine principles was that the monks, in addition to their devotions, should be employed in manual labour at certain times and at others in spiritual reading. This was to prove one of the corner-stones of Benedictine influence, as the spiritual reading took the form of transcribing the great works of ancient literature. It was at Monte Cassino, therefore, that there began that tradition, later adopted by other orders, whereby the monks took the place of the printing press that was not to be invented for another six centuries. To the monks of Monte Cassino we owe such works as Varro's *De Lingua Latina*, the most ancient work on grammar that we have, and much of the work of Cicero, Horace, Ovid, Virgil, Seneca, and many others. The originals of these manuscripts are among the priceless collection of documents, archives, and manuscripts that are Monte Cassino's especial pride.

Thus the monks spread not only the word of God through their teaching but some of the more inspired words of man through their dedicated copying. They therefore supplied a vital link in the passing on of civilization to the still barbaric west. In the dark days of the broken Roman Empire they provided the nursery in which the shoots of Christian ethic and Hellenic culture were fused, preserved, and nourished before being disseminated through the Benedictine missions that were all the time moving out into Europe from the parent establishment. At this time, therefore, Monte Cassino was the paramount cradle of western civilization.

This golden age reached its peak in the eleventh century under the celebrated Abbot Desiderius. Desiderius practically rebuilt the Abbey. He called in the greatest artists and craftsmen of the day from Constantinople to decorate it. (The heavily ornate Baroque tradition which has influenced all subsequent restorations dates from this, and is the reason why the interior of the Abbey, like its exterior, has always been spectacularly impressive rather than aesthetically pleasing.) He formed a group of scribes and illuminators that became famous throughout Europe, and the Cassinese script they developed is regarded as one of the greatest schools of mediaeval writing. In the year in which William the Conqueror invaded Britain, Desiderius brought his programme to a climax by starting to build within the monastery precincts a large cathedral, and when it was finished this cathedral—richly decorated with mosaics, gilded stucco, highly ornate marble inlays, frescoes, and wood-carvings—was one of the architectural wonders of the day.

But once again the Monastery was due to be destroyed, and this time the hand of man was not to blame. In 1349 it was wrecked in an earthquake. But rebuilding began immediately and was completed before the end of the century. It was less easy, however, to restore the spirit and influence that had risen to its high-water mark under Desiderius. Monte Cassino fell into a decline during the next two centuries.

In 1503 it had a narrow escape from yet another destruction, and this unexpectedly proved a long-term as well as an immediate blessing. Gonzalo Fernandez de Cordoba, the great Spanish general who, among other things, introduced gunpowder to European warfare, was fighting the French in this region. With the connivance of the monks a French garrison had occupied the Monastery. Gonzalo's men, finding a partial breach in the walls, managed to force an entry and drive out the French soldiers and the monks. But a natural fortress of such strength could not be left intact. Gonzalo prepared to destroy it with his gunpowder. On the eve of putting this plan into execution he is said to have had a dream in which St. Benedict appeared, standing between him and the Monastery entrance, reproving him. Whether or not the story of the dream is true, the fact is that Gonzalo not only decided to spare the building but from this time on became noticeably absorbed by the Order of St. Benedict and all it stood for. First he moved southwards towards the sea along the valley of the Rapido (which becomes known as the Garigliano after its confluence with the Liri) and on the banks of the Garigliano he defeated the French. That business being completed he concerned himself with badgering the Pope to reform the Monastery of Monte Cassino. A year later this was done and the Monastery was given a new lease of life in the charge of a fresh community provided by the monks of St. Justina of Padua. The story is interesting as an example of the spell which Monte Cassino has cast on so many of those who have come to it as soldiers. Gonzalo was not the last to be so affected.

During the Renaissance something of its former glory was recovered, and it became a favourite rendezvous of artists from all over the country. In 1866 the Abbey was again in danger, when the Italian government suppressed the monasteries. On that occasion it was, of all people, Mr. Gladstone and a number of prominent English friends of Monte Cassino who came to the rescue. Urgent representations were made to the Italian government and in consequence the Benedictine community was allowed to continue there.

In 1944 there were no trees on the slopes of Monte Cassino. That year the spring was late. Monte Cassino, towering guardian of the road to Rome, happened once again to lie in the path of a war. A new army, marching along the *Via Casilina*, had reached the bend in the road by Monte Trocchio. And when this new generation of soldiers looked across the valley at Monte Cassino, few of them knew that they were merely the latest manifestation of a rhythm of violence that for centuries had been breaking like a tide over this natural fortress-sanctuary.

But this time there was a difference. The soldiers who in 1944 subjected Monte Cassino to its fourth and greatest destruction had to do so because the ideals for which it stood were in peril. Benedict's monastery had to die once again in order that his ideals might have another chance to survive in a world that had largely abandoned them.

2

IT is not until afterwards that a modern battle acquires a shape. The word battle is itself misleading. It suggests a coherent clash between orderly formations of men and machines. It is a word that belongs to the past. Operations, though formal and abstract, is a more appropriate term.

A modern battle is not an isolated event existing in a vacuum. It is a phase in a continuous integrated process. It develops logically from what has gone before, and relates to what follows. The beginning is often hard to pinpoint, the end is seldom final—unless it is the last battle of a campaign. It is convenient to speak of this or that battle, but what is really meant is operations between this date and that. A battle is generally without identity until it is viewed retrospectively within the context of a campaign.

A battle is exceedingly complicated. It is a patchwork of tiny operations carried out by groups largely unaware what similar groups on their left and right are doing. It is a way of life extending for days, weeks, or months. It may be thirty miles wide, or two. A company theoretically in the thick of the fight may spend two days resting, eating regular meals, and enjoying a normal night's sleep because it happens to be temporarily in reserve, and the area where it is lying up is not receiving the immediate attention of enemy guns.

The layman's difficulty in gaining a realistic impression of what a major battle is like is increased rather than lessened by the conventions of war reporting. The correspondent has to describe and interpret complex events while they are still in confused progress, and reduce them at high speed to a few sentences. He is subject to censorship, the unresolved outcome of the events themselves, and the fact that he cannot be in more than one place at a time. Inevitably there has come into being a convenient idiom for these necessarily perfunctory accounts. Inevitably they can give only the general outline of events.

The newspaper reader learns that General X is 'throwing in his armour' or 'pouring in reserves' or 'launching a three-point thrust'. This descriptive shorthand may give a handy passing impression of the general course of events, but it gives no true picture of a battle. It is especially difficult for the soldier, picking up a newspaper several weeks after an action in which he took part, to relate himself to the account of that battle which he finds in it.

It comes as a genuine surprise to him to discover that the day the orders were changed three times in as many hours, and his unit eventually spent three days kicking their heels in a muddy farm area without a notion of what was happening, he was a reserve being 'poured in': it is difficult for Trooper Jones to grasp that on that unhappy morning when all but two tanks in his squadron were knocked out, he was part of a 'great armoured break-through'. It is no easier for a lonely platoon commander, recollecting in tranquillity a shambles in which his company commander dispatched him into the night without any clear orders about what he was to do, to realize that he was nevertheless an important contributor to a 'three-point thrust'.

A battle is a mosaic of just such experiences, confused and incomplete in themselves, and apparently unrelated. Even afterwards it is often difficult to say precisely when one battle ended and another began. A large operation may be preceded by one or more preparatory actions: the capture of a height required by the Artillery for observation, or the bombing of enemy airfields, or a series of patrols. Are these a part of the main battle, or not?

In the case of Cassino it is easier than with most battles to establish a precise identity in space and time. First, there was the place itself; a situation commonly considered to be the most perfect natural defensive position in Europe; a clearly defined battleground consisting partly of mountain, partly of river and valley, with one admirably complementing the other. The battleground shaped the battle, confined its crucial activity to a sector less than ten miles wide, so dominated and canalized operations that everything that happened beyond that sector became subsidiary.

In time the identity of Cassino is established by a consideration of the Italian campaign as a whole. Because of the nature of the country this was a campaign in which the initiative was always held by the defending army. It was the defender who dictated where it would be fought. Cassino was where the Germans chose to make their main defensive effort. Retrospectively, therefore, the campaign is seen to fall into three parts. Everything that happened before Cassino was a prelude to it: Cassino was the climax: everything that happened afterwards was anti-climax. For the battle of Cassino became the battle for Rome. Two days after the fall of Rome the Allies invaded Normandy and the Italian campaign became of secondary importance. Cassino was a climactic trial of strength fought to a finish at a time when Germany did not consider the war yet lost.

What came to be known as the Battle of Cassino may therefore be said to have started on the night of January 17th, 1944, when British troops of the American Fifth Army crossed the Garigliano and attempted to establish a protective left flank for a thrust into the heart of the Cassino defences by an American division three nights later. It ended on June 4th when the Fifth Army entered Rome.

It is certain, however, that when those British soldiers ferried themselves across the Garigliano, and the Americans splashed across the flooded valley to cross the same waterway where it is still called the Rapido, they had no idea that they were starting the battle of Cassino. They were merely continuing, after a few days' pause, a painful advance through mud, mountain, and river that had been going on for ever and would go on for ever.

3

THIS is the story of a battle, not the history of a campaign. But to understand the battle it is necessary to know something of the political and strategic background to the campaign which produced it, and the tactical factors which shaped it. And the essential point about the campaign in Italy is that it was handicapped from the start by a serious strategic difference of opinion between America and Britain, and by the peculiar tactical difficulty of the country as fighting terrain.

To Winston Churchill and the British High Command it seemed self-evident after the great victory in North Africa in 1943 that our land forces, at the peak of their power, should continue the momentum of attack by engaging the Germans again as quickly as possible. Italy seemed to be the country in which this could best be done. In Mr. Churchill's historic phrase it was the 'soft underbelly' of the Axis. An invasion of the Italian mainland via Sicily had much to offer.

It was at the time the easiest and most direct way into Europe. The establishment of an expeditionary force at all on the mainland of 'Fortress Europe'—on which Hitler had said that no Allied soldier would ever set foot—would in itself be a significant step forward. Italy was where the weaker member of the Axis partnership could most quickly be knocked out of the war. In its early phases an invasion of Italy would complete the clearance of the Mediterranean, give the Allied navies the important ports of Naples and Taranto, and the air forces the extensive Foggia airfields from which the air offensive against central Europe could be considerably strengthened. Later, the capture of Rome would be psychologically and morally of great importance. In addition, an Allied army in Italy would provide encouragement, and practical assistance in the form of bases and supplies, to Tito, still conducting an incipient and lonely resistance across the Adriatic in Jugoslavia. Later still it would be well placed for a jump into the Balkans should such a move seem desirable. But above all, with a year to go before the cross-channel invasion was launched, it was essential to help that operation by diverting and destroying as many German divisions as possible elsewhere. As Mr. Churchill himself put it to the House of Commons: 'We have got to fight them somewhere, unless we are just to sit back and watch the Russians.' Italy was immediately the most suitable place.

General Marshall and the American Chiefs of Staff thought otherwise. Fully engaged in the Pacific, they regarded the war with Germany as something to be finished off at the right time by an overwhelming thrust at the heart by the shortest route— that is to say by an invasion across the English Channel and a drive on Berlin. Nothing, in their view, should be allowed to divert men or materials from that final effort, scheduled for the following summer. Anything else would be a side-show and they were against side-shows.

'The Mediterranean,' General Marshall told a meeting of the Combined Chiefs of Staff in Washington in May 1943, 'is a vacuum into which America's great military might could be drawn off until there is nothing left with which to deal the decisive blow on the Continent.'

This was the essence of the disagreement. Whereas Churchill considered that, quite apart from its other advantages, a diversionary campaign in Italy was an essential strategic preliminary to the decisive blow, Roosevelt and Marshall insisted that the demands it made would weaken the final effort. It was a disagreement which reflected both the national temperaments and the previous experience of the two nations. As John Ehrman, a British official historian, has summed it up:

> To the British, nurtured and confirmed in the experience, and largely governed by the forms, of maritime warfare, strategy implied an

economy of effort, best achieved, if circumstances allowed, by a careful distribution of strength between a number of complementary targets. . . .

To the Americans, on the other hand, strategy implied concentration of effort, in the Napoleonic sense. Unused to long wars against numerically superior Continental powers, and rightly confident in their application of ingenuity to unparalleled strength, they had no need for or experience of the devious approach.

Politically the difference of viewpoint was one of intuition and historical insight. To Churchill, a European statesman-historian, it not only came naturally to 'think Mediterranean' in matters of strategy, but his political insight and sense of history enabled him to see farther ahead than the immediate military consideration. 'War,' said Clausewitz, 'is the continuation of state policy by other means.' Policy, Churchill alone saw at this time, was likely after the Second World War to prove a continuation of war. His instinct told him that the right area in which to meet the advancing Russians was central Europe: and the way into central Europe was through Italy and the Balkans. Post-war history lost little time in proving painfully and drastically how right Churchill had been. But the reaction of the American leaders at the time was to develop profound suspicions that the subtle and mercurial Prime Minister was 'up to his tricks' and must be restrained from dragging America into dangerous Balkan adventures. Indeed 'Balkan adventures' became a bogy phrase that constantly clouded the top-level exchanges between the two governments during this crucial year in which the final phase of the war was being planned.

This summary of the Anglo-American disagreements, out of which the Italian campaign was born, is necessarily brief because the present work is concerned less with causes than effects. In the event the Americans agreed to the campaign but only on a compromise basis. They declined to put their full weight behind it. From the outset they regarded it as a secondary front, a sideshow. With the result that a campaign not exceeded by any in the war in natural difficulty was launched with one hand tied behind its back. Only once—and then not until it had dragged painfully on for eight months—was there a sufficiency of men and the right materials in Italy. But even when this had resulted in a considerable victory, Washington, by a crowning stroke of irony and despite the urgent pleading of Churchill and the American commanders in Italy, insisted on diverting from Italy to the south of France large forces with whose help the Italian victory might well have been made decisive.

These disagreements existed only, of course, at the highest level. The American Commanders on the spot did everything possible to influence the build-up of the Italian effort once it had started, and as the campaign wore on they were partially successful: sometimes at the cost of being labelled too pro-British. But the basic strategic reluctance always remained. Washington was a long way from Cassino. The American divisions who fought so well in Italy could justifiably have felt that they were to a large extent America's forgotten army.

The German High Command took it for granted that an invasion of southern Europe would follow the African victory, but they expected it to be directed against the Balkans. In their view 'domination of the Balkans as an integral part of the Fortress of Europe is decisive from the point of view of winning the war for tactical, military-political and economic reasons'. They had made their dispositions accordingly. Throughout the summer they had twice as many divisions standing by in southeast Europe as they had in Italy. The Allied invasion of Sicily did not change the German view, nor even the invasion of Italy itself: they assumed these were preliminary moves to facilitate a Balkan venture, and it was not until the Italian campaign had reached the end of its first phase that they accepted that Italy was in fact the chosen objective.

Meanwhile, as the Sicilian campaign was drawing to its successful conclusion, an event took place which radically changed the outlook of the Allies for the better, and thoroughly vindicated Mr. Churchill's inclination to move into Italy. On July 25th

Mussolini fell and emissaries of Marshal Badoglio—representing a new Italian order that wished to continue the war at the side of the Allies—began to pay secret flying visits to discuss an armistice. One of the campaign's major objectives—the elimination of Italy from the war—was to be achieved without a shot being fired.

This development might have been expected to succeed, where other arguments had failed, in persuading General Marshall and the American Chiefs of Staff to revise their views on the value of the Italian campaign. This was not the case. They did, however, agree to the stepping up of the initial invasion effort. Whereas the original plan had provided only for the Eighth Army to land on the toe of Italy the new plan included in addition an assault landing seven days later in the Naples area by the Fifth Army.

It took the whole of August for the details of the armistice to be settled, and in the circumstances this could hardly have been otherwise. Before changing allies in midstream, Marshal Badoglio not unnaturally wanted a solid assurance that Anglo-American forces would be landing in Italy in strength—his idea of strength being fifteen divisions. Before welcoming so recent an opponent as a full partner, General Eisenhower, who was in charge of the negotiations, not unnaturally had a few stipulations of his own to make as well as needing time to consult with London and Washington. In addition he did not feel disposed to mention that the initial invasion effort, limited by availability of shipping, would be undertaken, not by fifteen divisions, but by eight. As a result the armistice was not signed until September 3rd, a few hours after the invasion had actually started. This time-lag between the collapse of the Fascists and the signing of the armistice deprived the Allies of some of the advantages they might have expected from it. The Germans, acting with customary swiftness, were able to take over the country and immobilize the Italian army. But the net gain was still considerable. The Axis partnership had been broken. Thirty or forty Italian divisions, which might have fought well on their own soil, had been removed from the opposition without a shot being fired. Their replacement by

German divisions from other fronts would fulfil one of the long-term Allied objectives. The Italian people, sickened by a war they did not want and now under a ruthless German occupation, would regard the Allies as liberators.

That, in broad outline, was the strategic and political background to the Italian campaign. Tactically there was one factor which dominated all others, the geography of the country.

Italy is a peninsula about 1000 miles long and a little over 100 miles wide. Down the greater part of its length runs a central backbone of mountains, some of them as high as 6000 feet, and these are generally about twice as far from the western coast as they are from the eastern. Branching out from this backbone is a succession of mountainous ribs. On the eastern side they tend to run tidily down to the coast in straight ridges: on the other side they are more frequently in the shape of a dog's leg: for a few miles they run almost parallel with the central range, then they jerk southwards towards the sea. In the centre of the country the mountains form a continuous mass, but in the coastal belts they abut on to small plains.

The few roads in the centre of the country are narrow, winding, and from a military point of view virtually useless in winter. In the southern half of the country there are only two major lateral highways: that between Naples and Termoli, and the one which runs between Rome and Pescara. As a result, a military advance up the peninsula will automatically be split between two coastal fronts. On the western side the practicable front is twenty to twenty-five miles wide, on the eastern side it is rather narrower, varying from five to fifteen miles. Because of the lack of roads through the central mountain mass, the armies on these two fronts will to all intents and purposes be fighting separate wars.

No profound tactical knowledge is necessary to appreciate that this country is ideally suited to defence. No sooner has one river or mountain barrier been crossed than another bars the way. Plains are few and far between and too small for the decisive use of tanks. A defender can fight an unlimited number of delaying actions from one end of the country to the other. As an officer put it: 'Every 500 yards there is a new defensive position for a company, every five miles a new line for a division.' In simple terms an advance up Italy against a strong enemy resolves itself into an interminable process of 'one more river to cross, one more mountain barrier to overcome'. Strategically Italy might be a soft under-belly: tactically it was a scaly, pachydermatous backbone.

Shortly before the Second World War Captain Liddell Hart, the military critic, put forward the theory that the power of modern weapons was such that infantry offensives on a large scale must be considered obsolete. No army, he contended, could hope to overcome another of similar quality, unless it had a superiority of three to one. He argued that since this superiority would be impossible to achieve on the western front, a German attack on the French Maginot Line—at that time the hope of Europe—could only end in stalemate, and was therefore unlikely to be undertaken.[1]

His estimate of a necessary three-to-one superiority was sound, but his deduction was wrong. What he overlooked was that in addition to greatly increasing its weapon-power, the modern army had through mechanization also increased its mobility. With the aid of this mobility it would be possible to achieve three-to-one superiority at a chosen part of the front, and there make a breakthrough. The fallacy of this theory of the ascendancy of defence—a theory to which the French General Staff were wholly committed—was demonstrated in the early part of the war by the Germans with the stratagem that became known as the blitzkrieg.

The blitzkrieg consisted in just this. Overwhelming forces were secretly concentrated opposite one small section of the opposing line—preferably a sector discovered by reconnaissance to be weak.

[1] "If we can credit the German Staff with a sense of realities, the possibility of a serious German offensive in the West becomes more than doubtful." *The Defence of Britain*. Liddell Hart (1939).

A breakthrough was achieved. Armoured forces were then poured through the gap, and wheeling left and right would swiftly fall upon the rear areas of those parts of the line that had not been attacked, thus throwing the whole defensive system into confusion. This was how the German army achieved its early victories, and how the 'impregnable' Maginot line was disposed of in a few days during the summer of 1940.

But the key to this pattern of attack is manoeuvrability. In order to build up local superiority of three to one and make the overwhelming thrust at the chosen point, the attacking army must have the power to manoeuvre swiftly and secretly so that the enemy is taken by surprise. The geography of Italy is such that even in dry weather power of manoeuvre is severely restricted, but between November and April it is non-existent.

These two correlated tactical factors—the geography of the country and the consequent absence of the power of manoeuvre —are at the very root of what happened in Italy. All failures and all successes were directly related to them. And, coupled with the additional handicap of America's strategic reluctance to throw its full weight into the campaign, they produced as their logical outcome the long and costly battle of Cassino.

4

FOR the new phase of the Mediterranean war, the invasion of Europe, the supreme command remained with General Eisenhower and Allied Force Headquarters in Algiers. But with the passing of time, and with Sicily and large territories of North Africa now under Allied control, the supreme command tended to become increasingly political and administrative. The active prosecution of the Italian campaign was entrusted to the 15th Army Group under the command of General Sir Harold Alexander. This formation consisted of two armies: the British Eighth under General Montgomery, and the newly-formed American Fifth, commanded by General Mark W. Clark. The composition of the Eighth Army remained for the time being entirely British: the Fifth, though under American command, initially consisted of three American and three British divisions, organized in two corps.

The invasion was carried out in two phases. On September 3rd the Eighth Army crossed the three miles of the Straits of Messina and landed on the toe of Italy. On September 9th the Fifth Army made an assault landing at two points of the Gulf of Salerno. The Eighth Army's task proved unexpectedly easy. There was no opposition to the landing. The Germans had withdrawn some days before. The Italian soldiers who met the Eighth on the beaches cheerfully assisted with the disembarkation. The subsequent advance up the southernmost two hundred miles of the country was nothing more than an exercise in organization and rapid movement. For the Fifth Army it was another matter.

The Italian armistice was signed, as we have seen, a few hours after Montgomery's men landed. It was left to General Eisenhower to announce it at the moment he thought it would be most helpful to the invasion. He made the announcement, and broadcast a proclamation to the Italian people, on the night of September 8th, as General Mark Clark's invasion fleet lay in readiness off the Gulf of Salerno. In the early hours of the following morning the British and American corps of Fifth Army simultaneously stormed the beaches at two points near Salerno, and immediately ran into the heaviest opposition.

The Germans at this time had sixteen divisions in Italy. They were organized in two groups of eight: one in the north, commanded by Field-Marshal Rommel, the other south of Rome, under Field-Marshal Kesselring. Kesselring was not deceived into thinking that the landing of two Eighth Army divisions in the far south represented the full extent of the Allied invasion. (The nature of this stretch of country made it impracticable to deploy more than two divisions.) With the Allies in command both of the sea and the sky, he correctly guessed that an amphibious assault would follow up the first landing, and he correctly guessed where it would take place. This was not very difficult. There are three prerequisites which govern the choice of a landing beach. The beach itself must be suitable for the actual landing: it must be near a major port that can be brought into use within a short time of the landing being established: it must be within range of fighter cover by the invader's air forces. Only the sandy beaches around the Gulf of Salerno—thirty miles south of Naples and at the extreme range of Sicily-based fighter aircraft—satisfied these requirements. So confident of this was Kesselring that he sent a Panzer division to the Salerno area to carry out anti-invasion exercises. The division actually underwent one of these exercises on the day before the Fifth Army landed. The following morning, as General Clark's men went in, the Germans, comfortably established on the heights which overlook the beaches, were waiting for them.

The British and Americans both established small beachheads, but once the landing had taken place, Kesselring lost no time in

rushing more divisions to the scene to drive the invaders back
into the sea. With a semi-circle of high ground overlooking
the beaches, the battlefield resembled half a saucer with the
Germans sitting on the rim. For four days the issue hung in the
balance. General Clark, anxiously waiting for news that the
Eighth Army were approaching from the south, was feeling
towards General Montgomery much as Wellington felt about
Blücher during the crisis of Waterloo. More than once it seemed
certain that the beachhead would not be held. But on the fifth
day, thanks to the stubbornness of the infantry, a continuous
offensive by the Allied air forces, and the tremendous bombardments carried out by the supporting naval forces, the tide turned
and the beleaguered Anglo-American forces began to push out-
wards. Afterwards, it was generally thought that the turning-
point had followed Admiral Cunningham's bold decision to send
the battleships *Warspite* and *Valiant* dangerously close inshore to
pound the German positions with their sixteen-inch guns. By
the seventh day the beachhead was secure and the Fifth Army,
after its fearful blooding, prepared to advance towards Naples.
The greatest weight of the continuous German counter-attacks
had been thrown against the British Tenth Corps. This was
reflected in the casualty lists. The seven-day battle had cost the
British 4,007 casualties, the Americans (with fewer men engaged)
1,667—and the *Warspite* had been disabled by one of the new
German glider-bombs. It was an ominous indication of things
to come. All of a sudden the Italian armistice seemed strangely
insignificant.

Meanwhile, by concentrating on resisting the Fifth Army
landing, the Germans had left the Adriatic side of the country
wide open. General Alexander was able to take advantage of this
by ordering the Eighth Army to land its reserve divisions and
open up an east coast front that would relieve the pressure on the
Fifth Army, while the original Eighth Army landing force caught
up with the Fifth and consolidated its advance in the centre.
Taranto and Bari on the east side were quickly occupied and the
78th Division of Eighth Army raced ahead to capture Foggia,

whose dozen airfields were important initial objectives of the campaign. Foggia was occupied on the 27th, as the Fifth Army prepared for the final stages of its attack on Naples. On October 1st the King's Dragoon Guards entered that city, and four days later the Eighth Army took Termoli on the east coast. With both terminals of the Naples–Termoli road—the only major lateral highway in southern Italy—firmly held, and Foggia and its airfields occupied, the Allied armies had in baseball parlance reached First Base. It was to be many months before they reached Second Base—Highway Five—the next important lateral between Rome and Pescara.

At the beginning of October the German High Command were still prepared for an Allied switch to the Balkans, and strong forces were accordingly held there in readiness. But in the meantime they had made a firm decision regarding their plans for the winter in Italy. Kesselring was to establish a winter line south of Rome and, until it could be completed, conduct a fighting withdrawal designed to bleed the Allied armies as much as possible. The northern group of divisions under Rommel would be positioned to defend Rome itself and resist any amphibious landings the Allies might attempt in that area or farther north. Kesselring's winter line was to run along the Garigliano and Rapido rivers through Cassino into the central mountains, and thence along the River Sangro to the east coast.

Between early October and November 20th the Eighth continued a methodically opposed advance up the narrow eastern front—always there was one more river, one more mountain spur—until they reached the Sangro. The Fifth, crossing the Volturno on October 15th, battered away on the wider western front until they ran into a series of mountains that might have been specifically positioned to act as crippling baffles in the way of an army approaching Cassino along the main road to Rome. The Eighth's more rapid advance was like a succession of sharp dagger thrusts: that of the Fifth was like a bull, tiring but still game, butting its way head down into attack after attack, under a continuous shower of banderillas. During this period the pattern

of battle seldom varied. The Germans would hold a position for
a time until it was seriously contested: then pull back a mile or
two to the next defendable place, leaving behind a trail of blown
bridges, minefields, and road demolitions. There was always a
new defendable place at hand. The Allied armies would begin
with a night attack—ford the stream or river after dark,
storm the heights on the far side, dig themselves in by
dawn, and hope that by that time the Sappers, following on their
heels, would have sufficiently repaired the demolitions and
removed the obstacles to permit tanks to follow up and help
consolidate the new positions. The Germans, watching these
proceedings from their next vantage point, would attempt to
frustrate them by raining down artillery and mortar fire on their
own recently vacated positions.

In the middle of November two significant things happened.
The Italian winter, about which travel agencies are inclined to be
reticent, broke in all its icy drenching fury; mud became the only
alternative to mountains; transport became virtually useless in
the forward areas. The other thing that happened was that the
Germans decided that there was now no danger of an Allied
jump into the Balkans before the following spring, and they
adjusted their ideas and dispositions accordingly.

Whereas in the middle of September there were thirteen Allied
divisions to eighteen German, the balance was now eleven Allied
to twenty-five German divisions. (It had been part of the original
plan that two Allied divisions must be withdrawn and returned
to the U.K. after the first phase of the Italian invasion.) The
German command was reorganized into two armies under
Kesselring as Commander-in-Chief South, Rommel being trans-
ferred to a new command in north-west Europe. The Tenth
Army faced the Allied advance, the Fourteenth was distributed
between Rome and the north in readiness for any amphibious
landings the Allies might attempt. Work on the winter line,
especially in the Cassino sector, was intensified. And with the
Balkan worry out of the way and the winter weather now on his
side, Kesselring set about making the Fifth and Eighth armies

fight for every yard before they even reached the main winter line so as to gain time for its completion.

In the first half of November, the Fifth began a series of difficult and costly attacks for possession of what became known as the Mignano gap. This was a stretch of six miles in which the main road passes through a corridor of mountains before it passes round Monte Trocchio and debouches into the open expanse of the Rapido valley. The Mignano gap was the entrance corridor through which an army must pass before emerging into the arena of the Cassino battlefield. It was a defender's dream as relatively small forces could ensure that each mountain mass on either side of the road had to be overcome in turn. In appalling weather conditions the Fifth Army addressed itself to this thankless task and it was not long before it began to find frostbite and exposure responsible for nearly as many casualties as shells and bullets. By mid-November General Clark had to call a temporary halt, to rest and reorganize divisions that had been fighting continuously since Salerno.

It was now the turn of the Eighth Army and an attempt was made to outflank the projected German winter line from the right by crossing the Sangro and pushing on to Pescara—linked with Rome by a main lateral highway. This was Montgomery's last operation in Italy. It was prepared and launched with his customary care and power. For a time it made good progress, but soon it became slowed down by the invariable curse of every pursuit in Italy—the endless succession of new obstacles. As a war correspondent put it: 'Our men battled across the Sangro, but behind the Sangro was the Moro, and behind the Moro was the Foro, and behind the Foro was the Pescara.' In addition to the succession of rivers there was also Ortona, a small port for which the 1st Canadian Division had to fight street by street, house by house, and even floor by floor. It took them a week, and they spent Christmas Day doing it, and in the end they took it. But that was the end of Eighth Army's effort. Pescara was still ten miles away: the weather and the ground were worse than ever:

the Army had temporarily shot its bolt. After Ortona the Canadians became the acknowledged experts in street-fighting. For the rest of the war officers who had been at Ortona toured the Allied military schools lecturing on this subject. Ortona is a small piece of Canadian history. But it was the end of the Eighth Army's effort to break through on the Adriatic front.

On December 1st, while the Sangro battle was at its height the Fifth Army renewed its attack on the Mignano Gap, and in particular on Monte Camino, a predominant mountain that had stubbornly defied it. This time a combined Anglo-American effort succeeded, but at a great cost in casualties and after an expenditure of more than 200,000 shells—which caused the Americans to rename the mountain Million Dollar Hill. The pressure was kept up on both sides of the road, and gradually the entire Army edged forward, hill by hill, until the gap had at last been captured and there was only one more mountain beyond, an isolated height named Monte Trocchio. The Americans occupied that one, too, on January 15th. The war had reached the bend in the road by Monte Trocchio, the 'last height before Cassino'.

Battling through these outposts of the winter line—they were no more than that—had cost the Fifth Army nearly 16,000 casualties. It had given an ominous foretaste of how useless machines can be when climate and terrain conspire to make them so. It consummated the pattern of fighting in Italy: the monotonous, heart-breaking, exhausting, seemingly pointless battle for one great obstacle only to be faced immediately afterwards by another. It had taken eight divisions six weeks to advance seven miles at a cost of 16,000 casualties. Yet from the German point of view this was only a delaying action. The Germans never meant to hold these positions, but only to stay in them long enough to harass and bleed and delay the Fifth Army before it reached their real winter line—and to give themselves time to complete that line. They were playing for time while they put the finishing touches to a line a few miles farther on in which they did intend to remain.

If the cost of breaking this temporary line is remembered, and the time it took to do it, an idea may be gained of what was going to be involved when the finest German troops, the geography of Italy, and the full fury of mid-winter conspired together in defence—as now they were about to do.

5

IT was not through any exceptional tactical percipience that the Germans chose Cassino as the hard core of their main defence line. It was already well known. Truthfully the German commander might have said, 'I got it from a book'. For many years the Italian Military College had held it up to students as an example of an impregnable natural defence barrier. Generations of officers had fought imaginary battles of Cassino as a part of their military studies. Had the Allied commanders happened to ask an Italian senior officer where he thought the Germans would be most likely to make a stand south of Rome, he would have replied without hesitation: 'Why, at Cassino, of course.' It is not on record whether any responsible Italian military men were so consulted. On the whole it seems unlikely as there appears to have been no awareness among the higher Allied echelons that Cassino might prove any more difficult than what had gone before.

The defence of this sector had been entrusted to the Fourteenth Panzer Corps of Tenth Army commanded by General von Senger und Etterlin. The essence of the position was its situation of a steep mountain massif towering above the angle made by two wide valleys meeting at right angles. To enter the Liri Valley (along which the road to Rome passes) it was necessary to cross the Rapido valley with which it formed an L. Monte Cassino, in the angle of the L, commanded the approach across the first valley, and the entrance to the second. If a force managed to break directly into the second valley away from the immediate vicinity of Cassino, it would still be overlooked at every stage of its progress. That was the heart of the matter.

Monte Cassino and the adjacent heights completely controlled the approach to Cassino and the route past it. From the summit of Monte Cassino an observer could watch every move in either valley. Even in moonlight it is possible from this vantage point to pick out the shapes of hills four miles or more away.

It may be as well to make it clear at this point that when we speak of commanding heights—and in any account of the Italian campaign the phrase recurs on every page—it does not necessarily mean that soldiers must sit on them to make them so. Heights are commanding because of the observation they afford. Observation is the key to the modern land battle. The combination of modern gunnery techniques and wireless communication means that one man—quite literally one man—with a good view and a wireless set can direct the guns of an entire army within a few minutes on to any target he can see. The seizing of a dominant height is not undertaken merely in order that it may be garrisoned, but primarily in order that an observation post may be established on it. A modern campaign is largely a progress from one desirable line of observation to another.

Conversely, having picked out a height on which the enemy will obviously have established observation posts, it becomes necessary to do everything possible to make such posts untenable, by shelling and bombing them and generally making the practice of observation as unpleasant as possible. If some feature such as a water tower or a church steeple presents itself as a vantage point likely to be used by the enemy, it will be necessary to try to destroy it. If a vantage point on a hill feature is proving particularly tiresome as an enemy observation post, it may be necessary to mount a brigade or even a divisional attack against it merely to deprive the enemy of it.

The importance of observation is stressed because every soldier who ever sees Monte Cassino at once recognizes it to be just about the finest natural observation post he has ever encountered. This is a key matter in the battle of Cassino, and one which has a considerable bearing on subsequent events.

The decision to defend the Cassino line having been made when the Fifth Army was still sixty miles away, General von Senger could set about improving on this natural defence barrier methodically.

He blasted emplacements in the solid rock of the mountains. Natural caves were enlarged and adapted to house guns and men. Artificial caves were created and camouflaged to conform with the appearance of the mountainside. Machine-gun nests were constructed behind rocky outcrops, so that they had concealment, protection, and good lines of fire. The zig-zag road up the eastern face of Monte Cassino began to bristle with gun positions, as did the heights which crowd in on the mountain on its northern and western sides. In the deep ravines which run between these ridges and crests mortar emplacements were constructed—for mortars fire at a steep angle and can therefore be hidden away in deep gullies from which they can fire without much danger of being hit back. On the mountainsides the stiff gorse thickets were laced with barbed wire and sown with mines. Approaches to all prepared posts were guarded by trip wires that would set off flares or mines or both.

In the valley both sides of the Rapido were heavily mined, and more trip wires were laid. Gun positions were buried in the banks on the enemy side of the river, and in the ditches, and mounds, and hummocks which are numerous at the entrance to the Liri Valley. Farm buildings were fortified, pill-boxes and tank turrets were ingeniously submerged in the ground and camouflaged so that they were invisible. All these positions were most carefully constructed and reinforced with steel and concrete so that they would resist the great artillery concentrations which always preceded the Allied attacks. The Germans were used to them by this time and determined to endure them in security if not comfort. In fact the Allied troops were repeatedly disappointed to discover afterwards how relatively little damage even their heaviest barrages inflicted—so skilled had the Germans become at constructing positions that would afford them protection.

Cassino town was heavily fortified. Buildings were turned into strongpoints. Cellars and ground-floors were reinforced. Tanks were concealed inside some of the larger buildings. Tunnels and connecting trenches were constructed between a cellar strong-point on one side of the road and a shelter on the other. Many buildings, strong in themselves, were made stronger by the in-clusion of a bunker or pill-box inside.

To the north of the town, where the Rapido has its source, they dammed it and created diversions so that when the heavy rains came the whole valley was turned into an area of flood and marsh.

The work went on day after day while the rearguards kept the Fifth Army at bay, playing for time, weakening the advancing troops, tiring them, making them fight for every yard of ground. For three months the Fourteenth Panzer Corps worked at these defences and to help them they had a large detachment of the Todt Labour Organization.

They did not at this time enter the Monastery itself. An army order had placed it out of bounds and a military policeman saw that this was enforced. But they were all round it, on the heights close by, and along the zig-zag road, and near the crest of the mountain.

This was Cassino—the hard core of what the Germans called the Gustav Line—a natural mountain barrier made infinitely stronger by the ingenuity of military engineers: a natural river barrier made infinitely stronger by steel and concrete fortifications and artificial flooding of the wide valley approaches.

6

AT the beginning of January, when the Eighth Army had run into a dead end on the narrow Adriatic front and the Fifth had at last battered its way to the edge of the valley approach to Cassino—to be rewarded by the sight of yet another natural obstacle more formidable than anything it had so far experienced—a natural break in the progress of the campaign had been reached.

It was not only desirable that the tired Fifth should stop to lick its wounds, reorganize, and rest, but it was essential. It had been fighting, almost without pause, for four months. It had had to contend not only with country which entirely favoured the defender, but also with exceptional extremes of winter weather. Wet and frozen, continuously in action, these men had known nothing but mud and mountain for weeks. Sickness brought on by too much exposure to wet and cold was claiming as many casualties as wounds. More divisions had arrived in the country, but there were never enough to arrange a system of regular reliefs. Every formation was needed all the time. On top of this the British divisions were badly under strength. British manpower was now stretched to the limit and reinforcements could not be spared for Italy. Battalions had to reorganize from four companies into three, companies from three platoons to two, and sometimes the word company was a courtesy title for a handful of remnants. The American divisions—numerically twenty-five per cent larger, anyway—were able to keep up the supply of reinforcements, but the continuous using of the same formations placed an increasing strain on the hard core of experienced officers and men. A system of reliefs was badly needed. But none could be arranged because there were no divisions to spare. Italy was a side-show.

Now they had reached the bend in the road. Looking across the great valley to Cassino they knew that they faced a barrier more powerful than anything they had yet tackled—and they had tackled a few by this time. It was essential that there should be a pause and a short rest—if only so that the next move could be properly thought out, prepared, and launched. But there was no pause.

Christmas Day, 1943, meant many things to many men. The Canadians of Eighth Army passed the day expending themselves in the fortified streets and buildings of Ortona: the Americans, British, and newly-arrived French soldiers of Fifth Army dragged their numbed bodies up a few more nameless heights on the way to Cassino: General von Senger, in charge of the German forces responsible for the Cassino sector, visited the Abbey of Monte Cassino and asked if he might attend Mass: but the most important event of that day was that Mr. Churchill, on his way from the Teheran Conference to a few days' rest at Marrakesh, had Christmas dinner with Generals Eisenhower and Alexander in Tunis in order to discuss what could be done about the Italian campaign.

No one—except perhaps those who are fighting it—can tolerate a slow campaign. Football crowds want goals. Governments and those whom they govern want victories. The farther away the campaign the more difficult it is to understand why progress is so slow. Critics of the Italian campaign were becoming vocal both in England and America. Was it worth it? What exactly was being achieved? If the initial object—as had been said—was to knock Italy out of the war, occupy Naples and the Foggia airfields, and draw into Italy a sizeable German army, why not now cut losses and stabilize the front for the winter? What possible good could come of prolonging this interminable, costly advance against country that gave the attacker nothing, the defender everything? No one was altogether happy about the standard answer that 'large German forces were being contained'. So were large Allied forces. General Alexander himself has remarked that he had to ask himself almost every day who was containing whom.

Mr. Churchill was particularly concerned about the way things were going in Italy. For him it was a personal issue. The campaign had been his idea in the first place, and now it was looking as though he was landed with it. Was this not precisely what the American strategists had feared when they questioned the advisability of invading Italy? They had argued that a secondary campaign in the Mediterranean could only draw in increasing numbers of men and materials and so weaken the decisive effort elsewhere. This, it now seemed, was just what was happening. Negative results were being painfully achieved at considerable cost. It looked as though the process would continue indefinitely.

Churchill now had to justify the consequences of his strategy to his American colleagues, to the House of Commons, to the British and American public, and even to Stalin. For Stalin never lost an opportunity to hint that Russia was still making most of the running against Germany, and that the Second Front was a long time coming. At Teheran the Prime Minister and the President had assured Stalin that the Italian campaign would be pursued more vigorously than ever. With characteristic verbal shrewdness, Churchill had redefined Italy as the Third Front— leaving the Second appropriately vacant. And now, almost by accident, Rome became the symbol of success.

Hitherto neither side had attached much military importance to Rome. The Allied High Command had been particularly insistent that the purpose of the campaign was to contain as many German divisions as possible to prevent their use elsewhere—and thereby materially assist the final decisive invasion of the following summer. Now both sides seemed glad to clutch at Rome as a symbol. Hitler had ordered Kesselring to build the Gustav Line through Cassino, and he had announced that the Allies would never break through to Rome. The Allies were now openly treating Rome as the next objective. 'If there were no God,' said

Voltaire, 'it would be necessary to invent him.' If there is no clearcut objective, the Allied High Command seemed now to be saying, it is necessary to invent one. For the time being Rome would do fine. So Rome became temporarily the official prize, and to decide how to accelerate its capture was the reason the Prime Minister, determined that his campaign should not stagnate, broke his journey at Tunis to discuss ways and means with Eisenhower and Alexander. The campaign was his baby. It was not doing well. It must be revitalized by a bold stroke.

In Italy there is only one way in which to avoid a frontal attack and that is to carry out an outflanking movement from the sea. A seaborne landing behind the German lines seemed the only solution to the present *impasse*. Indeed, such an operation had long since been envisaged. Plans had actually been drawn up for a landing near Anzio, a small port some thirty-five miles south of Rome and some sixty miles behind the German lines. There was just one difficulty. There were not enough landing craft in the area to mount such an operation in any strength. In fact there was an overall shortage of landing craft, and most of those that were not already in the United Kingdom in readiness for the following summer were in the process of returning there from all points of the compass. Enough could not be spared for Italy.

The story of how the landing-craft were eventually scrounged —the word is deliberately chosen—is long and involved, and an example of how the running of a war can be simplified when a British Prime Minister and an American President happen to be close friends as well as colleagues. It will be enough to say that Mr. Churchill telephoned the President from Tunis: signals flew in all directions: harassed staff officers were obliged to have rapid second thoughts about time-tables and schedules concerning the return and assembly of landing-craft in Britain: landing-craft sailing placidly through the Indian Ocean on their way from Burma to England were told to make, instead, for Naples. By one means and another ninety-five craft were eventually provided for the Anzio operation—enough to land an initial force of two divisions and some commandos and Rangers.

But arranging for enough landing-craft to be available was only half the story. It would also be necessary to hold on to them for at least a month as, in addition to landing the assault force, they would afterwards be required to shuttle between Naples and the beachhead (120 miles) building up supplies. This meant more arguments with the Chiefs of Staff about how long their return to the United Kingdom could be delayed. And this, unfortunately, ended with a rigid deadline having to be imposed on the launching of the operation. In order that the landing-craft could be ready to return to England at the end of February the Anzio landing would have to take place not later than January 30th. And because of moonlight, and other factors, January 22nd became the only suitable date.

The Anzio plan was simple. An Anglo-American force of two divisions would land and strike towards the Alban Hills—seventeen miles inland and fifteen miles from Rome. This hill mass dominates both the main roads—Highways Six and Seven—which were supplying the main German front. It was hoped that the landing in his rear and the threat to his main arteries of supply would cause Kesselring to withdraw forces from the Cassino front to cope with the beachhead, and so make it easy for the main force of Fifth Army to break through at Cassino and join up with the landing force. The full plan provided for the Fifth Army to launch a series of attacks on the main front at Cassino immediately prior to the Anzio landing.

This meant that the overworked and exhausted Fifth Army, which did not reach the bend in the road and occupy Monte Trocchio until January 15th, would have to resume the offensive without rest or even pause for breath, without time to reorganize, and without even a little time to plan its new operations properly. Mr. Churchill's Christmas Day conference was to have repercussions that were far from festive.

7

IT was unfortunate that, while these plans to give new life to the Italian campaign were being made, Generals Eisenhower and Montgomery were recalled to England to take over their new commands in connection with the Normandy invasion. The effect of this was to give the impression that Italy was more than ever a secondary battleground. Of the two the loss of Montgomery was probably the most keenly felt by the army at large—by the British element, anyway.

As a rule the rank and file are not excessively concerned about which particular general happens to be the top commander. Montgomery was an exception. The Eighth Army—both the old Desert divisions and those that had come to it from the First Army—were intensely aware of him.

Like all men who are both individualists and successful Montgomery has had his detractors. They will seldom be found among those who served under him, whether as lance-corporals or divisional generals. His appeal stemmed from two qualities, one professional the other personal. Professionally he had the rare gift of simplifying the business of war. At a time when operation orders were inclined to become great wordy dossiers of foolscap, packed with administrative detail, Montgomery preferred the direct briefing. He would personally brief as many officers as possible. He would summon a meeting of all concerned down to, and including, battalion commanders and say, in effect: 'All we have to do is this, that, and the other thing.' The battalion commanders would return to their units completely clear about what was to happen, and what they personally had to do. They would repeat what they had been told to their own officers—on many occasions commanders would assemble their entire battalions and brief the whole lot. The consequence of this was that a Montgomery operation always began with everyone knowing what was to happen, why it was to happen, how it was to happen, and what his own job would be. Montgomery hated written orders. He preferred to reduce a task to its essentials and explain it himself. The little tricks of showmanship that attended these briefings ('There will now be an interval of two minutes for coughing. After that there will be no coughing.') were incidental. What mattered was that men usually went into a Montgomery operation knowing what was happening. In war this is by no means a general experience.

The personal aspect of Montgomery's impact was the extent to which he could inspire confidence. The showmanship was a part of it, but it was only an outward manifestation. The plain fact is that his presence automatically inspired confidence at all levels. A personal mystique enveloped him. Montgomery's supreme gift was that when he made an appearance in the front line during the crisis of a battle, everyone who saw him immediately felt that everything would be all right. The interesting thing is that this applied not only to the privates but also to the generals. Anyone who saw it happen will testify to the immediate rise of spirits that would follow the appearance of the open car, with the general waving and beaming like a stand-in for a royal drive. It was not merely because he sometimes threw cigarettes to the nearest soldiers.

The commander of a celebrated division has told me how on one occasion, when a battle was at a critical stage, Montgomery suddenly appeared at his headquarters, talked for a while, then, almost as an afterthought, casually mentioned that he had moved a certain armoured brigade forward. 'I thought you might find it useful.' The point is that the divisional commander did not know that this particular armoured brigade was even in the country at the time. The one thing he badly wanted at that moment was some tanks and till then he could not for the life of him think where he could get hold of any. Behind the incident was the hard, correct judgment of an army commander who knew just what would be wanted and when. 'With Montgomery,' this divisional commander told me, 'you always knew that he would produce something out of a hat at the psychological moment, even an armoured brigade.'

The personal appeal that he exercised is all the more curious because outwardly he had none of the attributes that might be expected of a popular general. There was none of the buccaneering glamour, for instance, that characterized Rommel. Thin, sharp-featured, with a high rasping unattractive voice : austere in manner and tastes : ascetic : these are not the qualities normally associated with popular captains. It was commonly believed that Churchill, whose personality was the antithesis of Montgomery's, disliked him. The archetype of the innumerable Churchill-Montgomery stories is probably the one in which Montgomery is supposed to have said, 'I never smoke, I never drink, I take regular exercise, and I am a hundred-per-cent fit'. To which Churchill allegedly retorted : 'I smoke too much, I drink too much, I take no exercise, and I am three-hundred-per-cent fit.' Yet this curious sharp-faced, dry, ascetic man with the unattractive rasping voice and none of the qualities that commonly endear a man to other men, more than any other general of the war (except perhaps Rommel) conveyed to everyone who served under him, from generals downwards, that if he put in an appearance 'everything would be all right'. It was a kind of genius.

To the armies in general, Eisenhower was for obvious reasons less familiar, a remote, father figure. The level where his summons to new duties was felt was among the higher echelons of the staff. Eisenhower's greatness was not as a field commander but as a presiding chief at the head of a vast Allied enterprise.

The American regular army between the two world wars was not a natural breeding ground for field commanders, and Eisenhower never commanded anything higher than a peacetime artillery regiment. His talent from the beginning was for staff work, and most of his career had been spent on the staff. There is little doubt that his great contribution to the winning of the

Second World War was not as a military captain but through the exceptional talent he had for creating a harmonious alliance between the American and British forces. Running an alliance is well known to be one of the more difficult aspects of waging war. Eisenhower was a born president. As 'president', first of the Mediterranean alliance and then of the one that invaded north-west Europe, he was big enough to take the chair, accept the supreme responsibility, and leave it to the field commanders to win the battles. It was in the furnace of the Second World War that Anglo-American oneness developed from a beautiful dream into a tempered reality. History will remember General Eisenhower as one of the chief instruments of that mutation.

He was succeeded by General Sir Henry Maitland Wilson as Commander-in-Chief Mediterranean, and with the arrival of Wilson at Algiers, that appointment subsided more than ever into political and administrative remoteness. For all practical purposes the war in Italy was now under the complete direction of General Alexander.

Alexander was well fitted for a task which became increasingly difficult with the passing of time. Not only was he an outstanding soldier, but he was also a man of broad culture with the necessary imagination and diplomatic flair to manage what was becoming an increasingly international force—it now included American, British, New Zealand, Canadian, Indian, Polish and French divisions. Alexander was a professional soldier to the finger-tips. If he visited a unit in the front line, it was not to take tea with the officers nor to deliver a pep talk to the soldiers. It was strictly a matter of business. He would ask to be taken to the foremost positions, and there he would interest himself in such basic matters as lines of fire, positioning of Bren guns, siting of trenches, the location of reserve ammunition. General Truscott, an American commander who was to have a great personal success in the Anzio beachhead, tells of a time Alexander visited the beachhead and asked to be taken to the front. Truscott gave him one of his divisional commanders, Brigadier-General O'Daniel, as guide, and privately ordered O'Daniel not to take the Commander-in-

Chief anywhere dangerous. Some time later a plaintive message reached Truscott from a forward unit: 'If General O'Daniel and the guy with the red hat have to prove how brave they are, could they please do it some place else?' Their arrival had attracted the attention of enemy gunners who had thoroughly shelled the area immediately afterwards.

On his return O'Daniel was given a dressing-down by Truscott for taking Alexander too far forward. Replied O'Daniel: 'Did you ever try giving orders to an army group commander?'

Alexander was a general regarded with the highest degree of respect, admiration, and affection, not only by his own countrymen but by every one of the diverse nationalities which came under his command. He was the embodiment of all that is most admired in the English character. He was without a doubt the British general the Americans liked best, and without reservations. His avoidance of anything remotely resembling showmanship seemed at times to be an almost deliberate rejection of the methods of his talented but flamboyant subordinate Montgomery. But the professionalism and the modesty which he always displayed could not conceal the charm. He had a quality of glamour which was all the more telling because it stemmed from the man himself rather than from any sense of performance.

The problematical figure of the Italian campaign was the commander of the Fifth Army, General Mark W. Clark. Mark Clark was the antithesis of Alexander. A handsome, rangy American, his appearance suggested the kind of film star who excels in Westerns. He would have looked well in a ten-gallon hat. Though vain, he had considerable charm and Eisenhower seems to have thought highly of him. He was aggressively determined that the Fifth Army, his first field command, should do well and that the whole world should know it. This is a good way for an army commander to feel. Less becomingly he was equally anxious that his own connection with Fifth Army should never be overlooked. It was a standing joke among the war correspondents that Clark required all press dispatches to use the complete phrase 'Lieutenant-General Mark W. Clark's Fifth Army'. An American correspondent has reported how on one occasion an important dispatch was delayed for several hours in order that it might be returned to him for amendment. He had committed the sin of heading it merely 'with the Fifth Army'.

Clark's compatriot General Truscott had this to say:

'When Clark visited my Command Post, he usually arrived with an entourage including correspondents and photographers. . . . His concern for personal publicity was his greatest weakness. I have sometimes thought it may have prevented him from acquiring that "feel of battle" that marks all top-flight battle leaders, though extensive publicity did not seem to have that effect on Patton and Montgomery.'

Part of Clark's trouble may possibly have been an inferiority complex inspired by the greater experience of his British superiors and subordinates. His references in his own memoirs to Alexander, Montgomery, Freyberg and other British generals reveal a curious chip on the shoulder. He had a thankless task in Italy. But he did not make it easier for himself or others by appearing sometimes to approach it in a frame of mind more appropriate to an over-zealous school football captain.

On the German side, Field-Marshal Kesselring, Commander-in-Chief of the Tenth and Fourteenth armies was, like Alexander, a top-class professional soldier. He had the reputation of being a hard-worker, a man of simple tastes, and one who dispensed with showmanship. He was said to be popular with all ranks. The other commander who was to play a big part in the forthcoming Cassino battles was General von Senger und Etterlin, who commanded the Fourteenth Panzer Corps, the formation charged with the defence of the Gustav Line in the Cassino sector. The war in Italy was rich in irony, not the least being the choice of von Senger to defend Cassino. He was a former Rhodes Scholar and graduate of Oxford University; an Anglo-phile; an officer whose known anti-Nazi feelings resulted in his contribution to the defence of Cassino being played down by the German authorities. To cap everything, in this battle in which the Benedictine Abbey of Monte Cassino was to become so tragically involved, von Senger was, and is, a lay member of the Benedictine Order.

These were the men who faced one another across the Rapido valley in January 1944. In the Cassino sector, some ten miles wide, the Germans had five divisions in the line, three more in close reserve: the Allies had seven, with two others ready to embark for Anzio.

8

DURING those Christmas days and nights in which the Germans were putting the finishing touches to a winter line that was intended to be an immovable object, and the Fifth Army was preparing to set in motion what it hoped would be an irresistible force, there was another group of men who were intimately and fearfully concerned with the impending clash: the Benedictine Community of Monte Cassino.

For weeks there had been German soldiers in the neighbourhood. The monks had grown used to their being around. But as they carried on with their holy way of life in the detachment of the mountain top and the hallowed vastness of the great Abbey, they had not particularly related themselves to military events. A war was in progress. Allied armies were advancing from the Naples area. It was tragic, but it was no concern of theirs. To these monks the days passed as usual. Each day began at five o'clock in the morning: continued mostly in silence through a routine of prayer, study, and worship until the Gregorian chant of Vespers and Compline. The day was punctuated by three frugal meals, also taken in silence except for the intoning of the Latin reader, and it ended in meditation. To men following this way of life, the ability to comprehend the implications of war and to relate it to anything within their experience could not be expected to come easily. The cloistered remoteness of their monastery, sanctified by fourteen centuries of tradition, gave them not only a spiritual detachment from the everyday world but also, because of the exceptional situation of the place, a physical apartness too. The actuality of what was happening in Italy at this time was utterly beyond their grasp.

It was therefore a profound shock when on October 14th, 1943, these scholarly dedicated men, most of them elderly, were brought suddenly face to face with the possibility that they were personally involved in the war: that the seclusion from it which they had taken for granted was threatened.

The Fifth Army was more than fifty miles away, fighting in the neighbourhood of Capua. The autumn weather was still agreeable. The German garrison in the Cassino area was still inconsiderable, and it had not yet impinged on the life of Monte Cassino. Then, on the morning of the 14th, the Monastery had two visitors: Lieutenant-Colonel Schlegel and Captain Becker, a medical officer, both of the Herman Goering Panzer Division. They said that they had been sent by their divisional commander, with the secret acquiescence of the Italian Minister of Education, and they spent the day closeted with Abbot Diamare, an old man of eighty, while the monks wondered apprehensively what it was all about.

Schlegel said he had come to inform the Abbot that Monte Cassino would in the near future become involved in the fighting. The Germans therefore wished to evacuate all its transportable works of art, archives, manuscripts, and books to a place of safety. Schlegel, an Austrian catholic who felt the situation of Monte Cassino keenly, made a good impression on the monks who afterwards praised him for his courtesy and tact. As he himself has since explained, he could not, for reasons of military security, go all the way and tell the Abbot that the German front line would run right through Monastery Hill. But short of saying this, he did all he could during this first visit to persuade him that it would be best if Monte Cassino's treasures were removed.

The reaction of Abbot Diamare was one of extreme distress. He could not understand why the Monastery should be in any danger. It was unthinkable that he should part with any of the valuables entrusted to his care, or any of the property of the Abbey. This reaction was understandable if all the circumstances are taken into consideration, and he communicated it in no uncertain terms to the Community when he assembled them the same evening to tell them what the Germans had suggested.

Schlegel gave the monks two days to think it over. Then, on the 16th, he and Becker again visited Monte Cassino. This time they were firmer and more specific. Within a few days, they said, the Abbey would find itself in the midst of a line on which the Germans were to make their winter stand. 'Like Santa Clara in Naples and San Lorenzo in Rome,' Becker told a monk, 'your Abbey will be reduced. It is a sad thing for your monastery, beautiful and important as it is. Mais, c'est la guerre. The order is not to let them get beyond here. Rome, ils ne l'auront pas jamais!'

Again the Abbot said that he would not hear of it. The archives and certain other valuables were the property of the Italian Government. An inventory had been made a century before, and ever since that time they had been entrusted under State seal to the care of the abbots of Monte Cassino. He could not betray that trust. As for the priceless manuscripts and the famous library— these were Monte Cassino's own. He would not dream of letting any of them leave the Monastery.

They argued for a long time, and as the Germans became more insistent, the Abbot clutched frantically at every kind of objection he could think of. Finally, he stated in desperation that an evacuation was not even practicable. It would be quite impossible to pack up these articles satisfactorily. It would take a long time and it would require special packing materials which they just did not possess. But he counted without German efficiency.

That same afternoon army lorries started arriving, and from them soldiers began to unload great quantities of wooden boards, already cut to the necessary size, and other packing material. While Schlegel reassured the Abbot that the German Army would assume complete responsibility for the safe transfer, that the articles would be taken to a safe place and in due course handed over to the Italian Government, the treasures of Monte Cassino were methodically and expertly packed by his soldiers into crates. The first lorry-load went off the next day, and two days later two more lorries were dispatched in the direction of Rome, with two monks riding in each. For the next ten days loaded lorries left Monte Cassino, generally accompanied by monks or nuns from the neighbourhood.

An American nun who worked in Rome at this time, and later published a diary under the pen-name Jane Scrivener had this to say on November 5th:

A tremendous propaganda effort is now being made regarding the art treasures and the archives of Monte Cassino. The Germans claim that they have put them in a secret place of safety and that by so doing they are the saviours of civilization, etc. etc. Some say Spoleto is the place. They brought most of the monks by car and lorry to Rome. . . .

All stages of the evacuation were filmed at length by German Army film units.

Schlegel must have handled his own part of the job well. The monks appear to have liked him to the end. One of them, after recording the grief and shock which they all felt during the evacuation, praises the Colonel for the tact with which he supervised it. 'He even,' says the monk, 'managed to eject from the Monastery, by means which might well be called energetic, a group of S.S. who had made their way in with the object of seizing men and chattels.'

At first the Germans wanted the Abbey completely evacuated, but later they agreed to the Abbot, five monks, and a small caretaker party remaining behind. Before leaving, Schlegel informed the Abbot that the Monastery itself would not be used as a strongpoint in the German defences.

There were great welcomes whenever the fugitives from Monte Cassino reached Rome, and their arrival was always faithfully recorded by the German film units. As he tearfully blessed group after group of his monks before they boarded the lorries taking them to what they regarded as exile, the Abbot would reassure them—as though he were speaking of only the day before yesterday—that this exile was not exceptional: it was, after all, only what had happened to their predecessors in the sixth century a few years after the death of St. Benedict. Their predecessors had returned after a while. So would they.

The Department of Archives, the Directorate-General of Antiquities and Fine Arts, the Academies and the Libraries, Crown Prince Umberto, and of course the Holy See itself all concerned themselves with the fate of the valuable cargoes from Monte Cassino and it seems just as well that they did. The crates were taken to Spoleto, where the Germans had a large ordnance dump, and there appears to have been no great eagerness to hand them over until the Vatican and the other authorities had been insisting for a long time. When, some weeks later, the handover did take place, there were several crates missing, and their contents were eventually recovered, during the closing stages of the war, in Germany.

Miss Scrivener might well write in her diary on December 10th:

Strangely enough the Germans have made good their boast about saving the treasures of the Abbey of Monte Cassino. It is difficult to understand their motives, after their wanton destruction of the great library at Naples. Anyway, here are the treasures . . . archives, manuscripts, books, pictures, engravings and illuminated missals . . . about a hundred thousand volumes in all, not counting the manuscripts. The sight was striking and picturesque when the long line of heavily laden lorries came down the Tiber embankment and passed beneath the battlemented walls of Castel Sant' Angelo through the gate into the court of the old fortress. German officials made a speech or two, somebody answered them on behalf of the Ministry of Education, and the transfer was accomplished. These precious things will be housed in the Vatican library as soon as it is convenient. . . .

The photographers and film men were there too. 'A tremendous effort of propaganda. . . .'

The caretaker party that remained behind with the Abbot consisted of five monks, all youngish men in their thirties: five lay brothers, also young, except for one who, like the Abbot

himself, was eighty: the priest director of the diocesan administrative office: a few laymen who acted as domestic servants. In
addition the Abbot was given permission to take in a number of
local peasant families, who were allowed to occupy the buildings
and outhouses. In all about 150 people initially made up this new
community, but before long the number began to grow, as
numerous refugees made their way to the monastery.

At the same time, the evacuation of Cassino town was completed. The few thousand Cassinese who, citizens of Cassino, had
stubbornly insisted on their right to stay there, were forced by
the Germans to leave. From the beginning of December the
Rapido, Cassino, Monastery Hill and the adjacent heights were
no longer respectively a river, a town, and a spur of the Abruzzi.
They were the raw material of a conspiracy between man and
nature aimed at devising a perfect and impregnable military
defensive system.

While the Abbot and his five monks tried to keep as far as
possible to their daily routines—with the added burden of looking
after the refugees—they could hear the muffled echoes of distant
explosions as houses in Cassino were blown up and converted
into strong-points; as demolitions and excavations were carried
out; as the waterways were diverted to create floods. Nearer at
hand, on the very hillside on which their Abbey stood, they
could watch the industrious working parties busily fortifying this
and the neighbouring heights.

There was one small consolation for what was now developing
into a nightmare of unreality. Early in December the Germans
told the Abbot that in order to preserve so notable a monument
from the ravages of war, they had established all round the Abbey
a neutral zone 300 metres wide and out of bounds to all military
personnel. To ensure that this area was kept clear, they had posted
a guard of three military policemen on the main gate, the only
entrance to the Monastery.

But early in January, as the rumble of Allied guns was heard
for the first time, this neutral zone was formally declared abolished.
By this time the Germans were getting down to business. The last

of the villages in the surrounding neighbourhood were being ruth-lessly cleared of their populations. The people who had taken refuge in and around the Abbey were now peremptorily ordered to be cleared out. Whatever fancy ideas about propaganda their High Command might have, it is clear from this change of attitude that the local commanders were less happy about declaring the Abbey a neutral vacuum while the great mountain on which it stood was be-ing fortified. The abolition of the neutral zone round the Monastery was the first move. The second was an order to the Abbot to get rid of the civilian refugees. These people were accordingly sent away, permission being obtained to keep there only three peasant families, all of whose members were ill. The next move was to suggest that the Abbot and his small remnant leave as well. This they refused to do. The Germans told them that in that case they could not accept any responsibility for their safety.

On January 15th the first Allied shells began to fall on Monastery Hill, and a few hit the Monastery buildings without causing much damage.

From this time on, the Monastery was cut off from the outside world. By now there remained only the Abbot and his five monks, the secular priest, the three sick peasant families, and—to add a final touch that was almost grotesque—a servant who was a deaf mute.

From the deep coffers of their faith, the Abbot and his five monks steeled themselves in the dark emptiness of the great Abbey to face a calamity which they did not even begin to comprehend.

II

THE FIRST BATTLE

'The first quality of a soldier is fortitude in enduring fatigue and hardship: bravery but the second. Poverty, hardship, misery are the school of the good soldier.' NAPOLEON

I

THE point to be stressed about the first battle of Cassino is that it was not a prepared offensive against the Gustav Line, but a hurried resumption of a weary advance that had battered its way to a standstill. Exhausted by weeks of heavy fighting, severe casualties, and appalling weather conditions, troops badly in need of a respite were, in effect, merely ordered to keep going. A plan was devised which looked coherent on paper. But the fact remains that the first assault on one of the most powerful defensive systems of the war was an *ad hoc* affair, hastily undertaken without anything like proper preparation.

This was not the fault of the local commanders. It was entirely due to the deadline imposed by the Anzio landing. Because of the shortage of landing-craft, and the schedules under which most of those available had to return to the United Kingdom, Anzio had to be fixed for January 22nd. As the operations on the main front had to precede it, and as Monte Trocchio wasn't captured until January 15th, it will be seen just how little time the unfortunate Fifth Army divisions had. Everything had to be geared to this problem of shipping. The beginning of Cassino was therefore simply a continuation of what had been going on for weeks, and it was undertaken in support of Anzio. Anzio was the star of the show, the great masterstroke that would change the course of the campaign. At Army level and above no one seems to have anticipated that there might be any difficulty about romping past Cassino into the Liri Valley and joining up with the triumphant beachhead a few days later. A Fifth Army Intelligence Summary on January 16th viewed the prospects in these terms:

Within the past few days there have been increasing indications that enemy strength on the front of the Fifth Army is ebbing due to casualties, exhaustion, and possibly lowering of morale. One of the causes of this condition, no doubt, has been the recent, continuous Allied attacks. From this it can be deduced that he has no fresh reserves and very few tired ones. His entire strength will probably be needed to defend his organized defensive positions.

In view of the weakening of enemy strength on the front as indicated above, it would appear doubtful if the enemy can hold the organized defensive line through Cassino against a coordinated army attack. Since this attack is to be launched before SHINGLE (the code name of the Anzio landing) it is considered likely that this additional threat will cause him to withdraw from his defensive position once he has appreciated the magnitude of that operation.

It is notorious that enemy strength and morale often seem weaker to observers at Army Headquarters than they do to the platoon commander in more active touch with them. Even so, the Intelligence Summary just quoted must surely take a prize as one of the most remarkable pieces of wishful deduction in the war.

Following the Christmas meetings with the Prime Minister, General Alexander had ordered Fifth Army 'to make as strong a thrust as possible towards Cassino and Frosinone shortly prior to the assault landing to draw in enemy reserves which might be employed against the landing forces: and then create a breach in his front through which every opportunity will be taken to link up rapidly with the seaborne operation'.

General Clark's plan to implement this directive was in four phases. On January 17th the British Tenth Corps would force a crossing of the Garigliano near the coast and turn inwards to threaten the left approaches to the Liri Valley. On the 20th the American Second Corps would force a crossing of the Rapido five miles south of Cassino, and break directly into the Liri Valley. Simultaneously the Free French Expeditionary Corps would continue a turning movement already in progress through the mountains on the right and corresponding to the British effort on the extreme left. Two days later, on the 22nd, the American Sixth Corps (1st British and 3rd American divisions) would land on Anzio beach about thirty-five miles south of Rome. Anzio was to be the trump: the other operations the means of making it possible by engaging the Germans fully and drawing their reserves to the main front at Cassino.

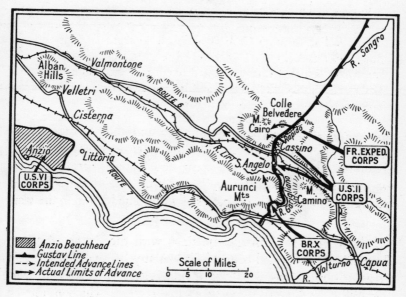

FIRST BATTLE

General offensive on main front combined with seaborne landing at Anzio

In the event the British on the left and the French on the right both achieved a limited success, but neither force was able to follow through decisively against the enemy flanks. But the key to the operation was what happened in the centre, where the Americans, having forced the Rapido, were expected to drive into the Liri Valley towards a link-up with the beachhead.

The battle of Cassino therefore began on the night of January 17th when, as a preliminary move, the British crossed the Garigliano: the main battle opened when the 36th (Texas)

Division of the United States Army splashed through flooded meadows, thickly sown with mines, to the River Rapido and a calamitous two days and nights which an American correspondent afterwards described, perhaps a little emotionally, as 'the biggest disaster to American arms since Pearl Harbour.'

There is an element of tragi-comedy about the manoeuvre of war known as the opposed river crossing. There is always something grotesque, if not pathetic, about the efforts of landsmen to handle boats. Even if this is being done under the most favourable conditions and in daylight, considerable difficulty and confusion can be expected. It requires no great feat of imagination to visualize what it must be like when the launching and manning of small boats has to be undertaken by amateur boatmen, not only weighed down by the boots and heavy equipment of the infantry, but at night and while being shot at. A night infantry assault is difficult enough without the journey having to be completed by boat; in boats, too, that have had to be carried down to the river by those who are to man them.

The boats themselves were no great help. They had to satisfy a number of conditions. They must be collapsible so as to be transportable by lorry in sufficient numbers: they must be light enough to be carried to the water's edge by the men who would be crossing in them: they must be sturdy enough to bear a load of six or seven heavily armed and equipped men. The compromise that resulted from these requirements was an ungainly flat-bottomed affair that barely lent itself to sailing on anything more formidable than a millpond in daylight, and was certainly not an ideal load for men to hump through the darkness (not to mention minefields) and launch satisfactorily while being shelled, mortared, and raked by machine-gun fire.

In addition to these canvas-and-wood assault boats, inflatable rubber dinghies were also used, but these—at the mercy of strong currents and amateur oarsmen—tended to be even more hazardous.

The organization of a river crossing varied in detail from one formation to another: divisions were constantly trying out new ways of making it less difficult: but the underlying principles were necessarily the same. The boats must in the first place be delivered by lorry to assembly areas as far forward as possible, but where cover would provide concealment. If, as in the case of the Rapido, the approach to the river was rather flat and open, the assembly areas would have to be some distance from the river. On the nights preceding the operation, the approaches to the river had to be thoroughly reconnoitred for crossing places and the best routes to them: these routes had to be cleared of mines, and lanes marked with white tape so that they could be identified in the dark. Guides had to familiarize themselves with the lanes and the crossing places so that the assaulting troops could concentrate on getting themselves and their boats to the river with the minimum of delay on the night.

Even when all this had been done with meticulous care over a period of several nights, the difficulty was still immense. Enemy patrols could slip across the river and lay more mines. Shelling could churn up the marked routes, destroying the tapes. Finally, it is not easy to carry cumbersome boats, in addition to arms and equipment, along slippery paths at night, and in silence.

Tactically it was necessary to carry out the crossing in normal battle formations so that when they disembarked units were for all practical purposes deployed and disposed exactly as if they had come all the way by land. This entailed a high degree of discipline, experience, teamwork, leadership, practice, and quick-wittedness. No soldier is likely to dispute the suggestion that the night crossing of an unfordable river against powerful defences is about as distasteful a manoeuvre as infantry are ever asked to undertake, and indeed only the most experienced formations have the slightest hope of accomplishing such an operation successfully; and these need to be rigorously practised in river crossing exercises shortly beforehand.

This was the task allotted the 36th (Texas) Division on January 20th. This was the main thrust designed to by-pass Cassino and break into the Liri Valley in conjunction with the Anzio landing.

Paradoxically it is easier to carry out such an operation over a wide river. If the river is wide, the vulnerable period of launching can be disposed of farther from the enemy. The width of the river will make it possible for the attackers' artillery to plaster the enemy bank during launching, and even for a part of the journey across. And it will be less easy for the enemy to detect what is going on and precisely where. The assembly dumps of the boats can be much nearer the river. The crossing of the Rhine, for example, was facilitated by the width of the river which made possible the maximum use of artillery, as well as amphibious armoured vehicles and rocket-projectors of a type that were not even available in Italy at this time. The Rapido was extremely difficult for just the opposite reason.

It is only sixty feet wide. Indeed, driving over it where it skirts Cassino, the peacetime motorist might well wonder if this could be the river there was so much fuss about.

The difficulty of the Rapido was threefold. Though narrow, it was nine feet deep: it had an eight miles an hour current: for most of its length in this particular reach it had vertical banks two to three feet above water level, an added disadvantage for launching.

The places chosen for the crossings were north and south of S. Angelo, a village built on a bluff forty feet high and dominating both reaches of the river where the crossings were to take place. The enemy positions, like those at Cassino, had been in preparation for weeks. They were dug into the bank of the river, and in the ditches and sunken lanes just beyond, and in the village itself. Many of them were shell-proof.

On the night of January 20th, at 2000 hours, the assault companies of two regiments (i.e. of six battalions) set off for the river with their boats. One regiment was detailed to cross north of S. Angelo, the other south of it. After securing their crossings, they were to converge on each other round the back of the village, pinching it out.

Continuous wet weather, assisted by the artificial flooding

carried out by the Germans, had reduced to marsh and mud the flat meadowland across which they had to advance. At the last minute the weather struck a final blow at the 36th Division: a thick fog developed shortly before the operation was due to begin.

As the leading troops groped towards the river a violent half-hour artillery bombardment hit the German positions in S. Angelo and along the river banks due to be attacked. Not for the first nor for the last time in this campaign, the attackers were to discover that sheer weight of shot and shell cannot by itself dislodge good soldiers who are dug into well-prepared positions. The bombardment bothered the Germans relatively little. They immediately started firing back, and the Americans were under heavy fire all the way to the river.

From the first they suffered heavy casualties from the enemy guns and mortars, and also from mines—for the preliminary clearing of routes through the minefields on the near side of the river had not been adequately carried out, and the tapes marking the lanes had been blasted away or buried by enemy shellfire. In one company the commander was killed, the second-in-command wounded, long before they reached the river. Shell fragments tore into many of the boats, rendering them useless. In the darkness and the fog guides lost their way; sub-units and individuals strayed from their formations and got lost; there were constant halts while desperate officers and N.C.O.s struggled to reorganize their groups and keep control over them. Many support groups lost those they had to support—a bridging party, for instance, was found hours later one and a half miles from the crossing site where they were supposed to go into action.

When the Americans reached the river, their own guns could no longer help to neutralize the Germans on the opposite bank as they were only sixty feet away. So they had to attempt the crossing without artillery support in the face of murderous direct fire from a skilfully dug-in enemy fully alerted by the noise of their confused approach, and able easily, despite fog and darkness, to pour fire into crossing places that they could identify by sound alone. Many boats were sunk as soon as they were launched; others went spinning downstream in the fast current; others capsized as men climbed into them under murderous fire.

Of the two regiments employed, the 141st, operating north of S. Angelo, were the more successful. By 2100 a few boatloads from two companies were across and attacking German positions. The Engineers began a night-long battle to erect footbridges on which the follow-up troops could race across. But of the bridges brought forward one was defective, one destroyed by mines, and enemy artillery fire knocked out the other two. Out of the remains of the four the Engineers, improvising gallantly under heavy fire, managed to assemble one bridge and get it across by 0400 and it survived just long enough to enable two more companies to cross. But by dawn there was no communication of any kind with the troops across the river—the life of a radio set is short in these circumstances—and only by the sound of firing had their senior commanders any idea of where they were or what progress they were making.

The 143rd Regiment, working south of S. Angelo, were initially more successful. They had men across shortly after 2000 and two footbridges were up before dawn, enabling the bulk of one battalion to make the crossing. But with the advent of daylight, and the area coming into view not only of the local observation posts but of Monte Cassino towering over the area even at a range of five miles, the bridges were quickly destroyed by the German guns, and the 143rd found themselves in a pocket, with their backs to the river, surrounded by German tanks and self-propelled guns. As the Germans began systematically to wipe out the American force, its commander asked permission to withdraw across the river. Permission was refused, but before the refusal reached him he ordered a withdrawal on his own responsibility. On the morning of the 21st, twelve hours after the battle had opened, there remained on the enemy side of the river only the remnants of the northern bridgehead force of the 141st: a handful of men from a single battalion, completely cut off from the rest of their division. All they could do was to huddle in what cover they could find, conserve their ammunition, and pray for survival until the next period of darkness in twelve hours' time.

Early in the day the Divisional Commander ordered the rest of the 141st to cross the river that afternoon under cover of a smokescreen. They were ordered to move at 1400 but it was 1600 before they were able to start. By 1830 they had a battalion over. A footbridge was erected and the Regiment's third battalion was across by midnight. During the night and early morning the 141st, with all three battalions across attempted to enlarge their bridgehead.

On the left the luckless 143rd who had withdrawn across the river that morning were again unsuccessful. At their second attempt to establish a bridgehead one battalion lost all their company commanders, the bridge they had erected, and all their boats. By noon of the third day, the 22nd, their remnants had been driven back across the river a second time—those, that is, who could swim.

For a time during the morning of the 22nd it seemed possible that the more successful 141st Regiment might be reinforced, and there was still the third regiment of the division in reserve. The morning was foggy and now the fog was on the side of the Americans, for it helped to mask their efforts to put up a Bailey bridge and so at last enable tanks to make the crossing. But the German artillery had the crossing place too well registered. The Bailey was never completed. By early afternoon, when the fog had cleared, all surviving boats, footbridges, and telephone wires were again quickly destroyed. Pockets of men held on for a time. Then the American volume of fire gradually died down. From this diminuendo of sound it became clear that they were running out of ammunition, although there were no wireless sets still working through which they could report this. By four that afternoon it was all over.

In an action lasting just under forty-eight hours the 36th Division had lost 1681 men, of whom the significantly high proportion of 875 were missing. As a fighting force the division was temporarily reduced to one regiment (the one that had been in reserve) and the badly-shaken remains of two others.

It would appear that this operation was badly mishandled by the Command and Staff of 36th Division. The American system of command at this time was much more rigid than the British. Operational plans were worked out in the fullest detail at divisional headquarters, and the regimental and battalion commanders had to follow implicitly the written orders issued to them. In the British Army a divisional commander, having allotted tasks and objectives to his brigade commanders, would allow them latitude in deciding how best to perform these tasks. The American subordinate commanders were not allowed this latitude. Everything was decided for them, and this added to their difficulties if things went wrong.

For the Rapido operation the regimental commanders were told by Division exactly how they were to handle their regiments —what battalions to employ, where their assembly positions were to be, their routes to the river, and their start-lines. Division's views on these matters were, to put it mildly, extraordinary. One regiment had a two-mile approach march to the river, the other had one mile to cover. They had to cross two hours after dark. This meant that their final preparations in the assembly areas had to be made in daylight. It would have been impossible for them not to be detected by the Germans, and of course they quickly were. They were under fire almost from the moment they moved forward.

The second mistake was that the near side of the bank was not properly cleared of mines. It couldn't be, with one regiment two miles, the other one mile back. The only way in which the cleared areas could have been kept clear of mines would have been to establish a holding force as near as possible to the river to do the clearing, and by their presence and patrolling ensure that the enemy did not slip across and upset these arrangements. This same force would also have provided a firm base through which the assault forces could pass on the night of the operation. It is an elementary rule of river crossing tactics that the first thing to be done is to establish a firm base as near the river as possible. On the occasion of the Rapido battle it was neglected. Right up to the battle the Germans were able to undo the mine-clearance carried out by the Americans.

A third error was the absence of any diversionary operation. It is obvious that a river crossing force is exceedingly vulnerable once it has been detected. It is essential that this vulnerability should be mitigated by the launching of at least one diversionary attack so that the enemy is prevented for as long as possible from knowing which is the real one.

The two regimental commanders who bore the burden of this operation could not help themselves. Their thinking had been done for them. They had merely to carry out an extremely difficult assignment, with little scope to influence the proceedings themselves, and it seems clear that their divisional staff had committed a number of elementary mistakes in planning the operation. For the Germans it was an easy thing. They knew where the crossings would take place; they knew the lines of approach that were going to be used; they knew when to expect the attack as they could see the final preparations in the assembly areas.

The Rapido disaster caused a great deal of bitterness among the men of the 36th Division, and they vented it against their Army Commander, General Clark. They considered that they had been unjustifiably expended in an operation in which they stood no chance. After the war the divisional association demanded a Congressional Enquiry into the battle. The Board of Enquiry completely vindicated Clark, and it is difficult to see how he could possibly be blamed for the execution of an operation that was merely part of a larger design imposed on him from above. The operation was a difficult one but not impossible. A successful opposed crossing of the Garigliano had been carried out only three nights before by the British Tenth Corps a few miles away. To get the Rapido affair into perspective it is necessary to remember that these American divisions in Italy were still relatively inexperienced in battle and this was an occasion when some sharp lessons were learned the hard way—as British divisions had had to learn them in the Desert three years previously.

In the early hours of January 22nd, as the last desperate efforts were being made on the Rapido, an armada of more than 200 ships—including the precious and elusive landing-craft—dropped anchor off Anzio, and the first of the assault boats moved silently into the beaches.

2

THE full story of Anzio, which was originally conceived as a minor landing behind the enemy lines but evolved through many ups and downs into a separate Italian front of major importance, needs a history to itself. Within the scope of the present work it is possible only to summarize the main events and their significance in so far as they affected the main front at Cassino.

As we have seen, the decision to undertake this long-contemplated landing was made at the Christmas conferences between Mr. Churchill and Generals Eisenhower and Alexander. It was Churchill's plan to end the costly deadlock into which the Italian campaign was drifting, and vindicate his 'soft underbelly' strategy which the Americans had disliked in the first place and were now liking still less after the expensive unproductive battles of the preceding three months.

It was a gamble, but it was the only means of turning the German flank. It was the only hope of a more conclusive development of the campaign. But it was also a personal affair, a determined effort by Mr. Churchill to fight for his baby—the strategy which had taken the war into Italy. Hence the energy with which he flung himself into the Christmas conferences, over-riding the scepticism that some of those present felt about the project.

'In the case of Anzio,' General Clark has written, 'political rather than military considerations dominated the decision made at Tunis. . . . On Christmas Day the decision had already been made at Churchill's insistence, as I understood it, before the Prime Minister turned to the Chief of Intelligence of Allied Force

Headquarters and said, "Now we'll hear the seamy side of the question." The G-2 of A.F.H.Q., Brigadier Kenneth Strong, was sceptical of the advisability of the operation. . . . In spite of all this Churchill was ready to accept the obvious hazards of the landing because the prize to be gained by seizing Rome justified a calculated risk.'

Anzio was a Churchillian enterprise.

'It was with tense, but I trust suppressed, excitement,' Mr. Churchill wrote, 'that I awaited the outcome of this considerable stroke. To Stalin I telegraphed: "We have launched the big attack against Rome which I told you about at Teheran. The weather conditions seem favourable. I hope to have good news for you before long".'

At 0200 on January 22nd the United States Sixth Corps under General Lucas landed at Anzio—the 3rd U.S. Division south of the port, the 1st British Division north of it. To their astonishment they met practically no opposition. Two hundred men of a couple of depleted battalions, resting after a gruelling on the Cassino front, were captured in their night clothes, and that was about the extent of the earliest opposition. By midnight 36,000 men and 3000 vehicles had been landed.

'We appear,' reported Alexander, 'to have got almost complete surprise. I have stressed the importance of strong-hitting mobile patrols being boldly pushed out to gain contact with the enemy.'

To this signal the Prime Minister replied:

'Am very glad you are pegging out claims rather than digging in beachheads.'

'But now,' continues Churchill, 'came disaster, and the ruin in its prime purpose of the enterprise. General Lucas confined himself to occupying his beachhead and having equipment and vehicles brought ashore. . . . No general attempt to advance was made by the commander of the expedition. By the evening of the 23rd (i.e. thirty-six hours after the first landing) the whole of two divisions and their attached troops, including two British commandos, the United States Rangers, and parachutists, had

been landed with masses of impedimenta. The defences of the
beachhead were growing, but the opportunity for which great
exertions had been made was gone.'

The German reaction, as always, was brisk. Without withdrawing any troops from the Cassino front, Kesselring dispatched
everything available to contain the beachhead while a major
force could be sent to the scene. This force soon began to
materialize, thanks to a defensive procedure that had been prepared for just such a contingency.

Realizing the futility of attempting to defend every beach on
Italy's long coastline where the Allies might attempt a landing,
the German Command had issued a comprehensive emergency
plan to cover the whole of the country. In it was laid down what
troops should move against the possible landing points, as soon
as a landing had occurred: on what roads and at what times they
should move: and what tasks they should undertake. It was only
necessary to issue a code-word to put these pre-arranged plans
into operation. To provide the troops for such operations, every
division in the country had to earmark a special mobile force—
usually drawn from its reconnaissance and light armoured
element—which was permanently at one hour's notice to rush
to the threatened area wherever it might happen to be.

This was why there were no substantial forces at Anzio on the
22nd, and why, without weakening the Cassino front as the Allies
had counted on their doing, the Germans were quickly able to
call out the fire brigade, as it were, and contain the beachhead
after it had made its first penetration of about seven miles over an
area some fifteen miles wide. On the 25th Alexander reported
that the beachhead was reasonably secure, but that neither he nor
General Clark was satisfied with the rate of advance, and that
Clark was going to the beachhead at once. To this Churchill
replied: 'I am glad to learn that Clark is going to visit the beachhead. It would be unpleasant if your troops were sealed off there
and the main army could not advance up from the south.'

'This, however,' adds Churchill, 'was exactly what was going
to happen.'

By the end of seven days the Allies had four divisions ashore, and the beachhead was eight miles deep and on a continuous front fifteen miles wide. But by this time elements of eight German divisions faced them, and every square yard of the beachhead was under enemy shell-fire.

Churchill's bitterness was reflected in his cables to General Wilson, C.-in-C. Mediterranean, who cabled back that 'Though General Lucas had achieved surprise he had failed to take advantage of it. This was due to his "Salerno Complex"—that as a prelude to success the first task was to repel the inevitable counter-attack.' General Wilson added that there had been no lack of urging from both Alexander and Clark in the first two days after the landing.

To this Churchill replied: 'My comment is that senior commanders should not "urge" but "order".' Later he made this point again in a cable to Alexander:

I have a feeling that you may have hesitated to assert your authority because you were dealing so largely with Americans and therefore *urged* an advance instead of *ordering* it. You are however quite entitled to give them orders, and I have it from the highest American authorities that it is their wish that their troops should receive direct orders. They say their Army has been framed more on Prussian lines than on the more smooth British lines, and that American commanders expect to receive positive orders, which they will immediately obey. Do not hesitate therefore to give orders just as you would to our own men. The Americans are very good to work with, and quite prepared to take the rough with the smooth.

Alexander replied on February 11th:

The first phase of operations, which started so full of promise, has now just passed, owing to the enemy's ability to concentrate so quickly sufficient force to stabilise what was to him a very serious situation. . . .

This exchange of signals in the first fortnight of the Anzio operation sums up Mr. Churchill's optimistic view of what should have happened, and his disappointment at what did. It was his opinion that a great opportunity had been thrown away.

Now consider the same events through the eyes of the most reliable man on the spot, the American General Lucien Truscott, who commanded the U.S. 3rd Division at Anzio until he was promoted to supersede General Lucas as beachhead force commander three weeks later.

Most British generals who came into contact with him rated Truscott the best American general in Italy. He was a blunt and forthright practical soldier with no time for frills, and in his judgments, both of his compatriots and his allies, Truscott was always outspoken. This is confirmed by all who had personal dealings with him during the campaign. It is self-evident in the memoirs (*Command Missions*) which he published after the war and which contain the most authoritative and balanced account of the Anzio operation.

This is what Truscott has to say.

I suppose that arm chair strategists will always labour under the delusion that there was a 'fleeting opportunity' at Anzio during which some Napoleonic figure would have charged over the Colli Laziali (Alban Hills), played havoc with the German line of Communications, and galloped on into Rome. Any such concept betrays lack of comprehension of the military problem involved. It was necessary to occupy the Corps Beachhead Line to prevent the enemy from interfering with the beaches. Otherwise, enemy artillery and armoured detachments operating against the flanks could have cut us off from the beach and prevented the unloading of troops, supplies, and equipment. As it was, the Corps Beachhead Line was barely distant enough to prevent direct artillery fire on the beaches.

On January 24th (i.e. on D+2) my division, with three Ranger battalions and the 504th Parachute Regiment attached, was extended on the Corps Beachhead Line over a front of twenty miles. . . . Two brigade groups of the British 1st Division held a front of more than seven miles. . . . We were in contact with German detachments with tanks and self-propelled artillery everywhere along the front. We knew that there had been a German division south of Rome and at least one other in easy reach . . . and we knew that the attempt to cross the Rapido River had ended in failure. Under such conditions, any reckless drive to seize the Colli Laziali with means then available in the beachhead could only have ended in disaster and might well have resulted in destruction of the entire force.

One must admit, I think, that the initial strategic concept erred in two respects: overestimating the effect that the landings would have upon the German High Command; and underrating the German capacity for countering this move. Our own High Command expected—or at least hoped—the landings would cause a hasty German withdrawal from the Cassino front. None of the commanders who landed at Anzio held any such belief, and we had learned through experience to respect the resourcefulness of our German opponent. Any reckless advance to the Colli Laziali without first establishing a firm base to protect our beaches would have been sheer madness and would almost certainly have resulted in the eventual destruction of the landing forces. Field Marshal Kesselring, the German commander, remarked to the Associated Press correspondent, Daniel De Luce, in an interview in January 1946: 'It would have been the Anglo-American doom to over-extend themselves. The landing force was initially weak, only a division or so of infantry, and without armour. It was a half-way measure as an offensive that was your basic error.'

It should be emphasized that Truscott had no personal axe to grind in committing himself to this view. From a personal standpoint he emerged from Anzio with nothing but credit. He landed as a divisional commander, and was therefore in no way responsible for the progress of the operation as a whole. Within a month he had been chosen to replace General Lucas as beachhead commander. Churchill, referring to this, said: 'Truscott, a young American divisional commander, whom everyone speaks of most highly, has now superseded Lucas.'

During the next few weeks Truscott proved himself a brilliant and successful commander. There was no reason for him to justify the policy which had cost his predecessor his job unless he sincerely meant it. It seems reasonable to accept his version of events as the view of a reliable military witness who was, after all, on the spot all the time. (It is a significant fact that the most outspoken critics of the Italian campaign—including Churchill— never saw the battlefields.)

A final answer to the Anzio critics was contained in Alexander's dispatch of March 5th, six weeks after the landing:

> From various reports I have read from home it appears that public opinion imagines that after the initial landing no effort was made to advance further. This is most distressing to me and the troops. Reference should be made to the many casualties sustained by the British in taking Campoleone where they were finally held at the foot of the Colli Laziali, and also the losses suffered by the Americans in trying to take Cisterna, where all attacks failed. After this, superior German forces attacked us in strength and threw us on to the defensive and we had a bitter struggle to maintain the bridgehead intact after being driven back from Campoleone. A man may enter the backdoor of a house unperceived save by the kitchenmaid who raises the alarm. But unless the inhabitants hide upstairs there will be a fight in the passage for possession of the house. We are now fighting in that passage.

From this it would seem to emerge that in his views on Anzio, the Prime Minister's temperament outweighed his judgment. His greatness as a war leader is unquestioned and it would surely be doing his reputation a disservice to ignore the possibility that like other human beings he could sometimes be subject to error.

One of Mr. Churchill's idiosyncrasies is known to have been a temperamental allergy to orthodox military men. He became impatient when the generals pointed out the practical aspects of any scheme on which he had set his heart. He had a strong buccaneering streak in him, which tended to favour irregulars —commandos, special forces, and their like—and was quick to assume that more orthodox commanders were unnecessarily making difficulties.

One recalls his singling out of the eccentric and difficult Wingate to take with him to Quebec to expound to the American President how the war in Burma should be won: yet by the war's end he had never met General Slim, the excellent orthodox general who in the end won the Burma campaign—on which Wingate's influence, viewed retrospectively, is seen to have been important but not decisive.

The conferences which preceded Anzio provide further examples of this attitude. During the one at which the detailed operational plans were concluded, the American commanders quite rightly insisted that it would be madness to undertake the landing without a full rehearsal. Time, however, was short and Churchill argued that a rehearsal was unnecessary. One of the Fifth Army staff officers who was present recorded that the Prime Minister maintained that all the troops were trained and needed no rehearsal. 'One experienced officer or non-commissioned officer in a platoon was sufficient.' Of course this was nonsense. Of all operations, an assault landing particularly requires most elaborate rehearsal. In the end they did have a rehearsal and it seems to have been a good thing that they did. It was an unmitigated disaster. No one reached the right beach. Quantities of equipment were lost in the sea.

Admittedly it is the duty of a war leader to chivvy his commanders and attempt to control the tendency of many generals to plan for every conceivable contingency when speed and boldness are called for. But there has to be a compromise between forceful leadership and acceptance of practicalities: especially such practicalities as the Italian winter, the Italian terrain, the tiredness of overworked troops, and the expertise of the German soldier.

In addition to marching on its stomach, a modern army marches on its petrol, oil, wireless batteries, spare parts, and technical facilities. The disposal of a sufficiency of these things to maintain 70,000 men in combat within a few days of landing on an open stretch of sand is a not inconsiderable task.

But the building up of supplies can be overdone, and it was at this time a weakness of American military planning—due perhaps to an instinctive admiration of abundance for its own sake—to over-estimate material requirements. The impression that the

American army had a jeep for every three men was not entirely based on the envy of America's less generously endowed Allies. Churchill undoubtedly scored a shrewd point in his Anzio case when on February 8th he demanded an exact statement of the number of vehicles landed by the 7th and 14th days, not including the 4,000 supply trucks which travelled to and fro in the landing-craft in order to arrive fully loaded and so save time in the ships' turn-round.

The answer was revealing. By the seventh day 12,350 vehicles had been landed, including 356 tanks: by the fourteenth day 21,940 vehicles, including 380 tanks. This meant that nearly 18,000 vehicles (exclusive of tanks) had been landed in the beach-head by the fourteenth day to serve a total force of 70,000 men.

This information produced from the Prime Minister one of his best combinations of the humorous and the pertinent:

'How many of our men are driving or looking after 18,000 vehicles in this narrow space?' he demanded. 'We must have a great superiority of chauffeurs. I am shocked that the enemy have more infantry than we. . . .'

There is little doubt that General Lucas, an excessively cautious man, was an unsuitable choice to command an expedition that called for dynamic leadership. It is possible that a bolder commander might have made more of the lack of opposition in the vital early hours of the landing, and, by resolute exploitation, extended the original boundaries of the beachhead and caused the enemy greater alarm and despondency.

Lucas fell out with his British divisional commander, dug in his heels, and stayed put with the persistence of the Athenian Nicias who made a name for hesitancy in the Peloponnesian war. A British general, Major-General V. Evelegh, was sent to Anzio with the deliberately nebulous title of 'assistant to the Beachhead Commander' to help straighten things out, and shortly afterwards Lucas was replaced by the able Truscott.

Even so, it is clear, if one accepts the views of the men on the spot (who alone can know what all the factors are), that there was never any question of immediately pushing on to the Alban Hills and Rome. Had this been attempted the force would undoubtedly have been destroyed, or driven back to the sea.

The opening phase of Anzio—the landing and its immediate exploitation—can therefore be summarized as follows.

It was in the first instance a political gamble hustled into effect by the Prime Minister to justify his strategic decision to take the war into Italy.

It was unavoidably launched at the worst time of year from a fighting point of view because it had to conform with the limited availability of shipping.

It over-estimated the consternation that a landing in their rear would cause the Germans—overlooking the fact that another army of eight divisions was uncommitted between Rome and the north. Mark Clark, for instance, told Truscott that if the force merely held a beachhead at Anzio, he believed that it would cause the Germans so much concern that they would withdraw from the southern front.

It underestimated the strength of the defences at Cassino in its assumption that relatively small forces could break through there.

It erred on the side of caution in giving initial priority to a supply build-up against counter-attack instead of allowing for an early landing of elements (e.g. light armoured forces) that could have exploited the immediate landing more rapidly.

On the other hand it must be said in favour of the unfortunate General Lucas that his much-criticized build-up against counter-attack paid off handsomely when the Germans eventually launched a series of tremendous counter blows.

In so far as it affected Cassino there are two points that need to be grasped about the opening stages of Anzio. First, it was primarily a political move initiated by Churchill with some intolerance of the military difficulties pointed out to him by the men who had to execute it. Secondly, the failure of the Germans to oblige by withdrawing from the Cassino front to meet the new threat undermined at the very start the whole basis on which the project was founded.

3

ON the main front—the attempt to force the Rapido and by-pass Cassino five miles to the south having failed— General Clark ordered the same corps, the U.S. Second, to try to pinch out the town from the north with its other infantry division, the 34th. The new battle began on January 24th —two days after the Rapido debacle and the landing at Anzio, where unloading and consolidation were making progress in spite of gales, increasing German counter-strength, and a renascent Luftwaffe which had come out of hiding to deliver some sharp blows, including the destruction of a hospital ship and a destroyer.

The only advantage the 34th had over the luckless 36th was that they were spared the boating. North of Highway Six, the Rapido is fordable. This single factor apart, the task was as difficult, if not more so. A dam blown by the enemy in the upper reaches of the river had achieved its greatest flooding effect in the section of the valley the 34th must cross. They were faced with the prospect of traversing a plain that was little less than a quagmire, and likely to be impossible for tanks. On the far side of the river they had to meet not only prepared positions, wire, and extensive minefields, but the great wall of mountains rising, almost vertically, immediately behind the river, and running southwards in a tight mass to Monte Cassino a mile and a half to their left. They would have to cross two miles of marsh, wade an icy river, and then attack the mountains head-on, while a comfortably entrenched enemy, watching them all the way across from a score of vantage points, could pick them off as he pleased.

It was the 34th, slithering across the flooded valley, who first experienced the uncanny and daunting sensation that every peak

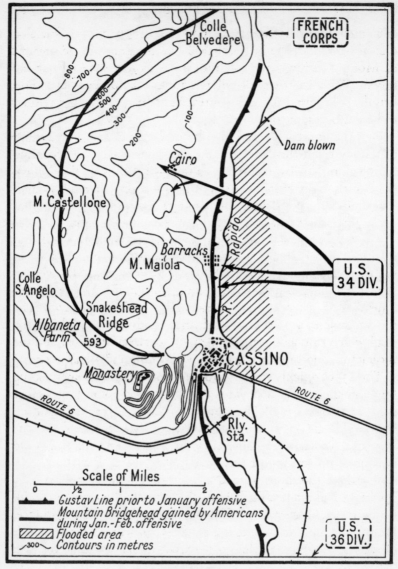

UPPER RAPIDO BRIDGEHEAD

Mountain salient gained by U.S. 34th Div. and subsequently the spring-board
for successive Allied attacks

contained eyes that were watching their every move: but that one in particular, the huge barrack-like building on the summit of Monte Cassino, was watching more closely than any of the others. With its rows of cell windows, its immense brooding length dark with rain, and its great battlemented base, it seemed to be daring them to come on.

First the approach across the flooded valley, then the wading of the icy river, then the pillboxes, dugouts, caves, and fortified houses along the lower slopes, and then—if they lived that long— they must fight their way up the mountains themselves and, wheeling left, bear *down* on Monte Cassino from the higher peaks around it: that was the task of the 34th Division.

They were given as their preliminary objectives two knolls and a large Italian barracks at the foot of the mountains. As soon as the 133rd Regiment had seized these objectives, the 168th were to pass through them and start the long climb, with Monte Castellone, Colle S. Angelo, and Albaneta Farm as their objectives. The third regiment, the 135th, would strike southwards and down the road which runs alongside the Rapido, between the river and the mountains, and capture Cassino town, a mile and a half away.

The 133rd quickly ran into trouble, one battalion being held up by a minefield only 200 yards past their start-point, long before they reached the river. The other two battalions reached the river but could not cross it in the face of heavy fire from the Barracks. Tanks were helpless on the muddy ground and could not move up to support the renewed attacks at dawn.

The three battalions pegged away throughout the 25th and by midnight had made a small bridgehead across the river, but with heavy losses, as the tanks still could not come to their assistance. During the night one company of the Regiment detailed to drive down the road into Cassino town reached the outskirts, but was pushed back.

On the next morning, the 26th, the attacks were again resumed but still without tanks. By now every battalion had lost more than a hundred men. On the morning of the 27th another attack was put in, the 168th regiment being ordered to pass through the

133rd, whose small bridgehead was the sole reward of three nights and days of fighting. Once again tanks tried to force their way across, and at long last four were over by 0930. But another squadron following them got bogged down and blocked the route, so that no more could follow, and by midday the four that were across had been knocked out. In the few hours that they survived they had succeeded in smashing a way through quantities of wire and fields of anti-personnel mines, and with their aid the infantry were able to widen their bridgehead and consolidate their scanty gains.

Meanwhile engineers worked desperately under heavy fire to make tank lanes across the mud with strips of wire matting used by the air forces for the construction of temporary landing strips on soft ground.

During the night the infantry made further small gains but still the minor hillocks that were only the first of their objectives were not yet taken, and they had to hang on to what they had got throughout the 28th, while the engineers were completing the tank tracks.

On the 29th the tracks were ready, tanks were able to cross in strength and with their aid the infantry reached the base of the two elusive hillocks, Points 56 and 213, and during the night both were captured. On the 30th they consolidated their gains, repelled counter-attacks, and on the 31st captured Cairo village, strategically situated in a defile leading up to Monte Cairo. As a bonus they captured, in addition to a large number of other prisoners, the headquarters of the 131st Grenadier Regiment, who for a week had caused them so much trouble.

It had taken eight days to gain this bridgehead, a small nibble into the mountain wall, and secure a gateway into the hills. But the worst was still to come. Now they had to force their way up these huge bare mountainsides, turn southwards, and fight towards Cassino along the mountain tops.

While the 34th had been fighting for their bridgehead in the waterlogged valley, the two divisions of the French Expeditionary

Corps two miles to the north were ordered to swing south-west and press hard on the right of the Americans so as to turn if possible the German flank between the mountain village of Terelle and the Rapido. On the morning of the 25th General Juin carried out a swift attack and on the 26th captured the two mountains, Abate and Belvedere. The Germans recaptured Abate on the 27th, but the French held on to Belvedere, despite furious counter-attacks thrown in by the Germans to arrest a movement which threatened to turn the left flank of the Gustav Line. To try to sustain the momentum of this turning movement the American Corps Commander sent the 142nd Regiment of the 36th Division (the regiment of this division that had not been committed during the Rapido crossing) to the French sector to form up between the French and the 34th, and cut down through the mountains on the right of the 34th, now ready to make their southward thrust towards Cassino and Highway Six through the mountains. A division, had it been available, might have succeeded. A regiment was not enough.

By January 31st the French were consolidated in a position from which they could no longer advance but which constituted a dagger in the flank of the German defence system. On the extreme left, near the sea, the British Tenth Corps, after a fort-night's hard fight to expand their bridgehead over the Garigliano had come to a halt, but threatened the German right as the French did their left. The 34th, with the single regiment of the 36th on their right, prepared to sustain the burden a little longer and make a positive and final attack on Cassino and its protective mountains.

These heights continue indefinitely from Cassino to the mountainous backbone running down the centre of the country, but the spur which provided the core of the natural (as well as German) defensive system protecting the road to Rome extended two miles west and about three miles north of Cassino. It was on the dozen or so peaks of this area, on a score of precipitous ledges and rocky saddles, on the slopes of the ravines, among the boulders of a barren volcanic wasteland that might have been a giants' graveyard, that the battle of Cassino was now to enter a new phase. The 34th, supported by the depleted 36th who had been placed under their command, were to be the first of many to take on a battlefield where Nature was as formidable an enemy as the opposing army.

Behind the town was Monte Cassino. Linked with Monte Cassino by a low saddle was Point 593: close to 593 was 569: to the west of 569 was Colle S. Angelo: between and around them were many smaller heights. Each of these features was so placed that it could be supported by fire from all of the others. Together they formed a coordinated line running parallel with, and overlooking, the main road after it has skirted the base of Monte Cassino and is running along the Liri Valley. To break through to the road it was necessary to force a way through these mountains, and as soon as one was reached fire from all the others could pour down on it. This was what the Americans were now about to attempt—by working up and along the two long mountains, Maiola and Castellone, towards the line of peaks running across at right angles from Monte Cassino to Colle S. Angelo.

The mountains were rocky, strewn with boulders and gorse thickets, laced with ravines and gullies on which you would come suddenly: and where there had been clumps of trees there were by this time only stumps blasted by shellfire. Digging was out of the question on these hard volcanic slopes. Only the Germans— who had had three months in which to blast holes in the rock, enlarge existing caves, and dynamite new ones—could man their guns in secure cover. The attackers in this country would have to forget about their spades, and rely for cover on the loose stones they could scrape together with their bare hands, and build into some kind of breastwork. There were no paths, only goat tracks, and all supplies would have to be brought up by mules. Not the least of the difficulties was that the line of advance, from north to south, would henceforth be at right angles to the line of fire of the Allied artillery. This made the task of giving close artillery support difficult and dangerous.

In the course of the next ten days the 34th made three major attempts to break through these mountains to the road, while one of their regiments, operating down the secondary road at the foot of the mountains attempted to force its way into Cassino itself.

This was the period when the news bulletins reported each day that patrols had reached Cassino, that the fall of the town was imminent, that the Americans were in the outskirts and so on. What was not appreciated was that in this particular country and defensive layout it would be possible to remain in the outskirts of Cassino indefinitely.

First the large hill masses of Maiola and Castellone were captured, and fighting their way forward foot by foot along the bare hillsides the 34th found themselves within 1,000 yards of the Monastery, 800 yards from Point 593, and a little farther from Colle S. Angelo. It seemed that they had not far to go now. But these interlocking positions were to prove impassable.

Working painfully along a ridge which, from its shape on the map, they called Snakeshead, they secured a foothold on 593. But it was only a foothold. The Germans, so far from withdrawing troops from this front to operate at Anzio, were reinforcing hard, and the Americans had to resist some fierce counter-attacks.

Between the 4th and 7th of February one battalion reached Colle S. Angelo, but was thrown off it. Another reached 445, a round-topped hill immediately below the Monastery, and not more than 400 yards from it, but their effort to take Monte Cassino itself from this point was broken by overwhelming machine-gun fire from the slopes below the Monastery.

Gradually it was dawning on the men fighting in those mountains that the key to the position was this Monastery Hill rather than the town of Cassino. Monastery Hill, commanding both valleys, protected on its northern side by a ravine, and on the west side by 593 and 569—hills known only by their surveyed heights on the map in metres but whose numerical designations were becoming more familiar than place-names. The reports they sent back now had a fixed refrain. 'The centre of resistance is Monte Cassino.'

Day after day, night after night, the Americans clung miserably to their bare slopes, and tried to inch forward. The slopes were becoming littered with dead that could not be removed in daylight, let alone buried. Platoons became reduced to small groups, numbed with cold and fatigue and exposure, hardly able to move but obstinately clinging to the positions they held.

At the end of January General Alexander had brought over the 2nd New Zealand Division and the 4th Indian Division from 8th Army, formed them into the 2nd New Zealand Corps under Lieutenant-General Sir Bernard Freyberg, V.C., and ordered them to be ready to follow up if the Americans succeeded in a last attempt to break through to the main road, Highway Six, only a mile away through the mountains.

Between February 8th and 11th the Americans made their last efforts to storm Monastery Hill and Cassino town, and the newly-formed New Zealand Corps stood by to exploit their success, if any.

The comments of General Kippenberger, commander of the 2nd New Zealand Division, illuminate this last gallant effort of exhausted men to continue beyond their powers of endurance.

'I attended with General Freyberg,' wrote Kippenberger, 'at a Corps conference where we were told that the American 36th Division was to join the 34th and deliver another attack on Cassino Abbey from the high ground north of the town. I told the General that the American infantry was worn out and quite unfit for battle without a thorough rest. He was disturbed and questioned the American commanders closely as to the condition of their troops and it was very plain that none of them had been forward or was at all in touch with his men.'

Nevertheless the attack was ordered to proceed and the New Zealand Corps made the necessary preparations to exploit it if it succeeded. Kippenberger continues:

'There was heavy rain all day, the attack failed as almost every-one expected, and we cancelled our own project. . . . The

Americans had battled since January with a stubbornness and gallantry beyond all praise, but they were fought out. Some of the eighteen battalions in the line had lost 80 per cent of their effectives and they were utterly exhausted. . . .'

The performance of the 34th Division at Cassino must rank with the finest feats of arms carried out by any soldiers during the war. When at last they were relieved by the 4th Indian Division fifty of those few who had held on to the last were too numbed with cold and exhaustion to move. They could still man their positions but they could not move out of them unaided. They were carried out on stretchers, and it was one of the final cruelties of this battle that some of them, having survived so much, were killed on their stretchers by shellfire on the long, tortuous way down to safety.

They had earned the praise which for soldiers is the best to receive—that of other soldiers who have moved in to relieve them and who alone can see at first hand what they have done, what they have endured. It was the British and Indian soldiers of the 4th Indian Division, moving in to relieve them, who proclaimed the achievement of the Americans the loudest.

Three years after the end of the war a party of British officers were walking over these same mountains, studying the battle of Cassino as a military exercise under the direction of officers who had fought there. As they clambered over the rocks, incredulous that anything resembling organized warfare had been waged there, they came at one point upon a grim sight. Crouched against some rocks, in the position in which an infantryman would take guard with his rifle, they found a human skeleton. At its side were the rusted remains of a rifle and steel helmet, both identifiable as American. It seemed a final comment on the endurance of the 34th U.S. Division and the men of the 36th who shared their ordeal in the later stages of the battle.

Fighting from their prepared positions, the Germans had won the first round. Before the final American attacks were over it became known in more detail just how prepared those positions were. A French soldier, captured during General Juin's great battle for Colle Belvedere, was with other prisoners made to work as an ammunition carrier by his captors. On February 4th, during an American artillery bombardment which sent his guards running for cover, he escaped. He brought back this information about the positions with which he had become familiar during the eight days of his captivity.

Along the ridges north and west of the Abbey (Points 444, 593, 569, Colle S. Angelo) there were machine-gun emplacements shielded on both sides and on top by armour plate, and with sandbags at their front and back. There were mortars at the crest of some ridges, camouflaged and protected by logs. (These weapons are normally sited in deep gullies or behind shelves of rock where they can make use of their high-angle firing to clear the obstruction, while remaining behind deep cover themselves.) The mortar crews of three men were dug in. The soldier reported that the artillery had little or no effect on enemy bunkers blasted and drilled into the rock, and protected by layers of logs and crushed stone, but it did cause casualties to troops in the less elaborate emplacements.

One of the Germans' most successful weapons was the *nebelwerfer*, a six-barrelled mortar which could fire six bombs simultaneously. In flight, these clusters of bombs emitted a distinctive cross between a shriek and a whine that added considerably to the effect they had on the nerves awaiting them at the receiving end. The *nebelwerfers*, shaped like small cannon, were deeply dug into the hillside, with clearance space for their projectiles cut out of the slope. The observer directing their fire was also provided with a deep hole, and did his observing through a narrow notch chipped out of the rock.

These were the defences which the Americans, and later many others, had to assault from positions that were not prepared because such field works can only be carried out with explosives and engineering equipment at a time when the enemy is not in residence a few hundred yards away. The Germans had had three months in which to do this.

Other new weapon developments were introduced by the

Germans at this time. A mortar bomb which burst just above ground after bouncing, so that its killing and wounding range was considerably increased. There was a development too in the construction of anti-personnel mines. Wooden mines were being used in increasing numbers, notably the unpleasant *schu* mine, the explosive being contained in a small wooden box which exploded when stepped on, blowing off the foot. The point about these wooden mines was that they could not be located by detectors. Mines were one of the most devastating features of the German defences at Cassino. When the Americans crossed the Upper Rapido they faced a minefield two miles long.

Another development was a portable pillbox, designed to contain a machine-gun and crew. The armour was five inches thick. The pillbox could be moved from place to place on a small wheeled structure drawn by a tractor.

For the Allies it was becoming harder all the time, and those who followed the Americans would find these defences not softened by the first assaults but strengthened, for in a battle of this kind the defender is able to add a little here, a little there, to his defences every night he is not under attack. A little more wire, a few more mines, some extra protection for that parapet which did not stand up too well to the night before last's shelling, a few more trip wires arranged to explode flares or small minefields when the attacker approached. Every night the defender can add to his strength, for he has nothing else to do or think about: every night he can build up his supplies of ammunition and food and comforts while he waits for the other side to make a move. For the Allies, whose forward base was still forced to remain on the far side of the Rapido valley, the problem was the very opposite. Every precious round of ammunition had to be carried by mule or men for several miles. Without the freedom to use explosives to blast trenches in their recently won positions in the mountains, they must start short, and replenish with difficulty as they went on. But for the well-established defenders there would always be an abundance of both ammunition and protective covering. Their problem was merely to stay there.

But if the Germans had won the first round it had not been a
picnic. Some of their companies had suffered 75 per cent casualties.
An N.C.O. in the mountains had the following entries in his
diary covering the period January 22nd—the Saturday the 36th
Division's Rapido ordeal ended—to January 27th when the 34th
Division's battle across the valley was four days old, and not going
too well.

Jan: 22. I am done. The artillery fire is driving me crazy. I am
frightened as never before and cold. During the day one cannot
leave one's hole. These last days have finished me off altogether. I
am in need of someone to hold on to.

Jan: 25. I am becoming a pessimist. The Tommies write in their
leaflets that the choice is ours, Tunis or Stalingrad. We are on
half-rations. No mail. Teddy is a prisoner. I see myself one very
soon.

Jan: 27. The lice are getting the better of us. I do not care any
longer. Rations are getting shorter—fifteen men, three loaves of
bread, no hot meals. They say we are to be relieved by some mountain troops. My laundry bag has been looted. Now ten men one
loaf of bread.

January had been no fun for the Germans either.

So ended—in another blizzard—the first battle of Cassino after
three weeks' fighting. From the first the offensive had never been
powerful enough to overcome the exceptional defences it had to
meet. It had been prematurely launched to support the Anzio
landing. It was an attempt to rush Cassino with a series of attacks
that were never overwhelming enough at one point. When the
hopes on which Anzio had been based proved to have been too
optimistic, each separate thrust spent itself alone.

By the end of the battle the British corps on the far left had
lost over 4,000 men among the three divisions, and had only a
close bridgehead over the Garigliano to show for it: the mountains
beyond had frustrated their plan to push on towards the southern
side of the Liri Valley.

The two divisions of the French corps on the far right had
spent themselves in their great capture of Colle Belvedere, but

there was no fresh formation to take over and press home the advantage. The fighting had cost them 2,500 casualties.

The 36th Division had been crippled in two days and nights trying to cross the Rapido and by-pass Cassino. The month had cost them 2,000 casualties, including those they later suffered when they reorganized and joined the 34th in the mountains.

The 34th had lost rather more than 2,200 men fighting for their mountain bridgehead—the one positive gain.

At Anzio the beachhead force had built up to 70,000 men and 356 tanks, but was now pinned down by superior German forces —with three and a half divisions faced by five German.

From the German point of view the battle had been profitable. The Gustav Line had been submitted to the test of battle and had held firm. Only once, in the last five days of January, did von Senger have any anxious moments—when the French turning movement from the north was making good progress and the Americans were simultaneously hammering at Cassino and Monte Cassino. From now on he could look forward to the future with confidence. Events had shown him where the weak points in his line were. As the Fifth Army successively attacked all sections of the line, von Senger was able to plug the holes as they appeared: reinforce weak points, fill in gaps, strengthen engineering works.

Throughout the last week of January and the first weeks of February, the sound of German working parties could be heard night after night, industriously strengthening the positions in the light of experience. Whoever next tried to attack them would find them not weakened by the battering they had received in the first battle, but stronger than ever.

The net Allied gain was the precious mountain bridgehead across the upper Rapido north of Cassino, and curling like an appendix through the mountain-tops to within 1,000 yards of Monte Cassino. It was a difficult bridgehead to hold because of the problem of supplying it, and the fact that it was overlooked from three sides. But it was a possible approach to Monte Cassino, now recognized to be the pivot of the whole defensive system.

There was one other capture—a German order of the day:

The Gustav Line must be held at all costs for the sake of the political consequences which would follow a completely successful defence. The Fuehrer expects the bitterest struggle for every yard.

After this even the Intelligence experts at Army and Army Group Headquarters were less inclined to assert that German morale was crumbling and that a withdrawal to the Po was more than likely.

The first battle of Cassino was launched under political duress to facilitate the Anzio landing. Now Anzio had fallen short of expectations; the Germans, so far from weakening their forces on the Cassino front had reinforced them, and the recent fighting had made it clear just how strong they were. By mid-February it would have been reasonable to conclude that no useful purpose could be served by renewing the Cassino attacks until the worst of the atrocious winter weather was over, and an offensive in overwhelming strength could be properly prepared against what was by this time known, beyond any doubt, to be as formidable a defensive system as it would be possible to encounter.

Unhappily the momentum of chain reaction could not now be arrested. From Anzio came ominous rumblings. There were clear signs that the Germans were preparing to launch an all-out counter-offensive with their fresh Fourteenth Army. The offensive would be opening in a few days. It was an ironical situation. Anzio had originally been designed to rescue the Cassino front from deadlock. Now it had become a liability, and was itself in need of rescue.

The first battle of Cassino had to start prematurely to pave the way for an Anzio masterstroke: the second had now to be launched even more prematurely to save Anzio from disaster.

III

THE SECOND BATTLE

'They gave their bodies to the commonwealth and received, each for his own memory, praise that will never die, and with it the grandest of all sepulchres, not that in which their mortal bones are laid, but a home in the minds of men where their glory remains fresh. . . .' PERICLES

I

AS soon as it became clear from the January battles of the Americans just how formidable the Cassino defences were, General Alexander decided to leave the moribund Adriatic front to the care of a holding force and move Eighth Army divisions across to Cassino to reinforce Fifth Army.

The first to come were the 2nd New Zealand and the 4th Indian Divisions, and later they were joined by the 78th (British). This *ad hoc* formation (which also included a combat group of the 1st U.S. Armoured Division) was named the Second New Zealand Corps, a title of convenience for a task force assembled with the specific task of taking Cassino and breaking into the Liri Valley.

The Second New Zealand Corps formally came into existence on February 4th. Initially it was given the task of exploiting the breach if the Americans succeeded in making one, but, as we have already seen, there was never any strong feeling that this would arise. By February 6th it was evident that the dwindling American attacks were finished. The 34th and 36th Divisions had shot their bolt. In the words of General Alexander 'It was clear that Second New Zealand Corps would be obliged, not merely to debouch through a gateway flung open for them, but to capture the gate themselves.'

This brought into the arena two of the greatest fighting divisions of the war, the 2nd New Zealand and the 4th Indian. They were utterly dissimilar in personality and method but alike in being able to claim a long record of success dating back to the earliest days of the war. Both brought to Cassino and the badly shaken Fifth Army an almost arrogant conviction of invincibility born of their great victories in the Western Desert. An aura of glamour invested these two divisions.

The situation of the New Zealanders was unique. They were more than just another division within the fabric of the British and Commonwealth armies. They were the business end of a tiny national army, the New Zealand Expeditionary Force. New Zealand was the first of the Dominions to mobilize its military forces on the outbreak of war for service abroad. (In the other Dominions, service overseas was initially voluntary.) The force that eventually served in the Mediterranean was not only a division, but a complete expeditionary force of some 25,000 which included all ancillary services—supply, ordnance, medical (including their own field hospitals) and welfare services run by their own womenfolk. It was a microcosm of New Zealand serving overseas, a family affair with a most potent clannish spirit. New Zealanders never served with other units. A man would rather remain a sergeant in a New Zealand battalion than be commissioned into an English regiment.

New Zealand is a small nation. The population at the beginning of the war was barely 2,000,000. It is a country where the *cliché* 'everyone knows everyone else' is nearer the truth than usual. Within the Expeditionary Force it was certainly true.

So when the New Zealand division went to war, it was a small hand-picked national army with a nation watching its every move, a national press reporting on every detail of every experience it encountered, a Government watching over its welfare and performance. The New Zealanders were under a permanent spotlight from their home country, 12,000 long miles away, to a greater and more personal degree than a British or American division, lost in the plurality of overseas forces. No wife in England, reading about the Cassino fighting, could know that her husband was involved, even though she knew he was in Italy. If a New Zealand paper announced that the New Zealanders were fighting at Cassino, every second family in the country would directly or indirectly be concerned.

The effect of this, coupled with the confident character of the men themselves, was almost to compel the New Zealand Division to take itself for granted as a *corps d'élite*, forced always to excel. If a man did well it would for a certainty get back to his home town or village. If he did badly it would get back too.

On top of this the typical New Zealander had qualities which are ideally suited to the vagaries and demands of infantry fighting. Tough, dour, sardonically humorous, physically robust (rugby football in New Zealand has something of the religious significance associated with cricket in England) they could claim, too, a high general level of intelligence, for New Zealand had for some time had an efficient system of universal state education that was ahead of its time. Like the Scots, from whom so many of them are descended, the New Zealanders are extremely education-conscious.

They had two other attributes invaluable to the infantryman. They were self-reliant and well able to act independently. Many of them were men who single-handed had run remote farms or sheep stations, a way of life that teaches a man to think and act for himself without relying on the facilities and assistance of others. They were for the same reason natural improvisers, and improvisation is fifty per cent of infantry fighting. A man who has started from scratch and worked up a farm with his own hands and his own ingenuity will take more readily to the business of modern war which calls for the maintenance of machinery, equipment and communications under extreme difficulties, and the ability to organize and administer a simple but efficient way of life in circumstances where individual tenacity and adaptability are constantly in demand.

Such was the New Zealand soldier. A quietly rugged man, a little sceptical of anything fancy; inclined to be affably mocking in his attitude to spit and polish; a man who liked to cut the frills and get on with the job: a product of a simpler, more down to earth mode of existence in which he had had to make a way for himself with his hands and his initiative: a man who was proud of his toughness but seldom flaunted it. Temperamentally he probably came closest to the Scots and the north-country English soldier who also had this quiet conviction of strength without any desire to show it off.

Because it was operated as a closed shop, this small New Zealand force also had the quality of an exclusive club for which there is a waiting list. This not only acted as an incentive to efficiency on the part of those who belonged, but made the competition for promotion keen and slow. Promotion vacancies would occur in other divisions through men being posted away for one reason or another. This did not occur in the New Zealand division. The units remained basically the same as they had been at the beginning of the war, with only the replacements occasioned by casualties and the Government system of turning over the force by bringing men home after a certain time on active service.

It was these qualities, and their application to battle, which led most English commanders to rate the New Zealanders at their best among the finest infantry soldiers in the world. Among their greatest admirers were the Germans, and their intelligence reports often showed this: 'The enemy is using New Zealanders, so he evidently means business,' was a typical reference.

Presiding over the New Zealanders was a personality whose situation was as unique as that of the esoteric formation he commanded, Lieutenant-General Sir Bernard Freyberg, V.C. Freyberg was more than a divisional commander. He was the G.O.C. New Zealand Expeditionary Force, Commander (except at Cassino) of the New Zealand Division in the field, the forthright representative of the New Zealand Government in the European theatre of operations, and the unofficial parent and guardian of every New Zealander overseas. Nothing was too good for them; there was nothing they could not do; he fussed over them like a father.

There was an endearing example of this when the New Zealanders were about to move from North Africa to Italy in October. By that time the crossing was a matter of routine. Convoys were making the journey regularly and uneventfully with a routine air and naval escort. This was not good enough for Freyberg. He asked the New Zealand Minister of Defence to raise at the highest level the question of the New Zealand force being properly protected on its journey. The Minister of Defence raised this with his Prime Minister, Peter Fraser, who took it up with Mr. Churchill, who told Admiral Cunningham, who in turn reassured Mr. Churchill, who then passed on to Mr. Fraser the Admiral's promise 'That every care will be taken of our old friends the New Zealand troops on their passage through the Mediterranean. We know their value too well to leave any precaution untaken which will assure their safe arrival where they can bring their weight against the enemy. The matter is receiving my personal attention.'

Freyberg was happy. And the New Zealanders set sail for Italy with exactly the same escort as they would have had anyway.

A huge, handsome man, with searching grey eyes and a strong jaw, Freyberg was in appearance the classic epitome of the soldier-hero: exactly what one would expect a man who finished the First World War with a Victoria Cross and three Distinguished Service Orders to look like.

The uniqueness of his situation lay in two things. First, he was the only senior field commander of the First World War (in which he ended up as a Brigadier) to hold an active field command throughout the Second. Secondly, the fact that he was directly responsible, not to Mr. Churchill, but to the Prime Minister and Government of New Zealand, gave him a measure of independence not enjoyed by any other divisional commander in Europe. This independence, which he did not hesitate to exercise, gave the New Zealand Division the additional status of a star performer that could not lightly be engaged without reference to its agent, Freyberg.

Freyberg accordingly had a much bigger say in the tasks allotted his division than any of his British or American colleagues. His division was not, like its British equivalents, available for use where and how the Army Commanders pleased. It was not expendable, though it was always willing.

'I knew,' General Mark Clark has written, 'that Alexander was

in a difficult position with regard to Freyberg. The British were
exceedingly careful in the handling of New Zealand Forces,
because they were territorial troops responsible only to their home
government.'

If you wanted the New Zealanders you had to sell the idea to
Freyberg first. I mention this not with any idea of suggesting
that they contributed less than others to the Mediterranean
campaigns—they contributed rather more than most—but as an
illustration of the special position they enjoyed: comparable,
perhaps, with that of the Brigade of Guards.

Because of his personal fighting record and his age, there
was a tendency in some quarters to think of Freyberg as a blood-
and-guts product of Ypres, Gallipoli, and Passchendaele. In fact,
the very opposite was the case. Like many men to whom courage
and physical strength come naturally, he was gentle, kindly
and warm-hearted, and he had a strong feeling for the culture
that had been denied him through orthodox educational
channels when he was a boy.

He was probably one of the few divisional commanders who
could quote Jane Austen as readily as Winston Churchill's
speeches. He must be one of the very few who have opened a
formal first interview with a newly-joined staff officer by asking
whether he got a First-Class Honours degree at Oxford, or a
second. A little surprisingly one of his greatest friends after the
first war was Sir James Barrie.

Geoffrey Cox, who served as an intelligence officer with this
division, has explained it in this way:

This intellectual interest arose possibly from the first war experience
when chance threw him, in the Hood Battalion of the Royal Naval
Division, into a mess which included Rupert Brooke, Arthur
Asquith, Denis Browne, Patrick Shaw Stewart, and Aubrey Herbert.
It is not difficult to imagine the profound effect of these men on the
rugged young New Zealander who came fresh from fighting in the
Mexican Civil War of 1913.

New Zealand education at that time had nothing to offer
in the way of intellectual stimulus. Freyberg was a product of

the philistine environment from which his contemporary Katharine Mansfield fled to Bloomsbury.

Oddly enough it was not until 1939 that Freyberg actually soldiered with his own countrymen. In the first war and during the years between, his service was entirely with the British army. When in 1939 the New Zealand Prime Minister, Peter Fraser, appointed him commander of the New Zealand Expeditionary Force, it was a rebirth. 'Freyberg,' to quote Cox again, 're-discovered himself as a New Zealander.'

His own rugged sense of independence and dry humour reflected that of the men he commanded. On one occasion a senior British general visited the New Zealand Division. At lunch he remarked with wry amusement, 'Your people don't salute very much, do they?'

'You should try waving to them,' replied Freyberg. 'They always wave back.'

On another occasion, when the division was relaxing after some heavy fighting, another senior general protested to Freyberg:

'You really must do something about this, Bernard. I have just followed a lorry load of your men—they were obviously drunk —and were hanging out of the back of the lorry offering me bottles of wine.'

'That's nothing,' said Freyberg equably. 'You should have seen what happened here the other day. They filled one of our water tankers with Chianti and ruined the thing.'

But these stories, which illuminate one side of the picture, should not deceive anyone into thinking the New Zealanders lacked discipline. Behind the superficial casualness the division had a hard practical discipline conditioned partly by the constant scrutiny of their activities from 'back home' and partly by a ruthless system of removing any man who failed in his job. They set themselves high standards, and those who failed did not keep their jobs.

There was one other unique feature of this division. This was what the New Zealanders themselves called their 'Cabinet'. The cabinet consisted of Freyberg and the senior brigadiers, and when an operation was being prepared plans would be fully, and even outspokenly, debated. Freyberg would listen carefully to everyone in turn, then sum up and make the final decision. These cabinet meetings constantly mystified British and American generals who had no experience of such a democratic approach to the waging of war.

Prominent in these councils was Brigadier Kippenberger (who, on the formation of Second New Zealand Corps under Freyberg, became Major-General, and took command of the N.Z. Division). Of Freyberg, New Zealanders always speak with affection, respect and humour, as men do who are discussing their former head-master. 'A difficult old cuss at times, but we'd do anything for him.' Of Kippenberger, they always say: 'Kippenberger is New Zealand's finest soldier.'

A solicitor by profession, Kippenberger served as a private in the First World War, survived the Somme, and was then so severely wounded that he had to be invalided out. Between the wars he was a territorial officer, and an indefatigable student of military history. In Italy he earned the high esteem of his British and American comrades both as a commander and a personality. As senior brigadier and later as divisional commander Kippenberger exercised a great influence in the 'cabinet'. This highly individual New Zealand H.Q. sometimes shocked Camberley and West Point men who saw it in operation but it was in practice brilliantly successful. The N.Z. Division was in the best sense a great amateur combination—a gifted civilian body that had learned the craft of war the hard way, and now excelled at it.

In its personality and its basic attitudes, the 4th Indian Division was almost the complete antithesis of the New Zealand Division. It was probably the most professional division of the Allied armies in Italy.

The Indian divisions were two-thirds Indian, one-third British. Each of the three brigades consisted of one British, two Indian battalions. The field artillery were entirely British—the Indians never, for some reason, seemed to master the more advanced branches of gunnery—but the Service, Ordnance, and Signals Corps were almost entirely Indian. The senior officers were British, the rest British and Indian.

The Indian Army was composed exclusively of volunteers. The martial races of India—the Sikhs, the Punjabis, the Mahrattas, the Rajputs, and the Gurkhas from neighbouring Nepal—joined the army because they loved the life. They loved everything about soldiering: the drilling, the spit-and-polish, the fancy uniforms. Unlike the British or American soldier who has to be persuaded that blanco and the barrack-square are necessary, the Indians revelled in it all as much as they enjoyed showing off their prowess as marksmen, signallers, or in the exercise of that field-craft which came to them naturally.

Because of this they automatically imposed on their British officers the necessity to live up to these standards. Between the British officer and soldier there could be an amiable spirit of give and take in discipline and military standards generally. But if, without persuasion, the Indian soldier insisted on achieving basic soldiering excellence, not because he was told to, but because he loved every minute of it, then the officer had to work overtime himself to keep up!

The result was that only the cream of the British officer corps found its way into the Indian Army. The rates of pay were higher: the qualifications were higher: only the best were accepted.

Between the world wars many Englishmen joined the army because at that time it could be approached as a pleasant, not too exacting, career with which went an agreeable social life. A man could do a useful, unspectacular job of work in a regiment, see a little of the world, and then retire with a pension and the respectable rank of Major. But only the pick of these men could transfer to the Indian Army, and then their soldiering became a dedicated existence imposed on them from below by the almost fanatical keenness of the men they commanded.

To an Indian soldier, the army greatcoat which he took with him into retirement was a source of incomparable prestige in his local village. And often these men would decline to take leave for the simple reason that they enjoyed their military life better!

The Indian soldier's joy in soldiering not only kept his officers up to the mark, but affected in precisely the same way the British regiments who served at his side. The British battalion in an Indian brigade had a compulsion to excel that was infinitely more powerful than the voice of any sergeant-major or martinet of a commanding officer.

This matchless professional excellence of the Indian division reached its natural apogee in war. War was the logical fulfilment of soldiering. And so, while formations that consisted largely of civilian soldiers approached active service as a nasty job of work that had to be got over as quickly as possible, the Indian division —the good one, anyway—saw it rather as the mystical fulfilment of the way of life it had chosen.

The 4th Indian Division reached Egypt shortly before the outbreak of the war, and at once began intensive training in desert warfare. In 1940, it had carried out, with the 7th Armoured Division, that rout of the Italian armies in Libya which is a classic of the few against the many. The following year it brought off the notable victory of Keren in Eritrea. In 1942 and 1943 it played an important part in the final Desert victory. Since then it had been resting and retraining in Africa.

Like the New Zealand Division, the Indians came to Italy with a great record of success and the same conviction of invincibility. Like the New Zealanders they had an exceptional commander. Major-General F. I. S. Tuker, C.B., D.S.O., O.B.E., was one of the star divisional generals. A scholar of war as well as a meticulous and successful field commander, Tuker was a man who combined to an exceptional degree the qualities of military academician and battle commander. He had written a number of books which are standard works: as an active commander he was a perfectionist who demanded the highest standards of professional efficiency. He was an individualist who, throughout his army career, had had a reputation for speaking his mind and going against the current of opinion, even if it meant making himself unpopular.

The story is told of an occasion when, a student at the Staff College, he was asked a question during a tactical exercise. Having answered it, he then added:

'That is the answer you expect me to give, and which you will consider correct. I will now tell you what I think ought to be done in that situation.'

Even the discreet official history of his Division is sprinkled with sentences beginning: 'General Tuker objected to this plan on the grounds that . . .'

Unlike many of the divisional generals of the war, Tuker was not the man to breeze informally into battalion cookhouses and drink a mug of tea with the troops: he lacked the easy informality with which many of the younger products of the Montgomery school of generalship were able to charm their divisions into achievement. He was personally austere, a rather aloof figure whose mind lingered restlessly on the job. But he had the complete respect and admiration of his division. He radiated and commanded total efficiency, and his division reflected this. He was in fact precisely the hundred-per-cent professional commander this professional division needed.

So they came together again, these two Desert formations: the great amateur division from New Zealand and the great professional Indian Division. Both brought to Cassino the easy confidence that this was just another occasion on which to demonstrate their invincibility. And then, in turn, they caught sight for the first time of the gaunt eminence of Monte Cassino with the huge fortress-like building sprawled across its summit: they saw the flooded valley and the universal grey-brown desolation and the hostile mountains packed tightly behind Monte Cassino. And they wondered.

General Freyberg's plan for the second battle of Cassino was in effect a continuation and elaboration of the American attack in the first. Cassino was to be assaulted from the north and south-east simultaneously.

From the bridgehead chiselled and clawed out of the mountain tops by the Americans, the Indian Division would storm the Monastery and Monastery Hill, and then sweep down the hillside to Highway Six. At the same time the New Zealanders would advance along the shallow causeway which carried the railway from behind the sheltering skirts of Monte Trocchio, and seize the station, a strongly fortified locality three-quarters of a mile south of the town.

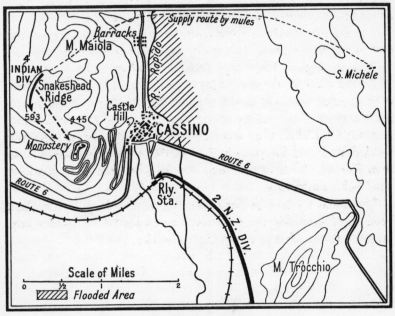

SECOND BATTLE

Pincer attack from north and south by 4th Indian and 2nd NZ Divisions

If both attacks succeeded, Cassino would be pinched out, and the rest of the New Zealand Division, and the 180 tanks of the U.S. First Armoured Division would burst into the Liri Valley. Even if the Indians failed, the capture of the railway station area would provide a springboard from which a further advance into the valley and against the town might be made.

It seemed at the time the best possible plan. To have attempted a crossing of the Rapido at S. Angelo (as the American 36th Division had done) would—with the number of troops then available, and the appalling flooded state of the valley approaches —have been to invite the same disaster and this alternative had been rejected.

This plan seemed the best available. But no one was under any illusions about it, and this was reflected in a conversation between General Freyberg and General Gruenther (General Clark's chief-of-staff) on one of those bleak February mornings.

'I guess this is where we throw the torch to you,' Gruenther had said a little wanly. 'What do you think the chances are?'

'Not more than fifty-fifty,' Freyberg had replied.

To the New Zealanders, whose great triumphs had happened in the golden wastes of the Western Desert, this grim amalgam of mud and mountain under the hypnotic stare of Monte Cassino was not a bit what they were used to. To the Indians, who had tackled mountain fortresses in Eritrea, this was going to be 'worse than Keren', the Eritrean battle that had become their standard yardstick of difficulty.

There was a job to be done and they would do their best. But both these divisions were far too experienced to be under any illusions about what it was going to be like.

2

IT is pointless to consider any battle critically without relating it to the precise circumstances and conditions prevailing at the time and place. This may be a truism, but military critics more often than not ignore it. Recollecting in the tranquillity of their studies an engagement at which they were not present, they will murmur placidly that 'more divisions should have been thrown in' or 'more boldness might have been shown'.

A commander's decisions can be properly appraised only if they are set against the background of the exact and peculiar circumstances, atmosphere, climatic conditions, and pressures under which they were made. This is especially true of Cassino which to an exceptional degree contrived at all times to be a conspiracy of difficulties. Consider, then, the context in which the responsibility for Cassino fell on the powerful shoulders of General Freyberg.

The Fifth Army was in a bad way: its commander, General Clark, sorely tried. Two of his best American divisions, the 34th and 36th, had been broken in two and a half weeks of fighting. One of them, the 36th, was not only temporarily finished as a fighting force, but it was in a state of rebellion. It believed, as we have seen, that it had been squandered unreasonably on the ill-fated Rapido crossing, and was proposing to raise the matter before Congress after the war. The fact that an experienced division should feel as strongly as this is indicative of the low spirits to which some of the overworked American units had been reduced by the heavy discouraging fighting of the previous months—culminating in their first trial of strength against

Cassino. On top of this the rest of Fifth Army at Anzio was in serious trouble.

Clark never took too kindly to his British subordinate commanders, whose experience of battle was considerably greater than his, and this is constantly evident in his memoirs. From the first there was little personal *rapport* between him and the forthright Freyberg, and this did not help an already difficult situation.

By this time the German defences, having survived the test of battle, were stronger than ever, and the winter weather was worsening every day. Rain, hail, and snow followed each other in monotonous succession. The battleground had been reduced to a universal greyness of fortified mountain wasteland protected by a moat of mud, marsh, and flood.

What use was a huge preponderance of aircraft if they had to spend most of the time grounded by the weather? Or six hundred tanks in ground conditions in which they could not move off a road without sinking to their bellies?

From the New Zealand and Indian Divisions, engaged in taking over from the Americans, came reports, almost hourly, of the extraordinary practical difficulties they were encountering in carrying out routine reliefs: the state of the tracks that had to be used, the need for more specialized equipment like bulldozers, the uselessness of the two-wheel drive transport to which the British formations were condemned; the difficulty of reconnaissance because every movement was under the direct observation of Monte Cassino and the adjacent peaks—the tale of woe was endless.

This was particularly the case with the Indians. The bridgehead which the Americans had driven into the mountain-tops at the back door of Monte Cassino created extraordinary difficulties. It amounted, in effect, to a forward and separate battlefield ahead of the main Allied front line. To reach it they had to make a seven-mile journey obliquely across the flooded valley of the Rapido and then continue up a succession of tortuous goat-tracks. Crossing the valley they were completely exposed to the glare of Monastery Hill, so that in effect this valley had become a sort of premature no-man's-land which had to be crossed merely in order to reach their own private front line.

The American remnants had managed to survive there in small packets. But it was another matter to set up a Brigade Group with the necessary supplies and equipment to launch a major attack.

The relief of the Americans by the Indians tells its own story. To reach even the forward base on the near side of the Rapido they had to borrow American four-wheel drive transport, which took them by a secondary road, two miles north of Highway Six, to San Michele. The road was badly damaged. On the way two lorries skidded on a bend and plunged over an embankment. They happened to be the lorries carrying the entire reserve of mortar ammunition and grenades of the Royal Sussex, the leading battalion. The ammunition was not replaced in time for the first battle five days later.

The next day was spent trying to raise enough mules to get the battalion and its supplies across the false no-man's-land to the mountain bridgehead. They could only get a third of the mules required. That night the Royal Sussex crossed the valley on foot and moved into a concentration area on the lower slopes of Monte Castellone. They arrived there at 3 a.m. and were shelled for five hours. Some of the shells were from Allied guns.

They were shelled all the next day. In the afternoon they were ordered to attack Colle Belvedere that night. This surprised them as Belvedere was supposed to be in the hands of the French. The attack was stopped half an hour before it was due to go in. The French *did* hold it.

The next morning the Royal Sussex were ordered to relieve the Americans that night. An American staff officer reported to the C.O. of the battalion to guide him to the positions in daylight. There seemed a good deal of doubt about just where the positions were, and it was not until he had led the colonel close to the German positions—which promptly opened fire—that the guide got his bearings, and the journey to the forward American posts was then safely completed. But the approach was made, somewhat hazardously, from the German side.

The British colonel found that the sector was held by remnants of four American battalions, from three different regiments, and two divisions. These were the survivors of the gallant 34th, and one regiment of the 36th, and they had regrouped themselves as best they could to hang on until relief came. Their positions were astride the irregular curving ridge named Snakeshead. That night, Colonel Glennie of the Sussex was joined by his battalion on Snakeshead, and it was then that it was found that fifty of the Americans who had hung on so courageously to these precarious gains were too numb to move, and had to be carried out of their positions on stretchers.

The nightmare of this relief by the advance guard of 4th Indian Division is explained by two things: the failure of the American higher headquarters to provide accurate information about what their forward troops held and did not hold; and the limitation on daylight movement (and therefore normal reconnaissance) imposed by the occupation of all the commanding heights by the Germans—especially Monte Cassino. As an officer put it, 'Wherever you went, there was the Monastery, looking at you.'

But there was an even more bitter blow reserved for Colonel Glennie's arrival on Snakeshead. The Indian Division had been told that the Americans held the all-important Point 593, the prominent height adjacent to, and overlooking, the Monastery. This feature is less than 1,000 yards from the rear entrance of the Monastery, and linked with it by a negotiable saddle of rock. The New Zealand Corps plan had been made under the impression that the Indian Division would assault the Monastery from the secure base of adjacent 593. It was not until the Royal Sussex actually got there that they discovered that the Americans did not hold 593, but merely had a footing on its nearer slope. The rest of this feature, including a fragment of a mediaeval fort, remained firmly in German hands. Instead of taking over the height that was to have been their jumping-off point for the attack, they would have to fight for it, and the attack was due on February 15th, three days later.

Meanwhile, the news from Anzio was worse. The red light was very red. The German counter-offensive was due in a day or two. Anzio was in danger. Anzio had to be saved. No matter how bizarre the difficulties, the new Cassino offensive must go in at once. So Wilson urged Alexander, Alexander urged Clark, Clark urged Freyberg, and Freyberg urged his two divisions to be ready to attack immediately. Once again there was too little time. Everything had to be rushed. Nothing could be properly prepared. Anzio was in serious danger.

This was the background of political and strategic pressure, tactical emergency, cumulative practical difficulty, ill-luck and in-adequate information by American higher headquarters that had handed over to him, against which Freyberg bluntly informed his superiors that he did not think an offensive in these circumstances and conditions had more than a fifty-fifty chance.

This was the background against which General Tuker—living every one of the difficulties, large and small, which his Indian division was doing its best to overcome in the limited time available—said: 'I must have the Monastery reduced by heavy bombers.'

On February 5th, while the Americans were making their last efforts in the mountains, and the New Zealand and Indian divisions were preparing to take over, a new burden descended on Abbot Diamare and his small party of monks and refugees in the Monastery.

That night, at the height of a thunderstorm, there arrived at the great wooden entrance door 150 more civilians. Driven by the ever-increasing artillery bombardments from the caves where for days they had been hiding like animals, they were led by some forty shrieking women who—numb with cold and starvation, and crazed with terror—pounded on the door till their knuckles bled, howling that they would set fire to it if they were not admitted. When the door was opened they swept uncontrollably through to the pitch black vaults and corridors and stairways of the Abbey.

The monks spent the next day calming them down, trying to get them into some sort of order. Some were lodged on the grand entrance staircase, others in the carpenter's shop beneath the monumental library, in the porter's lodge, or in the underground corridors. A number were directed to the rabbitry which had a separate doorway leading to the kitchen garden.

To control and organize 200 distraught people in this condition was, not surprisingly, beyond the capacity of an eighty-year-old abbot, five monks, a few brothers and a deaf-and-dumb servant. Water and food stocks were low: there was no form of lighting except candles. There was an infinite variety of places where people could stray and get lost in the miles of corridor: most of the refugees were hysterical and nearly demented by what they had gone through.

Meanwhile many shells were now landing on the monastery and in its courtyards from the ceaseless bombardments of the hill on which it stood. A man drawing water from the cistern in the central courtyard was hit: two old women hurrying along one of the cloisters were killed by blast: a boy, playing in another, was badly injured.

Within a day or two sanitary conditions were appalling and beyond control. Illness inevitably broke out and a disease, which could not be identified, caused an epidemic from which people began to die.

One of the younger monks, Dom Eusebio, took on the responsibility of looking after the sick, and he slaved night and day to combat an illness he could not even diagnose. His only absences from his patients were to go off to the carpenter's shop to make coffins for those who succumbed, and then—during the lulls between shellings—organize hasty burial services.

He carried on selflessly in this way for five days, then he caught the disease himself, and on the night of February 13th he died.

The other monks laid him in one of the coffins he had himself constructed in the carpenter's shop beneath the monumental library. They lit candles, and prayed over his body, and listened for a break in the muffled thunder of the guns, so that they could take him out and bury him. But that night there was no break in the continuity of the gunfire. The guns did not stop firing until morning and then the monks could do nothing, for they did not dare move outside the protective walls in daylight.

When General Tuker, commander of the 4th Indian Division, learned from the Americans that Monastery Hill was the key to the Cassino position: when he saw with his own eyes how it dominated the battlefield, and buttressed the entire system of mountain defences: when he felt, like everyone who experienced it, the almost hypnotic way in which the Monastery on its summit commanded every approach; he sent a routine request to Fifth Army Intelligence for all available information about this building.

The Intelligence Branch of Fifth Army had little to offer. So General Tuker, a determined and methodical man, carried out one of the stranger acts of generalship of the war. He summoned his car, drove to Naples, and spent the greater part of a day combing the bookshops of that city until at last he found what he wanted. That night he sent a memorandum to his Corps Commander, General Freyberg. This memorandum is not only a concise appreciation of the situation as it struck the man most concerned—the General whose division had to attack the Monastery Hill feature: it is a revealing insight into the character of General Tuker.

This was the memorandum:

1. After considerable trouble and investigating many bookshops in Naples, I have at last found a book, dated 1879, which gives certain details of the construction of the Monte Cassino Monastery.

2. The Monastery was converted into a fortress in the nineteenth century. The Main Gate has massive timber branches in a low archway consisting of large stone blocks 9 to 10 metres long. This gate is the only means of entrance to the Monastery.

3. The walls are about 150 feet high, are of solid masonry and at least 10 feet thick at the base.

4. Since the place was constructed as a fortress as late as the nineteenth century[1] it stands to reason that the walls will be suitably pierced for loopholes and will be battlemented.

5. Monte Cassino is therefore a modern fortress and must be dealt with by modern means. No practicable means available within the capacity of field engineers can possibly cope with this place. It can only be directly dealt with by applying blockbuster bombs from the air, hoping thereby to render the garrison incapable of resistance. The 1,000-lb. bomb would be next to useless.

6. Whether the monastery is now occupied by a German garrison or not, it is certain that it will be held as a keep by the last remnants of the garrison of the position. It is therefore also essential that the building should be so demolished as to prevent its effective occupation at that time.

7. I would ask that you would give me definite information at once as to how this fortress will be dealt with as the means are not within the capacity of this Division.

8. I would point out that it has only been by investigation on the part of this Division, with no help from Intelligence sources outside, that we have got any idea as to what this fortress comprises, although the fortress has been a thorn in our side for many weeks.

When a formation is called upon to reduce such a place, it should be apparent that the place is reducible by the means at the disposal of that Division or that the means are ready for it, without having to go to the bookstalls of Naples to find out what should have been fully considered many weeks ago.

General Tuker followed this up with an urgent request that softening-up of the Monastery and Monastery Hill be put in hand right away.

Shortly after this he suffered a bad attack of a tropical illness that had recurrently bothered him for years. For a day or two he managed to direct the planning of the battle from a sickbed

[1] In fact the last main restorations had been in the sixteenth and seventeenth centuries.

in his caravan. But several days before it was due to open he had
to hand over his command to Brigadier Dimoline.

It was a misfortune that on top of its other difficulties the 4th
Indian Division, facing its greatest test, had to be robbed at the
last minute of the commander who had made it what it was.

THE COMMANDERS
IN CHIEF

General Alexander

Field Marshal Kesselring

General Mark Clark, *Fifth Army*

General Leese, *Eighth Army*

THE ARMY COMMANDERS

General von Vietinghoff, *Tenth Army*

General von Mackensen, *Fourteenth Arm*

General Freyberg,
Second N.Z. Corps

General Truscott,
*U.S. Sixth Corps (Anzio
Beach-head Force)*

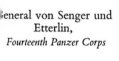

General von Senger und
Etterlin,
Fourteenth Panzer Corps

SOME
CORPS
COMMANDERS

General Juin, *French Corps*

General Anders, *Polish Corps*

German emplacement on reverse slope of Point 569

TYPICAL FIGHTING GROUND

Troops in action on Snakeshead Ridge

BATTLE CASUALTIES

AFTER THE BOMBING

BEFORE

Central courtyard of the Monastery showing the
famous Bramante Cloister

AFTER

Clearing a house

Point 593

View from the town ruins of Castle Hill with Monastery Hill immediately
behind in distant background

THE THIRD
BATTLE

New Zealand infantry and tanks attack Turreted House area. By holding on to this key position between Castle Hill and town outskirts, the Germans were able to prevent final clearance of the town and also to keep Castle Hill under constant fire

View from Continental Hotel of northern approach road by which New Zealander entered town. Castle Hill in background

BATTLE CASUALTIES

MONASTERY AND CASSINO TOWN TODAY

3

NO event of the war caused more heated and lingering controversy than the bombing, on February 15th, 1944, of the Abbey of Monte Cassino.

It is possible to understand the bitterness and bewilderment of the Cassinese monks themselves. The cloister is not the place in which a detailed grasp of military practicalities can be expected to flourish.

One can discount the naïve foolishness of the uninformed—like the English newspaper correspondent who spent a few hours at Monte Cassino after the war, and then published the complacent view that the bombing was 'vandalism' and the verdict on those who ordered it must be 'guilty but insane'.

It is more than a little surprising, however, that those who have emotionally wanted to believe that the bombing was a criminal act should have been fortified in their judgments by, of all people, the army commander who ordered it, General Mark Clark.

In his personal memoir *Calculated Risk*, published in 1951, General Clark wrote:

> I say that the bombing of the Abbey . . . was a mistake, and I say it with full knowledge of the controversy that has raged round this episode . . . Not only was the bombing of the Abbey an unnecessary psychological mistake in the propaganda field, but it was a tactical military mistake of the first magnitude. It only made the job more difficult, more costly in terms of men, machines, and time.

This might be read as an admission of error, but in the pages that follow Clark, who gave the order for the bombing, disclaims responsibility for the decision. If he had confined himself to a military reappraisal of the bombing, there could have been no objection to his being as outspoken as he liked. In fact, he ignores the special circumstances, conditions, and pressures prevailing at the time. He ignores the important psychological impact of the Monastery. He ignores the fact that two Commonwealth divisions were now being required to tackle a task that had just knocked the heart out of two American divisions. He makes little attempt to re-create the context in which the difficult decision had to be taken. He merely devotes himself to an angry apologia—disclaiming responsibility for an order which he himself gave, and blaming it on his subordinate commander, General Freyberg.

The great red herring that has been drawn across the bombing has been the relating of it to the question whether or not the Monastery was actually occupied by the Germans. It was afterwards reasonably well established that it was not. But this could not be known at the time. And in any case it is irrelevant.

The simple inescapable fact is that the building was an integral part of a physical feature that was not only occupied but to a high degree fortified. The fortified mountain and the building at its summit were in military terms a single piece of ground.

Ground is the raw material of the soldier, as weapons are his tools. Ground is the factor which more than any other eventually controls the shape of a battle. Like pigment to the artist and clay to the potter, ground is the material which the soldier must study, cherish, understand, and adapt to his purposes. This is the basis of all military tactics.

A mountain is one kind of ground. A mountain crowned by a building is another. If the building happens to be inordinately strong, the ground is something else again. To the soldier the mountain and the building are not separate things but together comprise a whole. Ground is indivisible. The mountain and the building are one and must be considered as one. Their relationship may be likened to that between a coconut shy and a tray of china set in its midst. It would be foolish to tell someone to aim as hard as he likes at the coconuts but on no account to hit the china.

The piece of ground called Monte Cassino comprised a 1,700-foot mountain with rocky sides: a zig-zag shelf of roadway twisting for five miles up one face of it, and providing both shelter and mobility for tanks and guns; and, at the summit, a building, more than 200 yards long, with the thickness, strength, design, and structure of a powerful fortress.

Occupation of a piece of high ground like Monte Cassino can take two forms. It can be garrisoned with soldiers. Or it can be occupied by one soldier equipped with binoculars and a wireless set through which he can accurately direct the fire of guns on to any point of the landscape within his view. There is absolutely no limit to the number of guns that can be so directed by one man. A trained observer is therefore an even more potent defensive garrison than a battalion of soldiers.

It follows from this that any high ground likely to be used by the enemy as an observatory is an automatic target for attack by the other side. The attacker must use everything in his power to make this observation point untenable until such time as he can deprive the enemy of it by seizing it himself. As we have already noted, the pattern of advance of a modern army is from one line of good observation to the next.

We have also mentioned that the relationship between the summit of Monte Cassino and the important main route which it commands is so exceptional that it invariably impresses military men as the finest observation post they have ever seen.

To observe from the summit of this particular mountain, a man might set himself up comfortably (and because of its thick walls, more safely) inside the building. Alternatively he might (to get a wider view) install himself in a trench outside it, with a telephone link to an orderly stationed securely inside the building. If an observation point is of exceptional quality, as is the case with Monte Cassino, there are likely to be a number of separate observation posts set up by the different artillery formations and headquarters who will want to use it. A prominent peak of this kind may well become a mass of observation posts providing eyes for the many different departments of the army it is serving.

Along the razor back of Monte Trocchio, for instance, where the
Allied armies had their main view of the Cassino front, there
were at one time more than a hundred observation posts.

The key to the German defence of the area for convenience
called Cassino—though it comprised a combination of river line,
mountain mass, and fortified town—was not the garrison, nor
was it the prepared system of fortifications, formidable though
both were, but the superlative observation which enabled such
good use to be made of them.

From the vantage point of the Monastery [reported Freyberg to the
New Zealand Government] the enemy can watch and bring down
fire on every movement on the roads or open country in the plain
below.

At New Zealand Divisional H.Q. [wrote Kippenberger] we felt
certain that the Monastery was at least the enemy's main observation
post. It was so perfectly situated for the purpose that no army could
have refrained from using it.

This famous building [recorded Alexander in his final report on
the campaign] had hitherto been deliberately spared, to our great
disadvantage, but it was an integral part of the German defensive
system, *mainly from the superb observation it afforded.*

The italics are mine.

Observation was the overriding issue at Cassino, not the
relatively unimportant question whether the Abbey was
occupied. And allied to the question of observation—in fact a
corollary of it—was the psychological impact of this altogether
exceptional observatory.

Because of the extraordinary extent to which the summit of
Monte Cassino dominated the valleys: because of the painful
constancy with which men were picked off by accurately observed
gunfire whenever they were forced to move in daylight within
its seemingly inescapable view: because of the obsessive theatrical
manner in which it towered over the scene, searching every inch
of it, the building set upon that summit had become the embodiment of resistance and its tangible symbol.

Everybody has experienced the sensation, when walking alone past a house, that invisible eyes were watching from a darkened interior. Hostile eyes can be sensed without being seen, and the soldier develops an exceptional awareness of this. Monte Cassino projected this feeling over an entire valley, and the feeling was being substantiated all the time by gunfire that could only have been so accurate and so swiftly opportunist through being directed by quite exceptionally positioned observers. Even in peacetime, Monte Cassino overwhelms the least imaginative visitor gazing up at it from below. In the cold desolation of winter and the fatiguing travail of unresolved battle, the spell of its monstrous eminence was complete and haunting.

This was the psychological crux of the matter. To the soldiers dying at its feet, the Monastery had itself become in a sense the enemy.

Only the generals on the spot could be fully aware of this. They alone knew what all the considerations were. It was their responsibility to order men to die attempting a task about which no one could feel optimistic. Theirs in the end are the only opinions which count.

I have quoted already the professional military summing-up of the situation by General Tuker before sickness compelled him to hand over to Brigadier Dimoline. We have seen the strategic and political duress under which, to save Anzio, the second battle of Cassino had to be precipitated at the most unfavourable time of mid-winter. This was the equally balanced, reasoned summary of General Kippenberger, the other divisional commander concerned.

Opinion at New Zealand Corps H.Q. and New Zealand Divisional H.Q. as to whether the Abbey was occupied was divided. Personally, I thought the point immaterial. If not occupied today it might be tomorrow and it did not appear that it would be difficult for the enemy to bring reserves into it during the progress of an attack, or for troops to take shelter there if driven from positions outside.

It was impossible to ask troops to storm a hill surmounted by an intact building such as this, capable of sheltering several hundred infantry in perfect security from shellfire and ready at the critical moment to emerge and counter-attack.

I was in touch with our own troops and they were very definitely of the opinion that the Abbey must be destroyed before anyone was asked to storm the hill.

It is difficult to see how Freyberg could have come to any other decision than that the Monastery must be destroyed whether occupied or not.

But since so much has been made of the question of occupation, it is worth examining the evidence available at the time to the Allied commanders, and it will be seen that there was a considerable doubt about this.

During the conference at which the Second U.S. Corps handed over to the Second New Zealand Corps, General Butler, deputy commander of the U.S. 34th Division (who made the first attacks on the Monastery feature) said:

I don't know but I don't believe the enemy is in the convent. All the fire has been from the slopes of the hill below the wall.

During the same conference a senior intelligence officer said:

With reference to the Abbey, we have had statements from our own observers who believe they have seen observing instruments in the windows. We have had statements from civilians both for and against. Some have said that Germans are living there but this is not supported by others. It is very difficult to say whether it is being put to any military purpose at this time.

Questioned further, the officer estimated that the Germans had a battalion-plus on top of the hill.

According to the official history of the U.S. Army Air Forces in World War II, the American Generals Eaker and Devers 'flew over the Abbey in a Piper Cub at a height of less than 200 feet and Eaker states flatly that he saw a radio aerial on the Abbey and enemy soldiers moving in and out of the building'.

There is one possibility, though it cannot be supported by evidence, which I think worth noting. Civilian refugees were lodged in the Monastery corridor being temporarily used as a rabbitry for the breeding of rabbits for food. This gave access to the open kitchen garden on the western, that is the German, side of the Abbey walls.

Anyone with experience of the more human side of front-line soldiering knows that no soldiers—lonely, uncomfortable, in danger, and bored—can be entirely restrained from making contact with any civilians within reach, either to exchange pleasantries with a woman or to barter cigarettes for a couple of eggs.

We know that three weeks before the bombing the military police guard was removed from the main entrance. For three weeks German soldiers were within a hundred yards or less of the kitchen garden to which the refugees had access. It can never be proved that some of them did not make contact with these civilians for one purpose or another, and that they were not seen doing so—thus giving rise to the reports that reached the Allies that German troops were in the Abbey: and perhaps explaining how it was that Generals Eaker and Devers were convinced during their flight over the Abbey that they had seen German soldiers moving about within its precincts.

Such unofficial excursions to a building which their Higher Command had formally placed out of bounds could easily have been accomplished without the monks' knowledge. The soldiers would merely have to wait until the sound of plainsong indicated that Abbot Diamare's small remnant community were safely inside their chapel in the depths of the building.

Finally, Sir D'Arcy Osborne, British Minister to the Vatican, had formally asked the Cardinal Secretary of State for an assurance that the Germans were not using the Abbey for military purposes. Sir D'Arcy's personal diary kept at the time shows that he received no reply until the evening of February 14th (the eve of the bombing) and then only a vague statement denying, on the authority of the German Embassy and German Military authorities, that there were any considerable ('grössere') concentrations of German troops in the 'immediate vicinity' of the Abbey. This was the only communication from the Vatican and it was hardly one on which action could be taken.

There remains the argument that a building becomes even more defensible after it has been destroyed. General von Senger, writing of the battle after the war, had this to say:

> As anyone who has had experience in street fighting—as at Stalingrad or Cassino—is aware . . . houses must be demolished in order to be converted from mouse-traps into bastions of defence.

This may be true as a general rule, but it is not necessarily so in the case of a building with walls ten feet thick, and the structural characteristics of a fortress. Nor had this consideration been overlooked by the New Zealand Command. They had discussed it thoroughly and had concluded that while the building would continue to be useful to the enemy after destruction, it would be more valuable intact. I again quote Kippenberger:

> Undamaged it was a perfect shelter but with its narrow windows and level profiles an unsatisfactory fighting position. Smashed by bombing it was a jagged heap of broken masonry and debris open to effective fire from guns, mortars and strafing planes as well as being a death trap if bombed again. On the whole I thought it would be more useful to the Germans if we left it unbombed.

It will be seen, therefore, that it was only after long and earnest deliberation, and after every aspect of the matter had been most thoroughly discussed, that General Freyberg reluctantly came to the conclusion that the destruction of the Monastery, by the only means powerful enough to have any effect on it, was tactically and psychologically necessary.

It may be added that General Clark was not in the closest touch with the Cassino front at this time. He was necessarily preoccupied with the bigger problem of Anzio, the crisis centre where a German counter-offensive was known to be due very shortly. His opposition to the bombing, of which he has since made so much, was mostly expressed at second hand through his Chief-of-Staff. He was not, like Freyberg, continuously on the spot. So that it became necessary for General Alexander, as Army Group Commander, to influence the situation by stating un-equivocally that he had complete faith in Freyberg's judgment.

And so, after days of doubt—the situation not being helped by the public airing of the pros and cons by the British and American press for the benefit of Goebbels and other interested parties—the decision was made, and General Clark gave the order for the bombing which he afterwards so bitterly repudiated.

If all the factors are considered dispassionately there can be little doubt that it was the only possible decision. The tragedy was that once the decision had been made, the matter became an Air Force responsibility. The Air Force, working alone without reference to the Army, projected it as a separate operation without co-ordinating it with the ground attack which was the only reason for its happening at all. The Air Force went ahead and carried out the bombing before the Indian Division could possibly be ready to make the attack it was intended to support.

So the bombing, when it happened, expended its fury in a vacuum, tragically and wastefully. It achieved nothing, it helped nobody.

4

FROM the Air Force point of view the timing of the bombing depended mainly on the weather and on operational requirements elsewhere. A forecast of twenty-four hours of good weather was the first stipulation.

This operation was something new. For the first time the heaviest bombers of the Strategic Air Force were to operate with the mediums in close support of infantry. Hitherto this had been the function of the mediums only. These aircraft, based on forward airfields and bombing from a relatively low level, were the ones whose job it was to attack at short notice targets designated by the forward troops. The mediums of the tactical air force were in effect another form of artillery under army control. The forward troops could indicate a target and the bombers would be over it within a short time.

The introduction of heavy bombers into an infantry battle created new problems. The operation had to be mounted from many airfields scattered through Southern Italy, Sicily, and North Africa. Many of the aircraft would have to travel a long way to the objective. The Flying Fortresses bombed from very high altitudes, and it was something new for them to be asked to attack a pinpoint target. Sustained good weather was therefore more than usual a factor in timing the operation.

The second factor—requirements elsewhere—meant, of course, Anzio. The combined air forces could not make a maximum effort at Cassino and Anzio simultaneously. It had to be one or the other. Anzio was at this time the major anxiety. The new German counter-offensive was expected to go in there not later than February 16th. (In the event, this forecast proved to be correct.) Cassino had to be disposed of before then.

It was inevitable in the circumstances that the timing of the bombing should have been a matter for the Air Commanders to decide. But this does not excuse the lack of liaison between the air and army. At the same time there seems to have been a failure on the part of General Freyberg to appreciate the difficulty the Indian Division were experiencing in getting ready to make their attack. Otherwise he must have requested that the bombing be delayed until they were ready to take advantage of it.

'Ask of me anything but time,' Napoleon once said. It is common to most operations that the subordinate commanders protest that they have insufficient time. It is the duty of senior commanders to treat such protests with some reserve. In this case Freyberg, himself under extreme pressure from above, appears to have carried scepticism too far.

The difficulties of the Indians were not being exaggerated. We have seen already the extraordinary hazards which attended the relief of the Americans by the Indians' assault battalion—the shortage of mule transport; the loss of their entire reserve of grenades and mortar ammunition; the laborious process of trickling the division across the Rapido valley, the false no-man's-land, to the remote and separate battleground in the mountain tops; the necessity to manhandle stores and supplies up the final stretches of the precipitous tracks; the limitation on daylight movement owing to the positions being overlooked; the impossibility of reconnaissance of the ground over which attacks were to be made; the constant casualties from shellfire, including the shells of Allied guns that had not yet mastered the intricacy of this isolated salient that, in relation to the gun lines, was *behind* the German positions.

There was the question of the all-important Point 593, the peak adjacent to the Monastery. As we saw, the Americans had claimed that they held it, and it was not until the Indian Division arrived to take it over that they found that the Germans still held this key piece of ground, and that it would have to be cleared before the attack on the Monastery could go in. This does not appear to have been understood at New Zealand Corps H.Q., which continued to show 593 in its Intelligence Summaries as held by the Allies.

An illuminating comment on this situation is that of General Kippenberger who, writing long after the event about the difficulties of his opposite number Brigadier Dimoline, had this to say:

> Poor Dimoline was having a dreadful time getting his division into position. I never really appreciated the difficulties until I went over the ground after the war. He got me to make an appointment for us both with General Freyberg, as he thought his task was impossible and his difficulties not fully realized. The General refused to see us together: he told me he was not going to have any soviet of divisional commanders.

So Dimoline protested that he needed more time: Freyberg insisted that he could not have any: and the United States Army Air Force waited with one eye on the meteorologists and the other on Anzio. On February 14th, after a great storm which raged throughout the 13th, the experts promised a twenty-four hour period of clear weather. The bombing was accordingly ordered for 9.30 the following morning, the 15th.

In the early afternoon of February 14th, the monks were preparing to take to his last resting-place Dom Eusebio, who had died the previous day of the unidentified epidemic[1] which had broken out among the refugees in the Abbey. Still in his monk's habit, he lay in one of the underground passages where the others had taken turns to maintain a twenty-four hour vigil over his body. Now they were ready to consign him to one of the improvized coffins which he himself had been constructing in the carpenter's shop for those refugees who had died of the same disease.

As the monks prayed for the last time over the body of Dom

[1] Subsequently diagnosed as paratyphoid fever.

Eusebio a group of refugees rushed up to them in high excitement. They brought with them leaflets that had just been dropped by an American aircraft. The leaflets, addressed to 'Italian Friends' and signed 'The Fifth Army,' bore this message:

We have until now been careful to avoid bombarding Monte Cassino. The Germans have taken advantage of this. The battle is now closing in more and more around the sacred precincts. Against our will we are now obliged to direct our weapons against the Monastery itself. We warn you so that you may save yourselves. Leave the Monastery at once. This warning is urgent. It is given for your good.

At once there was a great commotion. Alarm quickly spread among the refugees scattered in pockets throughout the vast building. They began to stream in to where the Abbot stood, reading and re-reading the leaflet. The best thing, the Abbot said, would be to find a German officer and see if it could be arranged for the Abbey to be evacuated.

Three young men volunteered to leave the safety of the Abbey walls and make a dash for one of the German posts not many yards away. This meant showing themselves in the open. They set off, but before they had travelled very far they were frightened by the shellfire and turned back. Panic broke out afresh, and while the Abbot deliberated and the monks and the refugees argued about what should be done, the Sacrist and half a dozen helpers quietly lifted Dom Eusebio into his coffin, and bore him off along the corridors to the Chapel of St. Anne where he was laid to rest in the central grave of the presbytery.

By the time the burial party had returned the refugees were barely controllable, still demanding from the Abbot a magical solution. One monk suggested a mass exodus under a white flag, but another opposed this with grim stories of massacres he said had taken place in similar circumstances. Another argued in favour of staying and making the best of it. Before long the un-certainty had prompted one of the men to start a rumour that the monks were in league with the Germans, and that the leaflet was a trick concocted between them to get the Abbey cleared of the refugees—whose relationship with the monks was always inclined to be strained. In desperation the Abbot ruled that it was everyone for himself. They could make a run for it or stay, whichever they preferred. Another effort would be made to get in touch with the Germans after dark.

Shortly after nightfall two men did succeed in making contact with a German armoured car troop which patrolled the road up to the Monastery entrance during the hours of darkness. They said that the Abbot wished to speak to an officer and were told that this could not be arranged before five o'clock the following morning. Then two representatives of the Abbot—but not more than two—could come along to their headquarters. So they resigned themselves to a night of fear and uncertainty, and from time to time, unable to bear the suspense, the refugees would shout from the rabbitry to the nearby German posts, which were in earshot—but the soldiers did not reply. At five o'clock, just as the Abbot's secretary and the man chosen to accompany him were leaving the building the officer they were to try to locate turned up. He was introduced to the Abbot and shown the leaflet.

The Abbot suggested that it would be convenient if he and the monks could be allowed to make for the Allied lines, and the refugees were removed to the German rear. There was a wistful irony in the old man's suggestion that his own small group and the refugees should move in opposite directions, and also, perhaps, in the choice of directions he proposed.

The officer, a lieutenant, said that there could be no question of anyone being allowed to walk to the Allied lines. He pointed out that it would be a risky business leaving the Monastery at all, and they would have to take full responsibility for any move decided upon. He added, however, that during the night he had discussed the situation of the Monastery with his commanding officer, and the latter had arranged for one of the paths leading down to Highway Six to be opened to the refugees from midnight until 5 a.m. the following morning, February 16th.

The Abbot protested that it might be too late then. The officer said that this was the best he could do and after being taken, at his request, into the Cathedral for a few moments, he left. It was still half an hour before daylight. Those civilians who were at hand dispersed to the various passages and corners that had become their temporary homes. The monks repaired to their small subterranean chapel in the *Toretta*, the oldest part of the building, the one link with St. Benedict's original abbey, and there they prepared to start the day's worship which in winter begin at 5.30.

Tuesday, February 15th, 1944, began, like any other day, with the celebration of Matins and Lauds.

5

THE morning of Tuesday, February 15th, was cold, but the sky was clearer than it had been for many days. In that part of their refuge which they had turned into a temporary chapel, the Abbot and the monks were addressing themselves as usual to the succession of holy offices which make up the Benedictine day: to that rhythm of prayer and psalmody and meditation precisely laid down for them fourteen centuries before by their founder in his *Rule*.

It had begun, after the departure of the German officer, with that part of the Divine Office that ended with Lauds. At 8.30 they recited together the psalms and prayers prescribed for *Prime* and the first of the Little Hours, *Terce*. And then, as it happened to be the week of the Feast of St. Scholastica—St. Benedict's sister, whose bones lay alongside her brother's in the great tomb below the high altar of the cathedral of Monte Cassino—they celebrated the conventual mass appropriate to this particular saint.

Not long afterwards they went to the Abbot's room to recite the next two, and then they returned to their temporary chapel. They had improvised an altar there, and on it they had set the little Madonna of De Matteis which normally rested on the tomb of St. Benedict in the cathedral. Kneeling before this altar, and chanting the antiphon of the Blessed Virgin, they invoked the blessing of the Madonna.

It was a little after 9.30 and they had just sung the words 'Beseech Christ on our behalf' when the first of a succession of great explosions sent a shudder through the thick Abbey walls and great gusts of thunder echoed along the vast stone passageways giving continuity to the crashes so that they were no longer a succession of explosions but a single great cataclysmic roar.

To these men whose lives had been passed in seclusion; whose scant conversation was in a low voice; whose meals were taken in silence; whose habitation was a mountain top that was the apotheosis of tranquillity; whose most violent acquaintance with sound was the Gregorian chant of the Divine Office; the bombing was, apart from anything else, an overwhelmingly terrifying baptism of sheer noise beyond anything they could conceivably have imagined. They huddled together in a corner on their knees, numb with terror. Automatically the eighty-year-old Abbot gave them absolution. Automatically they composed themselves for death.

The explosions seemed incessant. A great haze of dust and smoke was discernible through the narrow window, and great yellow flashes, as the bombs crashed about the building dispassionately destroying. All the time the thunder of the explosions echoed and re-echoed along the vaulted corridors and stone passageways, adding immeasurably to the noise.

After the first few minutes of petrifying shock there was a diversion, marked by that quality of melodrama which was never long absent from Cassino. A breathless figure, covered in dust, appeared suddenly at the side of the praying monks. He was gesticulating like a man demented, but he uttered no sound. It was the deaf-mute servant. In the sign language of the deaf-and-dumb, heightened by terror into almost maniacal convulsions, he was trying to tell them that the cathedral had gone. It had been one of the first parts of the Abbey to receive a direct hit. A bomb had passed through the frescoed dome.

The bombardment continued throughout the morning, and though only about ten per cent of the heavy bombers succeeded in hitting the Abbey, this was enough to wreck the interior.

Inside the cathedral the pipes of the ancient Catarinozzi organ, which had cost 10,000 ducats, were shredded like paper foil: the high altar, incorporating parts of an original attributed to Michelangelo, subsided into a mound of rubble about the tomb of St. Benedict: the wooden stalls of the choir, a masterpiece of the Neapolitan carvers who have no equals in this work, were reduced to a tangle of splinters. Fragments of marble inlay were scattered everywhere like outsize confetti.

One by one the five cloistered courtyards were shattered into dumps to contain the rubble of the elegant cloisters and the solid buildings which had formerly surrounded them.

The entrance cloister was a series of broken stumps amid a heap of debris that was knee-deep. The Cloister of the Priors, around which the boys' college had formed a square, had been totally submerged by the collapsed college, and nearly 100 refugees were buried under the ruins. The Bramante Cloister, the one unquestionable architectural masterpiece of Monte Cassino, no longer existed.

This cloister had been built round three sides of the central courtyard. Along the top of its arches ran the celebrated gallery known as the *Loggia del Paradiso*—and from the fourth side rose a magnificent stone stairway, sixty feet wide, leading up to yet another cloister, the Cloister of the Benefactors, decorated with the marble statues of seventeen Popes and Kings who had befriended the Monastery. This cloister led to the Cathedral. In the centre of the courtyard, too, was a cistern, decorated with a handsome pillared fountainhead.

By noon the central courtyard was unrecognizable. The cloisters were like broken teeth. The great flight of steps had vanished. The portico above the cistern had been levelled to the ground leaving only a gaping hole filled with water that was now coloured red.

Once during the morning, when there seemed to be a lull in the bombardment, the Abbot left his shelter to inspect the damage. He found that most of the upper storeys of the Abbey had gone and that all that remained of the Cathedral was its shell, wide open to the sky. He heard the groans of refugees buried under the ruins of the Priors' Cloister, and found that nothing could be done to rescue them. He saw other refugees making a dash for the open, and about a hundred got away during this interlude. And he was accosted by the three peasant families, who, from the earliest days of what might be termed the siege, had been allowed to stay on in the Abbey. They asked if they might now go down to the monks' refuge, and the Abbot gave them permission to do so. Then the sound of aircraft was heard again, and everyone hastily returned to his shelter.

The monks were safe in their chapel, and the lay brothers, it turned out, had been able to make themselves comfortable and secure in the bakery. Meanwhile the Sacrist had made a hazardous journey through the rubble and the half-collapsed walls to bring the Holy Sacrament from another chapel so that the monks could celebrate Communion.

The bombardment reopened. It was now the turn of the Mediums. They dropped smaller bombs, but they dropped them more accurately. The Mediums attacked from a low level in tight little formations of twelve, and their bombs fell in a compact carpet. Once again the Abbot, those monks who were still with him, and the three peasant families who had attached themselves to him, prepared for the worst. Soon an explosion more powerful than any they had yet experienced seemed to tear the heart out of the crumbling abbey. A great wave of debris thundered about the refuge, blocking the entrance to it, but the thick walls held.

To Allied observers, watching the bombing with a sense of uncomfortable awe, it did not for a long time seem as effective as they had expected.

Christopher Buckley, the British war correspondent, noted:

As the sun brightened and climbed up the sky I could detect little modification in the monastery's outline as each successive smoke cloud cleared away. Here and there one noted an ugly fissure in the walls, here and there a window seemed unnaturally enlarged. The roof was beginning to look curiously jagged and uneven . . . but essentially the building was still standing after four hours of pounding from the air.

Just before two o'clock in the afternoon a formation of Mitchells (Mediums) passed over. They dipped slightly. A moment later a bright flame, such as a giant might have produced by striking titanic matches on the mountain-side, spurted swiftly upwards at half-a-dozen points. Then a pillar of smoke five hundred feet high broke upwards into the blue. For nearly five minutes it hung around the building, thinning gradually upwards into strange, evil-looking arabesques such as Aubrey Beardsley at his most decadent might have designed.

Then the column paled and melted. The Abbey became visible again. Its whole outline had changed. The west wall had totally collapsed. . . .

The Mediums, operating in tight formation, had administered the *coup de grâce*, and this had been the explosion more powerful than any that had gone before, the one that had blocked the entrance to the monks' refuge.

(The wall, though breached, had not been split from top to bottom, as it had seemed to Buckley watching from a hillside five miles away. The lower part, the battlemented base, ten feet thick, was still intact. The Abbey had been wrecked, but there was still no easy way in for any soldiers who succeeded in storming their way up the slopes of the mountain.)

During the afternoon the Abbot and those with him dug their way out of the refuge they had been using, and made for the chapels under the largely intact *torretta*, which now seemed the safest place left. There they did what they could to help the injured. A little food was located and distributed. But there was no water. With the arrival of darkness, and periodical collapses of walls and ceilings—not to mention the artillery fire that was by this time following up the work of the bombers—a new kind of terror set in. Should they attempt to get away at once, risking the shells? Or should they wait for the German officer to whom they had spoken in the morning?

At eight o'clock this same lieutenant arrived at the Abbey. But it was not, as they had hoped, to guide them to the escape route that had been promised early that morning.

The lieutenant had come to say that Hitler, at the request of the Pope, was asking the Allies for a truce so that the monks and the civilian refugees might leave Monte Cassino. They would be taken away in German army transport, but owing to the state of the road, would have to make their way to the vehicles on foot.

Kesselring would ask for a truce that night. If the Allies failed to grant it the responsibility for the fate of the monks and refugees would be theirs.

The Abbot was then asked to sign a statement to the effect that there had been no German soldiers in the Monastery before or during the attack. The statement was already prepared:

> I certify to be the truth that inside the enclosure of the sacred monastery of Cassino there never were any German soldiers; that there were for a certain period only three military police for the sole purpose of enforcing respect for the neutral zone which was established around the monastery, but they were withdrawn about twenty days ago.

> Monte Cassino   (*Signed*) GREGORIO DIAMARE
> *February* 15, 1944.   Abbot-Bishop of Monte Cassino.
>
>   DIEBER
>   Lieutenant.

On the altar of the Chapel of the Pietà, his black habit still white with the clinging dust, the exhausted eighty-year-old Abbot signed the document and the officer left. Although his feelings were by no means pro-Allied at this moment, the Abbot and the remaining monks had little doubt that the statement about the request for a truce meant nothing. There is an innocent pathos in the way one of them expressed his doubts: 'The truce did not take place. It is indeed doubtful whether the request for it was ever even put forward, and whether it was not a case of deception.' But at this extreme time they needed some sort of hope to cling to, and the mention of a truce, however sceptically they felt about it, provided them with it. It was this hope of a truce that helped them to face the long twelve-hour night in darkness that was penetrated only by the flash of bursting shells, the moans of the wounded, and the fearful rumble whenever some further part of the ruins collapsed.

As they composed themselves to await the morrow there was one result of that day that affected the monks more profoundly than any other. In a devastation that had spared no part of the extensive monastery buildings except those below ground, the cell used by St. Benedict himself, and preserved through the ages, had unaccountably escaped. They would have been filled with even greater wonder had they known (what was discovered many months later after the war had passed on) that during the afternoon a large calibre artillery shell had landed within a foot of the Saint's tomb, but had failed to explode.

So it happened that in all this destruction the cell where Benedict lived in his lifetime, and the tomb in which his remains had rested during the fourteen hundred years since his death, were among the few places to escape injury.

That night the Air Command announced flatly that 142 B-17 Fortress bombers and 112 Mediums had by nightfall dropped 576 tons of bombs on Monte Cassino. The Monastery buildings had been wrecked and breaches made in the outer walls, but because of the great thickness of these walls the bombs had not breached them from top to bottom.

On this same Tuesday morning, February 15th, the foremost troops of the 4th Indian Division were facing their third day in the uncomfortable mountain salient. The conditions were unlike anything they had previously experienced. Only a shallow jagged hump separated their forward posts from those of the Germans seventy yards away. The whole of this isolated private front-line was overlooked from enemy-held heights on three sides, which made daylight movement out of the question. It had been difficult enough to relieve the Americans in the first place, and since taking over two nights before, it had been even more difficult to bring up the supplies they would need for the major attack they were being pressed to launch almost immediately. Living conditions were not improved by the presence of over a hundred unburied, and unreachable, bodies scattered about the area.

The best way to visualize this salient cutting into the crust of the German mountain positions, is to imagine a rocky, uneven ridge roughly in the shape of a boomerang and 1,000 yards long. From the British side the boomerang curved away to the left, with the Royal Sussex tenuously astride half of it, and the Germans occupying the remainder, Monastery Hill being just beyond the far end. At the 'elbow' of the boomerang

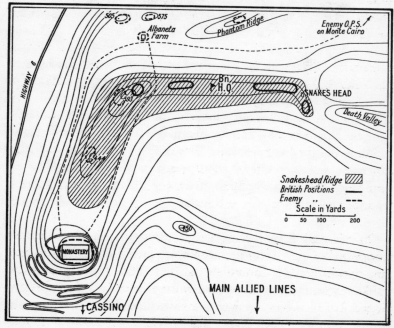

MOUNTAIN BATTLEFIELD

Snakeshead Ridge, mountain approach to Monastery Hill. Seventy yards separated forward troops of both sides here. American, British, Indian, and Polish infantry who successively occupied Snakeshead had to be maintained by mules and porters making round journeys of 14 miles each night. Allied positions were overlooked by enemy from three sides

was the dome-shaped mountain known on the map as Point 593. The Germans manned its forward slopes in strength.

The boomerang-shaped ridge, which the Americans had called Snakeshead, provided an approach to the Monastery, but blocking the way was the natural obstacle of Point 593. The sides of the ridge sloped away sharply, at times precipitously, and the only alternative to an advance along the ridge (taking 593 en route) was to cut directly across the open 'elbow' to Monastery Hill, giving Point 593 in the middle a wide berth. This, however, would entail crossing a chaos of slopes, gullies, ravines, boulders, gorse thickets, and shattered walls where shells had churned up the terracing. On the whole the approach along Snakeshead seemed the lesser of the two evils, but first Point 593 would have to be captured.

Two basic (as well as a score of minor) difficulties influenced the projected operation over this unpromising ground. The first was supply. Everything, including water, had to be brought seven miles across the valley on mules by an oblique route, and then manhandled for the last few hundred yards up the final steep paths to the forward positions. This supply route took five hours to cover, was constantly shelled so that only a proportion of the mules actually got through on many nights. The wounded had to endure the same long and hazardous journey in the opposite direction.

The second basic difficulty was that the ground itself—this tangle of rocky ledges, slopes, ravines, boulders, narrow ridges, and gorse thickets—was such that only a few troops could be deployed on it at a time. To adapt itself to these conditions, the Division's plan had been to establish one of its three brigades (the 7th) in the forward area as a firm base and assault force, and to feed battalions of a second brigade (the 5th) into the 7th as required. The 7th Brigade would therefore act as a funnel not only for its own jug of water, as it were, but also for that of the 5th Brigade. The third brigade of the Division, the 11th, would be used as a corps of porters, carriers, and labourers to keep the other two supplied.

By Tuesday morning the 7th Brigade were just beginning to become acclimatized to their spearpoint position. The 1st Royal Sussex were astride Snakeshead Ridge, seventy yards from the Germans, 1,000 yards from the Monastery. The 4th/16th Punjabis were echeloned down the slope to their left. The 1st/2nd Gurkhas were in reserve a few hundred yards behind.

To the Royal Sussex, who were the point of the spear, the focal point of the landscape was, of course, the cream-coloured Abbey on which they looked slightly downwards from this height. But what worried them more was the rocky dome of Point 593 rising up immediately to their front. While everyone else could talk of nothing but the Monastery, the Royal Sussex were doing their best to make it clear that Point 593 would have to be captured first. No 593, no Monte Cassino. At the Headquarters of the Second New Zealand Corps across the valley this had not been fully appreciated. Thus it was that the 4th Indian Division, now gloomily aware of all the local difficulties, was thinking in terms of a preliminary clearance of Point 593, to be followed by an attack on the Monastery: while Second New Zealand Corps, constantly being urged to get a move on, was visualizing an immediate direct attack on the Monastery as soon as the bombing had taken place.

While the officers were preoccupied with these problems on that Tuesday morning there was nothing for the soldiers to do but to make themselves as tolerably comfortable as they could in the circumstances. They would try to sleep, or read, or even shave if they had saved the dregs of their tea—for when water had to be brought seven miles by mule it had also to be severely rationed. They would clean their weapons, but not themselves. They would smoke, if they had not run out of cigarettes, for ammunition had to take precedence over comforts while mules were still short. They would write letters. They would stare at the Monastery.

When, shortly after 9.30, the formation of Fortresses passed high overhead, no one paid any attention. Except when the weather was bad, Fortresses were always flying over, so high that they were only just visible, to those regular assignments—marshalling yards, railway bridges, communication centres—that to the soldier seemed always so remote and useless. Then the bombs began to drop on the Monastery and some of them quite a distance from it and a few of the soldiers were wounded by flying rock splinters before they had quite grasped what was happening.

As the first salvo crashed down Colonel Glennie, C.O. of the Royal Sussex, picked up his telephone and called his Brigade Headquarters, but before he had time to speak the voice at the other end said: 'We didn't know either!' No one had remembered to tell the ground troops primarily concerned that the bombing, which they had been warned to expect on the 16th, had been brought forward a day. 'They told the monks,' remarked Colonel Glennie, 'and they told the enemy, but they didn't tell us!' Of this curious lapse, perhaps it may be said that army-air cooperation was still in its adolescence, if not its infancy, and that this was yet another occasion when the lessons of war were learned the hard way.

For the soldiers, the bombing was a spectacular diversion in the monotony of the front line day—albeit a nerve-racking one, for many of the bombs fell close to their positions and caused several more casualties. For the officers it was the background to a day of feverish planning, for it wasn't long before the order came through that, however unexpected the advancing of the date of the bombing, however unready they might think they were, an attack must be made that night. The preliminary clearance of Point 593 must be disposed of immediately. The Royal Sussex must deal with it that night.

The factors were brutally simple. The nearest German posts were seventy yards away: too close for the British battalion to employ direct artillery support. The peak of 593 was only another hundred yards farther on. The ground was rock hard, and littered with loose stones, making silent approach virtually impossible. There had been no time to build up a picture of exact enemy dispositions through patrolling and continuous observation. This was a battle that would be settled by grenade, bayonet, mortar, and light machine-gun, and the unfortunate Sussex would now have bitter cause to regret the loss of their mortar and grenade reserves on the journey forward, when the two lorries carrying them plunged off the road. (In passing, one may wonder why the Divisional Staff failed to make good this loss.)

This must have been one of the few battlefields of the Second

World War which reproduced the close conditions of 1914–18. The Flanders phrase is entirely applicable. What the Royal Sussex had to do was to go 'over the top'.

In view of their limited knowledge of both the ground and enemy dispositions the Sussex decided to make their first attack with one company only. That night, about the time that Abbot Diamare, propping himself against the altar of the chapel of the Pietà, was signing the document declaring that there had been no German soldiers in the Monastery, a company of the Sussex, three officers and sixty-three men strong, moved stealthily forward astride Snakeshead Ridge towards Point 593 at the 'elbow' of the boomerang.

They moved in normal formation of two platoons abreast, the third following behind in reserve. They moved very slowly. On this ground there was a danger at every step of a stone being dislodged and rattling against another: and in these high places sounds of this kind were audible a long way off. On this ground, too, it was fatally easy to turn an ankle, or stumble. It was especially easy for a man laden with something heavy, such as a Bren gun. With every single step there was a danger of breaking the silence that was essential to their approach, with an alert enemy a bare seventy yards away.

The leading troops had advanced no more than fifty yards when they came under a withering fire of machine-gun and grenade. They went to ground. They wriggled across the sharp, stony ground from one position to another, trying to work round to the flanks. Time after time individuals and groups made a new effort to find a way round, a way closer to an objective that was so near and yet so inaccessible. But the steep ground defeated them. And their grenades began to run short, though the Germans, sending them over in showers from their positions up the slope, had unlimited quantities. To help them out grenades were collected from the other companies of the battalion, and passed forward, but long before dawn these too had been used up.

If they had remained in the open after daybreak they would have been wiped out to a man. Before first light they were therefore ordered to withdraw. February 15th, a calamitous day for Monte Cassino, had not spared the Royal Sussex either. Of the three officers and sixty-three men who had undertaken this exploratory trial of strength against a preliminary objective, two officers and thirty-two men had been killed or wounded no more than fifty yards from their start-point. It was a foretaste of things to come.

6

DURING the morning the Sussex were ordered to try again that night, using the whole battalion. At the same time it was learned that the counter-offensive against the Anzio beachhead had started, as expected, a few hours before.

The Germans had massed four infantry divisions on a 4,000-yard front and were making an all-out effort to cut through the heart of the beachhead to Anzio, eight miles away. This was their biggest offensive operation of the campaign. It was supported by 452 guns. Following up the infantry divisions and their supporting tanks, ready to exploit their success, were two Panzer divisions, each reinforced by a battalion of the newest and heaviest tanks, the Tiger and Panther.

There was no doubt at all where the Allied Air Forces were going to be needed for the next few days. Everything that could fly would be wanted at Anzio. Cassino could look for no help from the air for a few days. The bombing offensive that had started the day before with the destruction of the Monastery had to end with it.

Poor Abbot Diamare and his reduced party of monks and refugees could not know this, however, and they spent a forlorn day in the Abbey ruins waiting in vain for the Germans who had promised to return and help them to get away.

By now the party was reduced to about forty. Most of the able-bodied survivors of the bombing had got away during the night or at dawn. There remained the three dogged peasant families who never left the Abbot's side now; some children— three of them badly injured—who had been deserted by their parents; a number of other injured including an old woman whose feet had been blown off; about half a dozen able-bodied men, and a few of the lay brothers. Only two monks remained. One, as we saw, died in the epidemic. Two others were killed in the bombing.

Apart from one brief visit from fighter bombers during the day, there was no air activity, but there was a great deal of artillery fire. Quite early in the day the Abbot decided that he could expect no further help from the Germans and that he must organize the evacuation himself. He decided that first light the following morning would be the best time, as he had noticed that there was generally a lull in the fighting then. Once again he and the monks had to resign themselves to another long night in the ruins.

There were two small comforts in a day of otherwise un-relieved fear and hopelessness. One of the lay brothers managed to rescue a breviary from the rubble: it enabled the Abbot and the monks to celebrate the divine offices as usual. The other, and more earthly comfort, was the discovery that a small water tank was undamaged in the ruins of the kitchen.

The first thing the Sussex C.O. did when he was ordered to attack 593 again that night was to send a strongly-worded SOS for grenades. The company battle of the night before had confirmed that grenades more than anything else were what were wanted for this close-quarter fighting among the rocks. Then he planned his attack.

B Company, reinforced by a platoon of A Company were to undertake the main effort: they were to attack 593 from the left and take it. Simultaneously the depleted A Company were to make a diversionary effort on the right, to distract the German defences. When B Company were on the hill, they were to send up a light signal, whereupon D Company, fresh and carrying as much ammunition as they could, were to rush through, relieve B on the newly-captured height and immediately prepare to repel the inevitable counter-attack. C Company, the one halved in strength by the battle of the previous night, would remain in reserve.

With the objective beginning only seventy yards away, it was not possible to have it shelled in advance.

The shortage of ammunition for the mortars was solved by salvaging the bombs (of a different calibre from the British) left behind by the Americans. These could be fired through some captured German and Italian mortars which the Sussex had brought back from North Africa as souvenirs.

No one was happy about the operation. The trial of strength the previous night had shown how strongly defended 593 was. The impossibility of prior reconnaissance made night movement over this broken and difficult ground a dangerous gamble. Ammunition was still far from adequate—it would take many nights to build up the necessary stocks. But Anzio was facing its gravest crisis and the Cassino attack had to go in. It would be something if the all-important grenades arrived in time. For the Royal Sussex it was a day of tension.

The attack was ordered for 2300, because that was the earliest time by which the mule train bringing the grenades could arrive. By 2300 the mules had not arrived. The supply route had been heavily shelled that night, and many mules had been lost. The attack was postponed for half an hour. By 2330 the mules had still not arrived, and the attack was postponed for another half-hour. A few minutes later the mules did arrive, but owing to losses on the way through the shelling, they brought only half the number of grenades required.

The attack at last started, calamitously, at midnight. As we have seen there could be no direct artillery support on an objective so close to the attackers. Instead the task of the artillery was to neutralize the adjacent peaks, especially Point 575, 800 yards to the right of 593. From the point of view of the guns—firing from the far side of the valley, 1,500 feet below the altitude of these hills—the ridge along which the Sussex had to advance was a crest only slightly below that of Point 575. To hit the latter, it was necessary for the shells to skim the top of Snakeshead by a few feet, and gunnery as precise as this allowed no margin for error. The tiniest fraction of a variation in elevation and the shells would hit the top of Snakeshead instead of Point 575, 800 yards beyond.

This is precisely what happened. As the two leading companies, closely followed by Battalion Headquarters and the Reserve Company, formed up on the start-line of the attack, the artillery opened fire on Point 575. But several shells failed to clear Snakeshead, and burst among the leading companies and Battalion Headquarters. It is axiomatic that the most demoralizing beginning to any operation is for the attacking force to be shelled on its start-line. It is not less disturbing if the shells happen to be from its own guns. Only one company—the one that was to take over and consolidate the hill if it was captured—escaped.

After a hurried reorganization the attack went in according to plan. As on the previous night fifty yards were covered before the advancing troops ran into a withering fire. The reinforced main-effort company worked round by the left, as they had been ordered, while the smaller company set about creating their diversionary display of fireworks on the right. This company at once ran into trouble. Just in time they stopped on the edge of a forty-foot precipice not indicated on the map. There was no way round by the right, so they edged leftwards, and then found themselves faced with a crevice fifteen feet deep and twenty feet across. There was nothing they could do except go to ground and give fire support.

Meanwhile the main-effort company on the left, thanks to a number of individual feats of valour which destroyed some of the German machine-gun nests, did succeed in forcing their way on to the main part of the feature. But the Germans, defending ruthlessly, could not be dislodged from well-prepared positions in which they were determined to stay. A hand-to-hand battle then raged, and in the confusion a number of the Sussex pushing through to the rear of the objective went beyond it, and fell down another of the small precipices in which the area abounds. They were wounded and taken prisoner. Another party, driving through to the rear of the peak, unluckily ran into a more numerous party of German reinforcements on their way in. As on the previous night it turned into a grenade battle, but while the Germans were sending them over in showers, the British battalion soon began to run out. After about two hours of this, the right-hand company had had all their officers killed or wounded, and the reserve company went to reinforce them. On the left the main effort force was rapidly running out of ammunition, and all of their officers had been wounded.

The one fresh company—the one that had been intended to exploit the captured position—was sent in as a last resort, but it came up against the deep crevice that had halted the one on the right, and at the same time it was caught in a murderous cross-fire.

The attack had failed and there was nothing for it but to withdraw the remnants of the four companies to the point from which they had started.

Out of 12 officers and 250 men that had taken part in the attack, 10 officers and 130 men were killed, wounded or taken prisoner. In the two nights, therefore, the Sussex casualties had been 12 out of 15 officers, 162 out of 313 men. In two nights a fine battalion that had fought since the earliest days of the war and to which success had become a matter of routine and habit had been cut to pieces.

The casualties speak for themselves. The battalion could not have tried harder or more gallantly. It wasn't their fault that they had to attack before they were ready. With the supply line what it was—the night was barely long enough for the mule trains to make the round journey of fourteen miles—they had no chance to build up their ammunition stocks to the level required.

At dawn on Thursday (by which time Tuesday's bombing seemed an age ago)—while the Commanding Officer of the Royal Sussex was reorganizing the remains of four powerful companies into three small ones; while General von Mackensen's Fourteenth Army, after a non-stop attack which had driven a mile and a half into the Anzio beachhead, was approaching the climax of its tremendous onslaught—Abbot Diamare, summoning up the last reserves of his strength, prepared for the final stage of his long ordeal.

He called the surviving monks and refugees together by the entrance arch of the Abbey (above which the inscription PAX was still intact) and gave sacramental absolution to each one of them. Then, taking hold of a large wooden crucifix, he led the way through the rubble on to one of the bridle paths leading westwards through the mountains. Before the party of forty left there was a last distressing decision to be taken. Three small children, a sister and two brothers, had been found in the ruins. All three were injured. Their mother had been killed in the bombing and their father had since abandoned them. It was clear that the girl and one of the brothers had a very short time to live. When an attempt was made to lift them they screamed with pain, and it was thought kinder to leave them. To have carried them up and down steep mountain paths would only have made their last moments more painful. The other brother was less badly hurt, he was only paralysed in both legs. A lay brother hoisted him on to his shoulders. A ladder was found which could be used as a stretcher for the old woman whose feet had been blown off, and two of the very few survivors who were not either sick or wounded carried her at the rear of the column.

Progress was slow and painful, the paths being steep and rough. But the Abbot, supported by the monks and lay brothers, insisted on holding up the heavy crucifix as they stumbled down the mountainside. Whenever they came to a German post the Abbot asked for permission to pass, saying that he was abandoning the Monastery with the consent of the German High Command. For the most part (one of the monks recorded) the soldiers just stared open-mouthed at this strange company and said absolutely nothing. Inevitably the little column straggled and after a time there were shouts from the rear. The men carrying the ladder bearing the woman who had lost her feet shouted that they could not keep up, the track was too steep and too difficult. Those in front shouted back encouragement. There was not much farther to go, they must keep up. After they had been walking for some

time they came to a level piece of ground and the Abbot called
a halt so that they could rest a little, and to give the stragglers a
chance to catch up. It was discovered then that the two men who
had been carrying the old woman had given up some way back
and abandoned her. They were too exhausted to carry on, they
said. The column moved off again and after a time they came to
a cottage in which the Germans had established a medical post.
There the injured were given some attention, but when the
Abbot asked to be put in touch with a Headquarters he was told
that the telephone line was cut. The Germans said it would be
better for the party to keep moving until they were farther to the
rear. They would receive help there. They pointed out a suitable
path and suggested that it would be safer (there was a certain
amount of shelling) if they moved off at intervals in small groups.

This was arranged and one by one the groups moved off. The
last to leave were to be the Abbot and the Sacrist. For the time
being these two rested inside the cottage as the Abbot was by
this time close to collapse. While they were there a messenger
arrived to say that an urgent search for the Abbot had been
instituted and all forward units had been warned to look out for
him. As soon as he had reported back that the Abbot was found
a further message was sent to the medical post ordering them to
look after him until he could be picked up. The ambulance
arrived during the afternoon.

The German Corps Commander, General von Senger has
described the end of the story:

I had the Abbot picked up there by car and brought to my Headquarters. . . . I lodged the venerable old priest, who was accompanied by a solitary monk-companion, for one night.

While the Abbot was my guest I received orders from the German
High Command to induce him to make a radio statement regarding
the attitude of the German troops and their respect for the neutrality
of the Monastery. I decided to comply, as the destruction of the
Monastery was an event of historic importance in which my personal
honour as a soldier and as a Christian was involved. After a conversation with his companion the Abbot agreed, and we conducted a

dialogue into the microphone which went even further than I had intended, complaining of the deplorable ruin and destruction of many valuable and irreparable works of art. After the broadcast I had him taken by car to Rome, appointing an officer to deliver him safely to Sant' Anselmo, where he informed me he wished to go. Sant' Anselmo on the Aventino is the centre of the Benedictine Order. . . .

My plan to convey the Abbot safely to Sant' Anselmo was thwarted. On the road to Rome the car was waylaid by agents of Goebbels, the Propaganda Minister. Goebbels had no intention of missing this excellent piece of propaganda and according to the methods of the Fuehrer Principle meant to act with complete disregard of what others might do in the same line. The frightened old priest was accordingly brought to a radio station, kept waiting a long time without food, and finally induced to make another statement as prescribed by the radio columnists. . . .

But this was not sufficient. Hitler's most stupid and most arrogant henchman, the Foreign Minister, also wanted his share of the cake. The statement which he required was shaped upon distinctly political propaganda lines. The unfortunate old priest at last broke down, refused to make any more statements and asked to be released, as he now understood that he was no longer a protected guest but a prisoner.

War exacts its wages indiscriminately. In the mosaic of suffering and endurance created by the battle of Cassino, Gregorio Diamare, eighty-year-old Abbot-Bishop of Monte Cassino, has an honourable place. So, it may be thought, has the old peasant woman with the severed feet, whom they carried part of the way to safety on a ladder, and then left to die alone on the cold mountainside. For it was her fate to be a battle casualty without even knowing what the battle was about.

That evening, the German propagandists having completed their work, the Tenth Army was able to make some small adjustments to its dispositions on and around the summit of Monastery Hill by establishing posts in the Abbey ruins.

For the 4th Indian Division and the New Zealanders it was a

day of urgency. Both divisions were at last ready to make the concerted attack originally designed to follow the bombing. That night the Indians would attack not with one battalion, but with three.

At midnight the 4th/6th Rajputana Rifles would pass through the Royal Sussex and attempt to storm Point 593. If they succeeded where the Sussex had failed, the depleted Sussex would then follow up the success, and sweep along the ridge to Point 444 at the far end of the 'boomerang'.

At 0215, with the help of the moon which would then be rising, two battalions of Gurkhas, the 1st/2nd and 1st/9th, starting from the left of the Sussex would sweep across the slopes and ravines in a direct assault on the Monastery. It was an appalling route that they had to cover, but the Gurkhas, born and bred in the foothills of the Himalaya, were the most expert mountain fighters in the Commonwealth armies. If anyone could negotiate the impossible mountain terrain, the Gurkhas could. Two entire reserve battalions of the division were organized into carrying parties to provide the necessary replenishments of ammunition and other essentials.

While the Indians projected themselves at these mountain strongholds, the 28th (Maori) Battalion of the New Zealand Division was to advance from the direction of Monte Trocchio along the railway causeway and take Cassino Station.

The New Zealanders had not had the same difficulty as the Indians in getting into position, but like the Indians they had found themselves on ground where few troops could be deployed at a time. Owing to the flooded state of the valley, the causeway was the only usable line of approach.

On the heels of the Maoris would follow a company of sappers to remove mines, deal with the demolitions that the Germans had left behind to make the causeway impossible for transport, and to erect Bailey bridges over two water-ways—a canal and the Rapido—which lay between the start-point and the station. The success of the operation depended on the sappers making the route fit for transport by dawn, so that tanks and anti-tank guns could join the Maoris on the objective by daylight. Massed behind Trocchio, ready to exploit the Maoris' success, was a force of 180 tanks, and the rest of the Division.

The Maoris had a special place in the New Zealand Division. They were cheerful ebullient men, with a keen sense of humour and a natural fighting spirit: great soldiers in the assault and pursuit. Temperamentally, they were the 'wild Irish' of the New Zealand Division. The advance started soon after dark to give the engineers as long a period of darkness as possible in which to complete their vital bridging and repairs to the route. In the closing stages of the advance the Maoris came up against mine-fields and barbed wire, and they were continuously mortared. But they fought their way through, and shortly after midnight they had stormed into the sheds and buildings of the Station, and triumphantly taken possession of them—and also a number of prisoners.

Meanwhile, two thousand feet above them in the mountains— just faintly discernible from the Station in the dark—the Raj-putana Rifles edged along Snakeshead Ridge towards Point 593. But as on the previous two nights within an hour or so the battalion was pinned down by impenetrable fire as it crouched at the base, and on the lower slopes, of the rock. They tried every-thing they knew to work their way round the boulders and ledges, and more than one small party succeeded in reaching the summit, but they were invariably killed or wounded. It developed into the same story as on the two preceding nights: successive small individual efforts that made no progress but always cost a few more lives. By two in the morning one company commander had been killed, two of the other three wounded.

While the Rajputs fought it out on 593, the 1st/9th Gurkhas, only 300 yards to their left, set off on the rough direct route to the Monastery, about 1,000 yards away. Their preliminary objective was point 444 at the end of the 'boomerang'. Almost immediately they came under heavy cross-fire from 593, and points on their left, and their efforts to deal with these positions brought them up on the left of the Rajputs, but neither battalion could make any headway. The stronghold of 593, supported by the neighbouring high points, was well able to take care of both.

The second Gurkha battalion, the 1st/2nd, then moved off, but some way farther to the left, with a direct approach to the Monastery via Point 450. As they worked their way down to the steep ravine which was the final obstacle—the ravine at the bottom of the northern slope of Monastery Hill—they approached a belt of what looked like scrub. It stood out in a landscape that had been bereft of so much of its vegetation by shellfire. They remembered noting it on their air photographs, on which it showed up as a long, prominent shadow. As the leading platoons approached it, a shower of grenades came down on them from the higher ground behind, and swiftly they dashed forward to take cover in this patch of scrub.

There was a series of staccato explosions. The scrub was not scrub at all, but a thicket of strong thorn, breast-high. It had been laced with barbed wire, and was thickly sown with interconnected anti-personnel mines set to explode when any of the trip wires, cunningly placed across all approaches, was touched.

As the leading platoons dashed into what they took to be cover, half of them were blown up by the mines, those that weren't were mown down by the rows of machine-guns a little way to the rear, which had only to pour their fire into the cries and flashes and the silhouettes grotesquely lighted up on the thorn and barbed wire every time a mine went off. The Colonel, shot through the stomach, was among those who fell wounded at this place. Despite this setback, the follow-up companies tried to press on with the attack, but a line of machine-guns across the full width of Monastery Hill presented a curtain of fire through which they could not break though they did not stop trying. The Monastery was only 400 yards away, but they were 400 of the longest yards in the world.

The full story of these deadly night battles can never be known, because too many of its authors died writing it. Under-supplied, without sufficient time to prepare, these few fought a lonely battle in the mountains and no one in the rest of the army had

any idea of what they were facing. They had nothing to sustain
them except that potent imponderable, their regimental identity.
It mattered to the Rajputana Rifles that they were Rajputana
Rifles: it mattered to the Royal Sussex that they were Royal
Sussex. In the end it was probably this alone that enabled them
to keep on. His mother in a village near Katmandu would never
know about her stretcher-bearer son making sixteen journeys
across this inferno until, as he raised his last load, he fell dead
with a burst of tracer in his back. Like the English officer who
lay dead at his side, he had done what he had done not only
because it was his job as a soldier, but because over and above
that he was conscious of being a Gurkha Rifleman.

By first light on Friday the situation on Snakeshead was
exactly as it had been the morning before, except that there were
three battalions instead of one pinned down among the boulders
of this nameless three acres of mountain. Once again there was
nothing for it but to withdraw the survivors before daylight.

By first light in the area of Cassino Station, the New Zealand
sappers had almost completed the night's work. They had lifted
scores of mines, despite the additional time-wasting labour of
having to dispose of the blown up railway line. (It could otherwise not be known whether the mine-detectors were picking
up the metal of the mines or the line.) They had cleared wire,
and booby traps: they had thrown Bailey bridges across two water
obstacles, a canal and the River Rapido: they had spanned with
rubble or bridging material several smaller gaps the Germans had
blown in the causeway. By one means or another—and in spite
of being under shell and mortar fire for half the night—they had
managed to create behind the advancing Maoris well over a mile
of usable roadway along which the tanks and anti-tank guns
could race at daybreak. Now they were working desperately to
finish by the end of the night, which for sappers can never be
long enough.

They very nearly succeeded. But as the sky began to lighten
there was just one more gap to be bridged. They had been

beaten by a few minutes. The work could not be done in daylight. The Maoris would have to spend the long twelve-hour day without tanks or anti-tank guns.

To infantry who have carried out a successful night attack, the arrival of the tanks and anti-tank guns at dawn is a matter of life and death. Without these aids they are naked and exposed if the enemy counter-attacks with tanks. They would have the support of their artillery, but ordinary artillery can do little from long range against armour. Tanks have to be tackled with the armour-piercing shells of anti-tank guns firing from close range in the infantry area.

Like the Indian Division nearly 2,000 feet above them, the Maori Battalion had had severe casualties: 128 of them had been killed or wounded. But by dawn they were well established and dug in. The Station buildings provided plenty of cover and also room for manoeuvre. They cheerfully accepted the order to hang on, in splendid isolation, until the next period of darkness, twelve long hours away.

At daybreak of this same day, Friday, the German Fourteenth Army, now two and a half miles into the heart of the Anzio beachhead, committed its armoured reserves, an indication that this day was to prove the climax of their counter-offensive. Lowering black clouds there warned the hard-pressed American and British beachhead divisions that they could expect no help from the Air Forces that day. The Germans had also introduced a new weapon, the 'Goliath', a small tank filled with explosives which was directed by remote radio control into the Allied positions, and then exploded.

In Rome Miss Scrivener recorded in her diary:

All Rome is thickly placarded today with posters showing photographs of the ruins of Monte Cassino with monks and refugee civilians, and reproductions of handwritten signed statements by the Abbot and his administrator. This is certainly a trump card in the German propaganda game.

It was an uneasy morning all round for the Allied commanders.

In the mountains the Indian Division made a melancholy count of the night's losses. The Rajputana Rifles had lost 196 officers and men including all their company commanders. The Gurkha battalion, so many of whom had been crucified on the thorn and barbed wire of that mined thicket, had lost 7 British officers including their Colonel, 4 Gurkha officers, and 138 N.C.O.s and men. The other Gurkha battalion had lost 96 of all ranks. In three nights four crack regular battalions had been cut to pieces, without a chance to do anything but die well. Nothing whatever had been gained.

Its crest only a hundred yards away, Point 593, the intermediate rocky eminence they had hoped to dispose of with a preliminary clearing operation, had proved to be a major fortification in its own right—thanks partly to the fragment of an old fort which provided its forward slope with a steel heart: but also to the skill and tenacity of first-class soldiers who knew how to make the best use of it: and to the closely co-ordinated fire of the adjacent German-held peaks. If you attacked one, six others could come to its rescue with machine-gun and mortar fire.

Everything now depended on the Maoris. Could they hold on to the Station for a whole day without the means of dealing with tanks, if tanks should be sent against them? If they could, the battle could be saved. As we have seen, the Station area—a thousand yards from the town and half that distance from the corner where Highway Six swung round Monastery Hill into the Liri Valley—not only provided a means of by-passing the core of the Cassino defences, but made a jumping-off point for an armoured break into the valley. It all depended now on the Maoris.

At daybreak General Kippenberger went forward to visit them. He found them cheerful and confident. They are the kind of soldiers who thrive on success. Their leading companies were well dug in, and they had good cover from the buildings, for the Italians construct their stone buildings solidly, even in railway stations and yards.

The chief difficulty was Monastery Hill, its south-eastern corner a mere five hundred yards away, towering over the Station area so overwhelmingly that it made a man feel puny and helpless just to look up at it. There were tanks and artillery pieces at all the key points of that corkscrew road which cut across the face of the mountain, and many eyes to direct their fire. To be in the Station so near to the base of Monte Cassino was like being stared at hugely and malignantly. But the position must be held. If they could only hang on till nightfall, the engineers could hurry along the causeway, deal with the last gap, and the whole weight of the Division could then pile up behind the Maoris.

When he had seen the position for himself from a forward viewpoint, General Kippenberger decided to cut off the Station from the view of the Monastery by laying a smokescreen and keeping it going all day, and also by frequent concentrations of defensive artillery fire. There was no difficulty about making the screen, the Gunners said, but to keep it going all day would require many more shells than they had available. The Artillery do not usually lay much smoke—it is generally left to the mortars—and the normal proportion of smoke shells at the gun sites is small. Where were the nearest reserves, Kippenberger asked. In Naples, seventy miles away. Then someone must go to Naples and get some. The Service Corps rose to the occasion. A column of lorries was sent off to bring back the necessary quantity of shells (to keep the screen going all day would require about 30,000) and within a few minutes the Maoris were relieved to find themselves screened from Monastery Hill by a thick artificial fog.

There was nothing for it now but to wait. The hours passed slowly. By ten there had been no counter-attack. By midday there had been no counter-attack. One o'clock, and no counter-attack—but reports from the Maoris that they were being mortared. Two o'clock. Only four hours to dusk. The lorries

were back from Naples, and the Gunners were thickening up the
screen confident that they could now keep it going indefinitely.

But soon after three, the ominous grating of tanks was heard
in the Station. A few minutes later German infantry and tanks,
skilfully using the New Zealand smokescreen to disguise the
direction of their approach, burst through it into the Station
area from two sides. The Maoris had nothing to pit against the
tanks, their bazooka teams being early casualties. There was a
short sharp fight; the New Zealanders lost a number of prisoners:
a few more were killed or wounded; the remainder were pulled
back. The smokescreen had proved a two-edged weapon. But
without it few of the forward troops would have survived the
day.

The sweating gunners, who in relays had been pumping smoke
shells into their guns without respite for more than eight hours,
stood down exhausted. The battle was over. The single net gain
on both divisional fronts was a bridge over the Rapido.

Viewed from a distance, the Second Battle of Cassino may be
thought—especially after the world-wide commotion which
preceded and followed the bombing—to have been something of
an anti-climax. In the mountains a company attack on Tuesday
night, a battalion attack on Wednesday, and a three-battalion
attack on Thursday—all unsuccessful. In the valley, an attack by
a single battalion, also unsuccessful.

Commentators at the time and since have been inclined to
dismiss the failure as a simple case of attacking in driblets instead
of strength. The criticism is not valid. Ground and weather were
the factors which determined the number of troops that could
be used in this battle. We have seen already how these factors
controlled the Indian Division's operations. In the valley, though
the New Zealand Division did not have the same difficulty over
the supply line, ground and weather imposed the same limitation
on deployment. The valley was waterlogged, and the only
feasible approach to the Station objective was along the railway
causeway and on a two-company front.

It must also be realized that there are two ways in which the might of a division can be used. It can attack with several battalions on a wide front, in which case its action is that of a scythe. Or it may initially use a small force on a narrow front, in the hope of making a penetration which can be followed up by the rest of its battalions piled up behind. In that case the action is that of a chisel, with a large number of hammer blows ready to force it through in a series of sharp thrusts. The ground and the weather made the second method the only possible one in this battle, and the New Zealanders nearly succeeded.

It was subsequently known that the Germans had been extremely alarmed by the capture of the Station. They did not expect their counter-attack to succeed as is shown by the following conversation between Kesselring and Vietinghoff on the night of the 18th:

V: We have succeeded after hard fighting in retaking Cassino Station.

K: Heartiest congratulations.

V: I didn't think we would do it.

K: Neither did I.

Had the New Zealand sappers been able to bridge the final gap on the causeway, and make it possible for tanks to come up on the objective, it seems likely that it would have been held.

The second battle of Cassino was notable, also, for two other things.

It showed how, in the most mechanized war in history, conditions of ground and weather could arise in which machines were useless, and the battle had to be fought out between small forces of infantrymen with rifle, machine-gun and grenade. An army that could call on six hundred tanks, eight hundred artillery pieces, five hundred aeroplanes, and sixty or seventy thousand vehicles of all shapes and sizes found itself dependent on the humble pack-mule. In the mountains above Cassino in February a mule was worth a dozen tanks.

The other lesson was that when Army and Air Force are

working together there must be unity of command and the closest coordination of plans. Retrospectively this may seem too obvious to be worth mentioning. The plain fact is that in the last year but one of the war it was a problem that had still to be solved.

IV

THE THIRD BATTLE

'In this situation there is such a choice of difficulties that I own myself at a loss how to determine.'
GENERAL WOLFE

I

AS soon as it was clear that the pincers attack on Cassino had failed the battle was quickly called off, and General Freyberg at once began to devise a new plan so that the offensive could be resumed with as little delay as possible.

It happened that February 18th, the day the second Cassino battle ended, was also the climax of the German onslaught against Anzio. That day von Mackensen made his supreme effort. But thanks largely to the firmness of the U.S. 179th Infantry Regiment and the 1st Loyals, backed by a prodigious artillery effort, the attack was finally halted. The turning-point had been reached: the time had come to hit back. On the following morning the U.S. 1st Armoured and 3rd Infantry Divisions drove hard into the flank of the now extended enemy salient and by the day's end had thrown it into confusion. The offensive was broken. In four days it had cost Kesselring more than 5,000 casualties. The Germans had been no more successful in the offensive than the Allies. Those hoary old reservists, Generals January and February, had no time for attack. In Italy, in winter, it was definitely a defenders' war. With the Beachhead now out of immediate danger, General Alexander could concentrate for the moment on Cassino.

'In this situation,' wrote General Wolfe in his famous dispatch to Pitt on the eve of Quebec, 'there is such a choice of difficulties that I own myself at a loss how to determine.' Alexander, Clark, and Freyberg—debating how best to make one last winter effort to crack Cassino—were of much the same mind.

Outflanking it from the left by forcing a crossing of the Rapido had been tried in January with unhappy results. With the approaches to the river as hopelessly water-logged as ever, none of the generals was in favour of trying the river-crossing again until the ground had dried out. For one thing it would mean risking their only fresh division—the British 78th, newly arrived from the Eighth Army front to stiffen the New Zealand Corps—in an operation bound to incur heavy casualties. For another, the preliminary road work that would be essential on the approaches would cause considerable delay. A by-pass movement on the right through the mountains had also been unsuccessful and costly in lives.

In a bleak 'choice of difficulties' there remained only a direct attack on the centre—an attack from the north on Cassino town and Monastery Hill. The disadvantages were obvious enough, but there were certain advantages too.

The New Zealand and Indian Divisions would be working side by side on a narrow front, instead of converging from widely separated points as in the previous battle. The approach from the north offered three usable roads. As floods or minefields or both made the open ground near Cassino impassable to infantry as well as tanks, roads were essential. The 78th Division could be kept in reserve to follow through with tanks if the other two divisions were successful.

No one was infatuated with this plan. The New Zealanders would be tackling, head-on, the formidable bottle-neck formed by the end of the town and Monastery Hill: the Indian Division would have to storm its way up the steep mountainside. On February 28th Clark gave the attack a fifty-fifty chance. On March 2nd, Freyberg noted in his diary that he had never been faced with a more difficult operation.

But the Allied Command had one card up its sleeve which it was hoped would prove a trump. The attack was to be preceded by such a bombing as had never before been attempted in support of ground forces. For the first time in history an obliteration bombing of a small infantry objective was to be carried out by heavy bombers. Cassino, long since cleared of civilians, was now a fortified town approximately half a mile square. For four hours before the infantry and tanks moved in, it was to be pounded to dust, and with it (it was hoped) every German soldier unlucky enough to find himself defending any part of it that day. Cassino was to be wiped off the map.

This was something new in warfare. Alexander emphasized that it was an experiment. London and Washington—with an eye to future operations in North-West Europe—would be studying it closely as the guinea-pig test of a new development in army-air cooperation. But at Cassino all that anyone cared about was that it might turn the scale in an operation which—with winter still securely in charge of the battlefield—could only be regarded as a 'choice of difficulties'.

The plan provided for the attack to be initiated by the 6th New Zealand and 5th Indian Brigades—with the 4th New Zealand Armoured Brigade in support. The remainder of the 4th Indian and 2nd New Zealand divisions would be called upon as required. The 78th Division and a force of American tanks would be in reserve to exploit a breakthrough.

The New Zealanders, advancing immediately the bombing ended, would capture Castle Hill, the knoll which rose like a rocky excrescence out of the foot of Monte Cassino, and move on to clear the town of any survivors. In the evening the Indian Brigade would take over Castle Hill and use it as the jump-off point for their fighting advance up Monte Cassino.

The necessary changes in dispositions were put in hand: detailed orders were issued on February 22nd: everything was ready for Operation Dickens, as they called it, to go in on February 24th, six days after the previous battle had been called off. But once again it all depended on the weather. There had to be three successive fine days for the ground to become firm enough for the tanks, and on the day of the bombing there would have to be very good visibility. But on the 23rd the weather deteriorated. It poured with rain all day and Dickens had to be postponed. One of the worst features of this battle was to be the long wait for it to begin. For it rained the next day too, and the day after that. It rained every single day for three weeks. The suspense caused by these daily postponements, and its effect on men facing an unpleasant battle, can easily be imagined. At dawn every morning they were at twenty-four hours' notice. At four every afternoon the decision about the weather was made. The codeword was 'Bradman'. All day they watched the sky and wondered. At four they would be told 'Bradman batting tomorrow' or 'Bradman not batting' as the case might be. For twenty-one successive mornings they went through this performance. On twenty-one successive afternoons they were told 'Bradman not batting'. That redoubtable cricketer can never have spent such a long time in the pavilion.

While they waited in the exposed valley, wet, frozen and on edge with uncertainty, they had to endure the towering immediacy of the mountains (and in particular Monte Cassino) and shelling which took its daily toll of them. During that period of three weeks the three battalions of the 6th New Zealand Brigade lost 263 men. The Indian Division lost about the same number. And while the Indians in the valley waited to go into the attack, their 7th Brigade—the one that had borne the burden of the mountain attacks in the previous battle—had to remain in their exposed positions on Snakeshead Ridge. They were not due to take part in the new attack. But even without that to face, it was bad enough just trying to exist where they were. The dead from the previous battle, whom they could not yet dispose of, made the atmosphere scarcely bearable. But in the valley it was worse.

It was not difficult down there, waiting day after day for an order that never came, to feel the fortified ruin of the Abbey as an increasingly obsessive presence: to think of it as almost a living thing, a monster wounded but still malignant and powerful and mocking. *Nemo me impune lacessit* might have been scorched across its broken walls with a flame-thrower. In the valley it was easy to get ideas during the long wait. The Monastery more than ever brooded over the battlefield like a curse.

A little way back, in an assembly area behind Monte Trocchio the 78th Division waited for the word. Like the New Zealand

and Indian Divisions they brought to Cassino an exceptional record and reputation. They had fought continuously through the North African campaign as the spearhead of the small First Army: they had played a decisive part in the Sicilian victory: they had fought without a break up the Adriatic Coast of Italy. In their last sector—the mountainous centre of the Abruzzi— they had been contending with ten-foot snow drifts and blizzards. There they had read about the earlier fighting at Cassino and it had seemed part of another war, something they read about in the papers. Now they were to be in it themselves. And as they caught their first glimpse of Monte Cassino they were not sorry that their role, for the time being anyway, was to exploit the success of others: not, as was usually their lot, to create that success in the first place. The 78th waited in the mud for Bradman to bat. The New Zealand Armoured Brigade waited. The American tank force, which bore the unpicturesque but practical designation of Combat Command B, waited. They all waited for the news that Bradman would bat tomorrow. (The staff officer who chose an Australian name to herald a New Zealand enterprise no doubt acted on the usual English assumption that Australia and New Zealand are more or less the same place.)

For the New Zealand infantry who were to go first, there was something else to add to the strain. In the early hours of the morning on which the attack went in, the foremost units would have to pull back 1,000 yards to be clear of the bombing danger area. This withdrawal would have to be skilfully carried out so that it was not detected by the enemy. Psychologically it is obviously a bad thing for a unit to withdraw from ground it already holds at the beginning of a battle—and then have to advance the same distance merely to reoccupy its original positions. In the circumstances it was unavoidable—bombing accuracy is a wayward thing—but it was an additional worry factor for the New Zealanders. They would have to start the attack with a withdrawal.

On March 2nd, when the postponements had been going on for just over a week, the New Zealanders suffered a major blow when they lost their Divisional Commander, the admirable Kippenberger. He was on a routine visit to one of his artillery headquarters on Monte Trocchio. Walking down a path that was supposed to have been cleared, he stepped on one of the vicious little wooden 'schu' mines. One of his feet was blown off and the other had to be amputated.

It will be recalled that just before the Second Battle, the 4th Indian had lost Tuker. Now, a few days before the new operation, the New Zealanders had lost Kippenberger. It seemed the climax to the long series of misfortunes which dogged every Allied venture at Cassino. Both men had made an outstanding contribution to the success of their divisions. Both, in the view of the men who had served with them, seemed irreplaceable: all the more so because of the unique difficulty of what lay ahead.

With the temporary elevation of Freyberg to the wider responsibility of commanding the New Zealand Corps, the presence of Kippenberger was more necessary than ever to the New Zealand Division which was rich in junior officers but had virtually no men with the experience and qualifications for high command.

The link between a good division and a good divisional commander is an intimate one. The commander of a division is the one grade of general who is close to the forward troops, well known to them, a familiar member, so to speak, of the family. At higher levels, generals become remote figures. To the fighting troops they are with few exceptions anonymous eminences with red hatbands. But the divisional commander is someone they know. His loss is personally felt. Kippenberger was one of the personalities of the Eighth Army, a man whose reputation had spread beyond the confines of his own formation. To many men shivering in the mud, waiting for Bradman to bat tomorrow, it seemed to underline the malignant ill-luck which haunted this battlefield, that the New Zealanders, like the Indians, should now have to face their hardest test without their captain.

Within the New Zealand Division itself, they felt a sense of shock as well as personal loss, and that night more than one soldier said: 'There goes our best man. He is irreplaceable.'

The only good news during this time was that the German Fourteenth Army had made what was clearly its final serious counter-attack at Anzio. It had been made weakly. After two days, in which they suffered more than 2,000 casualties, they had called it off. Allied guesses that they would now go on the defensive were confirmed a couple of days later by the capture of the German Army order to that effect.

But it is doubtful whether anyone at Cassino cared very much. They had troubles enough of their own. They had been fighting under extreme difficulties for a long time now because Anzio was in danger. That was fine. So now it was no longer in danger. That was fine too. But they were not in the mood for celebrating. Anzio was a long way away. In another war.

Towards the middle of the month there was an improvement in the weather and by March 14th the meteorologists were at last satisfied that conditions were good enough. Bradman would at last bat—tomorrow, March 15th. As a final ominous touch the battle would open on the Ides of March.

The Fifth Army still faced the German Tenth across a front of some twenty to twenty-five miles—not counting that part of it which engaged the German Fourteenth Army at Anzio. But for the next week they were to fight one another to the death on a tiny section of that frontage barely 1,000 yards wide. During the period of the long wait the Germans had carried out reliefs and now their finest division, the celebrated 1st Parachute, was in charge of the Cassino sector. Seven battalions held the town, Monastery Hill and the Abbey. Against them Second New Zealand Corps could bring ten—hardly a sufficient superiority to overcome the German advantages of terrain and prepared fortifications. Against 200 guns the Allies would pit 600—but the Germans, holding all the commanding observation points could use theirs more tellingly. In aircraft and in tanks the Allies had a vast superiority—provided that the weather made it possible to use them.

To gain anything like a coherent impression of the confused battle of the next seven days it is essential to have a clear idea of the battlefield, and to relate it closely to the plan.

It will be remembered that Highway Six, at the end of its three-mile sweep across the Rapido valley and through the southern fringe of Cassino, turns sharp left (or south) to skirt the foot of Monte Cassino. At the corner where it turns south it is joined by a secondary road running into it from the north. It was along this secondary road (which they called Caruso Road) and a track (Parallel Road) about a hundred yards east of it that the initial attack was to be made.

Where Caruso Road met Highway Six, the advancing troops would be faced with a bottle-neck somewhat akin to Scylla and Charybdis. On their right, Scylla the rock—Monte Cassino: on the left, Charybdis the whirlpool—the fortified town. The ultimate object was to force a way through this bottle-neck, and continue the drive southwards to the Station and the entrance of the Liri Valley about a kilometre farther along. There a base would be established through which the pursuit could be carried into the valley. To achieve this it would be necessary to clear the town and capture Monastery Hill and the Monastery.

Let us now take a closer look at the two halves of this narrow battlefield within a battlefield—the town and the mountain to be attacked from north to south.

The town had a built-up area about half a mile square. The buildings were very strongly constructed of stone, as is usual in Italy. Those that dominated the scene from a tactical point of view had been additionally fortified. The area was thickly sown with mines. (Half a million were lifted after the final battle.) Numerous machine-guns covered every open space. Tanks and artillery pieces had been concealed among, and actually inside, buildings during the months of preparation. Concrete emplacements and shelters had also been constructed inside buildings. Tunnels had been made so that a shelter on one side of the road could communicate with a gun position on the other. On the lower slopes of Monte Cassino, a few feet above the level of the

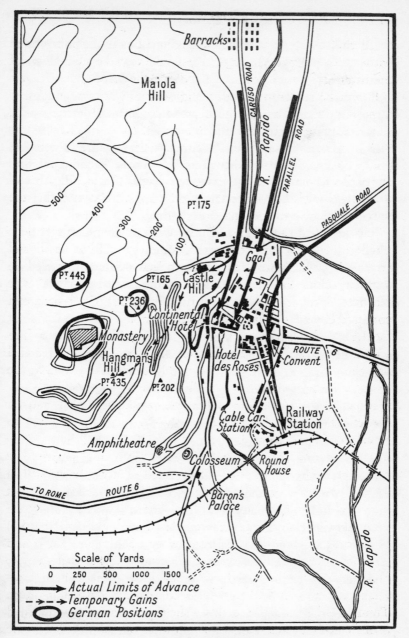

THIRD BATTLE

4th Indian and 2nd NZ Divs attack from north. Castle Hill and Station were captured but Hangman's Hill, daringly held for eight days, had eventually to be relinquished

rest of the town, were several larger buildings—including two hotels and a *palazzo*. Such an area could only be cleared with great difficulty house by house and at a great cost in lives. It was on this small area that the saturation bombing was to be unloosed in the hope that it would obliterate the German defences and reduce mopping up to a formality.

In the case of the right half of the battlefield, the mountain, there are three key places that need to be borne in mind. At the foot of the mountain, as we have seen, stands Castle Hill. This is a steep, rocky knoll, 300 feet high, crowned with yet another of the ubiquitous centuries-old forts which the Germans were finding so useful in this area. On its western side, Castle Hill is linked by a saddle of rock with Monastery Hill. It provides, therefore, a flying start to an ascent of that mountain. Indeed it was for precisely this reason that a cautious tenth-century Abbot of Monte Cassino had built on it this very castle as a protection for the Abbey against attack.

Three hundred and 600 yards above the Castle, the switch-back road which winds up to the Monastery makes a couple of hairpin bends (Points 165 and 236 on the map) which have been cut out of a dominating shoulder of the mountain. These corners, and the ledges of roadway winding about them, provide a natural defensive area about half-way to the top. This area of the hairpin bends—separated from Castle Hill by a gully—was the second objective on the Indians' uphill journey.

Above the hairpins, farther direct ascent would bring the climber into view of the Monastery. So the third stage of the climb was to be diagonally across the eastern slope to Point 435, about 600 yards onwards and upwards.

Point 435 was a jutting platform of rock with a convex slope below it. In altitude it was barely 250 feet below that of the Monastery: in ground distance to the Monastery walls it was about the same number of yards. Its overhang and the slopes and rocks below it provided a possible, if precarious, forming-up place for a final assault on the summit. On the rock platform stood the remains of a pylon that had formerly carried an aerial ropeway from the town to the Monastery. From the ground it resembled a gibbet. So Point 435 became known as Hangman's Hill.

These were the key points of Monte Cassino. Castle Hill, which could give the ascent a flying start: the hairpin bends, 300 and 600 feet higher: Hangman's Hill, 600 yards across to another shoulder of the mountain, the forming-up place for the final assault on the Monastery.

This was how they proposed to do it.

First the town would be bombed to extinction, then, behind a creeping barrage and led by tanks, the leading New Zealand Battalion would move down Caruso and Parallel Road on to the bottle-neck entry into the town, and fanning out to the left proceed to clear it as far south as Highway Six which would be their first objective line. On the way past Castle Hill, which is 300 yards north of the town, they would detach a company to capture that feature and an adjacent foothill. A second battalion would follow close on the first and assist in mopping up the town area. A third would cut through from Pasquale Road on a parallel axis 500 yards to the left and sweep on to the Station, the second objective. All this was to happen on the first afternoon, taking advantage of the paralysing effect of the bombing and the barrage.

That night the Indians would come forward by the same route, Caruso Road. They would take over Castle Hill from the New Zealanders, and using it as a gateway filter through on to the slopes of Monte Cassino to capture the hairpin bends and Hangman's Hill. Thereafter the battle would take its course, with the assault on the Monastery from Hangman's Hill as the climax.

The success of the plan depended on the first attacks being delivered swiftly and overwhelmingly while the Germans were still stunned and reeling after the morning's bombardment.

2

DIFFERENT official sources disagree about the exact number of aircraft that took part in the annihilation of the former market town of Cassino on March 15th, 1944. Some squadron adjutants in England, North Africa, Sicily, and Southern Italy appear to have been a little lax in their returns. It is agreed, however, that about 500 bombers, of which nearly 300 were Heavies, dropped more than 1,000 tons of bombs on the small target in three and a half hours.

During the preceding night the foremost infantry units filtered silently back to their prescribed safety line, leaving behind a few small suicide squads to fire occasional rounds of mortar or machine-gun between bombing waves, and so give a business-as-usual appearance to the temporarily vacated forward posts.

At New Zealand Corps Headquarters in Cervaro, five miles away, a V.I.P. enclosure had been established in a farmhouse on the hillside. There, shortly before 8.30, Alexander, Clark, Freyberg, as well as a number of eminent military tourists up for a morning's entertainment, assembled to watch the 'experiment'.

On the stroke of 8.30 the first formation of Fortresses appeared over the town. Christopher Buckley was among those who watched from Cervaro:

> Sprout after sprout of black smoke leapt from the earth and from the town itself, joined one with another and curled slowly upward like some dark forest of evil fantasy until three-quarters of the town was obscured in a widening and deepening smudge . . . one wave had no sooner started on its return journey than its successor appeared over the eastern skyline. Sometimes they flew in formations of eighteen, sometimes of thirty-six . . . again and again I saw them

turn and dip; again and again I watched that darkly evil smudge rise and spread over the town. . . . The enemy was strangely, horribly silent and very eerie it seemed. A little half-hearted ack-ack had greeted the first wave or two. Then we heard it no more. . . .

I remember no spectacle in war so gigantically one-sided. Above the beautiful, arrogant, silver-grey monsters performing their mission with what looked from below like a spirit of utter detachment; below, a silent town, suffering all this in complete passivity.

To those who were watching there was an additional touch of drama in the knowledge that some of these squadrons had flown from airfields in England to drop their loads and then fly on to North Africa to refuel. There was drama too of a more tangible kind. Despite the discreet periphrasis of Air Force communiqués, aircraft bombing from a considerable height are subject to error. One formation, mistaking Venafro, fifteen miles away, for Cassino, dropped its bombs there causing 140 civilian casualties. Another hit a Moroccan military hospital, killing and wounding another forty. There were forty-four casualties among the Allied artillery lines. And as if to indicate that the same law applied equally to the rich as well as the poor, a stick of bombs straddled Eighth Army Headquarters, wrecking the caravan of the Army Commander: General Leese was luckily not at home at the time. To the soldiers lying in wait near the target area it was a perilous as well as an impressive spectacle. Many times during the morning they echoed the sentiment if not the words of the Duke of Wellington when, after reviewing some of his troops, he remarked: 'I don't know how they will impress the enemy, but by God, they frighten me!'

At noon precisely the bombing ceased and 610 artillery pieces opened fire. At noon precisely the leading New Zealand Battalion, the 25th, moved down Caruso Road from their start-point about a mile north of the town. They moved in two columns of single file, one company along the right of the road, the other in the river-bed which runs along the side of the road. They were led by tanks, following close on the barrage, and more tanks moved along Parallel Road, 100 yards to the left. There was not far to go. Everything was going according to plan. As they approached Castle Hill, the company detailed to capture it was dropped off while the other three pushed on. Before one o'clock they were in the town and picking their way ruin by ruin towards the Convent on Highway Six, one of the key points in their objective line. But now they were meeting opposition. Germans, unaccountably and obstinately alive, began to shoot back from the ruins, and from the adjacent higher ground, including Castle Hill. The companies deployed and fought back but they could not for the time being get beyond Highway Six. But they had possession of a considerable part of the town already. And their tanks, though hampered by the craters, were in a position to help with their guns.

So far there was one shadow on an otherwise fair prospect (not counting the fact that some Germans seemed incredibly to have survived the bombing) and that was the craters resulting from the bombing. The column of tanks that had started off down Parallel Road had come upon one too large to span with their bridging tank, nor could they get round it. The other column, the one that had got into the outskirts, had only done so with great difficulty. Crews had had to get out and work hard with pick and shovel in order to get their tanks a few yards forward. It was slow work, and hazardous when the German snipers and machine-gunners began to come to life. In the outskirts the tanks had to remain until nightfall. That afternoon at all New Zealand H.Q.s the headline was 'craters'.

With the tanks stuck but the leading battalion having nevertheless made excellent initial progress, the next step seems clearly to have been to send in another battalion. The whole basis of the plan had been rapid follow-up before the German defences had had time to recover. The 26th Battalion were ready to go into the town 400 yards to the left of the 25th, and make for the Station. They were only waiting for the word. After the right lead, the left hook—to an Eighth Army division the left hook was almost a point of honour. This was not done, however. The three companies of the 25th Battalion were left on their own for that vital first afternoon, while the 26th kicked their heels on Pasquale Road waiting for the order to move that never came.

Meanwhile the detached company started its private battle against Castle Hill at one o'clock, as soon as the rest of the Battalion were in the town. They fought throughout the afternoon, and after an action which was a model of its kind had captured Castle Hill and the lower hairpin bend across the gully on Monte Cassino. It had cost them six killed and fifteen wounded. But in addition to the larger number of Germans they had themselves destroyed, they had forty-four prisoners to show for the afternoon's work. The time was 4.45. It was not until five o'clock that the first additional infantry reached the town to throw in more weight, and then it was not a battalion but only a single company of the reserve battalion.

Not until dusk was the 26th Battalion (the 'Left Hook') sent on its way. And then the rains came, torrents of rain, and the great black clouds hastened on the night so that 26th Battalion, supposed to go through to the Station, did not even reach Highway Six in the centre of the town until nine o'clock, having taken three hours to cover the last 650 yards in pitch blackness, each soaked man of them clinging miserably to the bayonet scabbard of the man in front. Some time before dusk and before the rain came it was clear that there would be no rapid breakthrough. Too few infantry had followed up the bombing and this error was now to be paid for dearly.

The generals had provided everything possible to make the task of the battalions easier: 500 bombers, 600 guns, 400 tanks. There was one thing beyond their power to provide—fine weather. They had postponed the operation for days waiting for a good forecast. Now, on the first evening of the battle, the weather had broken. Not only did the torrential downpour immediately turn the craters into lakes, and the rubble between into a sticky morass, but the clouds from which it streamed all night blacked out the moon which had been counted on to help the sappers in the prodigious task of clearing routes through the ruins on the all-important first night. Small wonder that a German commander, requesting help from the Luftwaffe for the following day added, reflectively: 'Rain would be even better than air support.'

Contemporary commentators have given the impression that the craters came as a great surprise to everyone. This was not so. The Air Force Commanders and the Engineers had made it clear that the craters would hamper tank movement in the early stages of the battle. It had been felt that the bombing would still be worth while and elaborate preparations had accordingly been made by the Engineers to deal with the cratering. If the first night had remained dry they might have succeeded. It was rain which hamstrung this attack on the first night—though it was not responsible for the failure to get more infantry forward during the afternoon.

During the night—by which time three New Zealand battalions were in the town or its outskirts, but without communications, their radio sets failing to survive constant immersion—the 5th Brigade of the Indian Division moved along the road taken earlier in the day by the New Zealanders.

Though the distance was well under a mile, this move proved to be an operation in itself. Men and mules of different formations were by this time streaming in both directions along the narrow road. It was raining heavily and pitch black. 'We could only force our way through by pushing and shoving', reported one of the three battalion commanders.

At half-past eleven the 1st/4th Essex (leading the 5th Indian Brigade column) arrived according to plan to take over Castle Hill and the lower hairpin bend from the New Zealand company that had captured those positions during the afternoon. Strung out behind them were the 1st/6th Rajputana Rifles. As the long single file of Rajputs jostled their way along the congested road, a heavy artillery concentration came crashing down among their two rear companies, causing many casualties and scattering the rest, who for the remainder of the night were hopelessly lost. The two leading companies continued alone to the Castle from which they were due to attack the upper hairpin bend (Point 236) nearly half-way up Monte Cassino.

Trudging along behind the Rajputs were the 1st/9th Gurkhas who reached the northern outskirts of Cassino an hour after midnight. Their task was to pass through Castle Hill and make for Hangman's Hill after the Rajputs were clear of the Castle on their advance to the upper hairpin bend. The Essex were to remain on Castle Hill and the lower hairpin and provide the firm base through which the other two battalions could successively pass. But on a night like this it was easier said than done.

The Gurkhas waited until 2 a.m. for news of how the Rajputana Rifles were faring in their attack. No news was forthcoming. So the Gurkha commander, Colonel Nangle, decided that he had better go ahead with his own allotted task and he led his battalion into the town in readiness for its move on Hangman's Hill. This was how he later described the scene:

> The place was in an unbelievable mess after the bombing. There was no vestige of a road or a track, only vast heaps of rubble out of which peered the jagged edges of walls. The whole of this mess was covered by huge, deep craters that needed hand and foot climbing to get in and out of . . . we could only make for that part of the jumble that seemed to be nearest to the Castle.

Eventually they found the track to the Castle, but as it was being shot up by a machine-gun post Colonel Nangle decided to find an alternative route well clear of Castle Hill. A route was picked out and after a time it divided into two paths which appeared to head in roughly the right direction. Nangle sent a company along each, and then devoted the remaining hours of darkness to shaking out the rest of his battalion into defensive positions, just north of the town, in which they stood a reasonable chance of survival when daylight came. Of the two companies ordered forward to Hangman's Hill one was immediately held up by opposition which it could not overcome. The other disappeared into the night.

Meanwhile at 0245, one of the Rajputana Rifles' companies

made an attack on the upper hairpin bend, but was thrown back. Soon after daylight they tried again, behind a smokescreen, both companies going into the attack. But the luck of the Rajputs seemed to be out. As they closed in for the final assault a mortar scored a direct hit on their battalion headquarters, knocking out everyone, including the C.O. and Adjutant. The companies withdrew to the Castle.

On this second morning of the battle the New Zealand battalions in Cassino sorted themselves out after their long confused night in the flooded shambles of the town. Routes and objective lines no longer meant anything. The bombing had had a catalytic effect on the layout of the town. It bore no relation to the aerial photographs and maps so carefully memorized during the long wait for the battle to begin. From now on it was going to be a yard-by-yard fight in mud and rubble and flooded cellars: a battle from ruin to ruin. Distances were meaningless. It might take a company all morning to get from one ruin to the next. Only one thing was clear. The German centre of resistance was concentrated among the buildings at the south-west end of the town: those buildings, a little higher than the rest of the town, which protected the base of Monte Cassino and the stretch of Highway Six which skirts it after it has turned left—buildings like the Continental Hotel,[1] the *palazzo* they called the Baron's Palace, and the Hotel des Roses. These buildings were major strongpoints, and between them stretched the hard core of the enemy resistance. All day the New Zealanders attempted to make ground, to improve their positions, to get to grips with these places, but the flooded craters and the mud were against them. Tanks could not move in the sticky mess, though some that were already in the outskirts of the town from the previous day could help with their guns.

During the day, there was one piece of good news. Since dawn the Gurkha colonel had been wondering what had become

[1] This hotel, which won a small place in history as the Continental, was in fact the Excelsior. The owners, with a fine disregard for the free publicity, have rebuilt it and persist in calling it by its original name, the Excelsior.

of the company he had dispatched to Hangman's Hill. There had been no word from it: none of the other units had seen anything of it. It had vanished off the face of the earth. Then, during the morning, suspicions were aroused when artillerymen reported that there were figures on Hangman's Hill. A faint wireless message confirmed the news shortly afterwards. This company, stumbling through the darkness, had just kept going, had threaded its way between the battle for the hairpin bend above it and the violent exchanges of fire between the New Zealanders and the Continental Hotel down on its left, and had finished up near enough to Hangman's Hill to occupy it after a short, sharp fight.

The Indian Division was therefore in the curious situation of having captured its second objective before its first, and this was going to make supply difficult, for the hairpin bend area commanded the route from the Castle to Hangman's Hill. It was nevertheless a triumph to have got anyone on to Hangman's Hill at all on that first night. The C.O. immediately made preparations to move the rest of his battalion up there as soon as it was dark. They set off at the same time as the Rajputs made another attack on the upper hairpin bend. The Rajput attack would keep the Germans occupied 'upstairs': the New Zealanders had undertaken to engage and hold the attention of the Continental Hotel Germans 'downstairs'. Through this steep and narrow corridor between two battles, the Gurkhas edged their way up the mountainside platoon by platoon, and it took them the whole of the night before the last of them had reached Hangman's Hill. Their arrival, just before dawn, was timely. It coincided with the Germans' first counter-attack. With the aid of the new arrivals the attack was broken up.

During the night the Rajputs established themselves on the elusive upper hairpin bend, but at dawn they were again chased off it. The problem now was going to be to maintain the Gurkha battalion on Hangman's Hill, since the Germans would obviously try to retain control of the passage through which their supplies would have to be taken. This they could best do from the upper hairpin bend. In addition the paratroopers succeeded in filtering back into the northern outskirts of the town and taking up positions from which they could fire on Castle Hill and make this Indian gateway to the mountain precarious. This also prevented a proper junction between the Indians' base on Castle Hill and the New Zealanders in the town.

But an entire battalion on Hangman's Hill, 250 yards from the Monastery, was a great gain. Things looked even better later that day (the 17th) when the 26th New Zealand Battalion led by tanks managed to run the gauntlet of the snipers and capture the Station.

The battle had started on Wednesday morning. It was now Friday afternoon. With the New Zealanders securely in the Station and the Gurkha battalion on Hangman's Hill the first phase of the operation was over. It remained to dispose of the German resistance in the Western end of the town and to take the Monastery.

3

THE Allied task was now clarified. Down below, the New Zealanders had to crack this hard core of German strongpoints between the Continental and the Hotel des Roses, 400 yards along the eastern base of the mountain: 1,500 feet above them the Indians must take the Monastery which was the control tower of the battlefield.

By this time, however, the German task was equally clear. The Monastery was the final key to command of the whole position. The Allied gateway to the Monastery was Castle Hill. All Allied traffic, whether for assault or supply, had to pass through this precarious bottle-neck. The obvious German policy, therefore, must be to deprive the Allies of the use of this gateway. They could afford to ignore the garrison on Hangman's Hill. It would be helpless without the gateway through which it had to be maintained. The other thing the Germans had to do was to maintain their interceptor posts on the outskirts of the town—between Castle Hill and the New Zealanders.

On the night of Friday the 17th, a few hours after the capture of the Station, the New Zealanders, not letting up for an instant, tried to take the Continental from the rear. A strong company, without greatcoats in order to enable them to carry more ammunition, was ordered to make its way via Castle Hill and the lower hairpin bend to Point 202, an as yet untroubled hairpin 700 yards along the mountain face, below Hangman's Hill. It was a difficult approach requiring careful contact with the variety of other units who now cluttered up the mountainside each night. On Point 202, they would be near Hangman's Hill and would need to establish with that garrison that they were not Germans.

In the event they narrowly escaped being shot up by a Gurkha patrol encountered *en route*. The Gurkhas have an exceptional talent for silent night movement. They are also good soldiers. Seeing, but unseen, they let the New Zealanders approach close enough to be identified. Less good soldiers would have fired first and asked the questions later.

From this new hairpin, Point 202, the New Zealand company swept downhill on to the rear of the Hotel. Their leader got close enough to an entrance to throw in a grenade, but it failed to explode. An answering burst of machine-gun fire killed him and several of those at his side. The small force was compelled to withdraw from a position far too strong for them. They returned to Point 202, and remained there for the rest of the battle—another lonely detachment on that mountainside, about half-way between the Castle and Hangman's Hill.

While this battle was in progress and the usual violent exchanges of fire were raging about the more familiar hairpin bends above the Castle, a supply party of Rajputana Rifles wove their way, with much courage, between the various commotions to carry supplies to the isolated garrison on Hangman's Hill—who by this time were short of everything, especially food.

The Rajputs had started the evening as a two-company escort for a party of Pioneers who were acting as porters, and therefore needed to be spared the burden of arms. On the way to the Castle the group was shelled and lost nineteen of its number, so it did not reach the 'gateway' until after ten. There it had to remain for an hour and a half while the Essex disposed of a raid on the lower hairpin bend. By this time the Pioneers had had enough and refused to go on. So the Rajputs decided to carry as much of the cargo as they could themselves, and fight their way through the various night battles. It was 2 a.m. before they could start, and three hours later a message was received that they had got through to Hangman's Hill—but they had lost eight men getting there. As they could not return in daylight, the gallant remnant of the party took up temporary residence with the Gurkhas.

The episode seems worth mentioning because it gives an idea

of what these nights on the mountain were like. Largely as a result of this particular experience, General Freyberg decided that future supplies would be dropped on Hangman's Hill from the air.

On Saturday the 18th, Freyberg decided to make his climactic effort on the following day. At dawn on Sunday a fresh New Zealand battalion, the 28th (Maori), would attack the Continental Hotel: the Gurkhas and the Essex would storm the Monastery from Hangman's Hill. The New Zealand Corps was going in for the kill.

The surprise factor designed to help the infantry on their strenuous uphill assault against the great fortress was to be the 'impossible'—a simultaneous tank raid from the rear. For weeks New Zealand sappers had been making a tank track through the heart of the mountain mass. As the route was overlooked by distant enemy observation posts they had first had to construct a protective screen of camouflage to conceal both their working parties and the completed sections of road. The route, which they called Cavendish Road, was now completed. It gave access to a usable defile and track sweeping round to the rear of the Monastery. It was hoped that the appearance of tanks from this direction would cause something like the consternation that greeted Hannibal's elephants after their Alpine crossing.

So Saturday was a day of preparation and hope and suspense. For many of the troops it was also the day the smoke became an active nuisance. Since the capture of the Station and the greater part of the town area, the sappers had been able to step up their efforts to complete the necessary bridging and clearance of roads. To enable them to work by day a continuous smokescreen was now being laid across the town area throughout the daytime. This was fine for the sappers, but an insufferable nuisance to everyone else. Twice the Germans made counter-attacks which were thrown back. In both cases heavy losses would have been inflicted on them had they not been able to disappear rapidly into the New Zealand smoke. At the same time the troops in the town had to double their daylight sentries in case the Germans made further raids under cover of the smoke.

On the mountain the problem was slightly different. The artillery smoke shell achieves its purpose with the aid of a small explosive charge which ejects the base plug of the shell during flight, permitting the smoke-producing canisters to drop to the ground at the desired point. The empty shell then proceeds on its way. Any troops who happen to be in the line of flight get plagued by these empty shells, and on Saturday they were causing a number of unpleasant wounds: for to be hit by one at all meant to be killed outright or to have a limb severed. One man, struck by the descending base plug of one of these shells, ran crazily down the mountain screaming, then dropped dead. Others lost a leg or an arm.

Every headquarters kept sending back complaints, but the smoke went on. A British artillery officer on Hangman's Hill, viewing the matter with professional disdain reported:

> The smoke nuisance now became acute. Our shelling continued throughout the afternoon with such accuracy that the Gurkha commander's *sangar* received three direct hits from the shell itself. Attempts by the battery commander, urged by the Gurkha C.O., to shift the target proved fruitless. Relations in all directions assumed an atmosphere of strain. The galling aspect of the whole business was that the smoke so placed screened nothing from nobody.

To take their minds off the smoke the garrison had a welcome diversion during the afternoon when fighter bombers flew low over the mountain dropping supplies by parachute. Inevitably, with so small an area to be aimed at, many of the canisters bounced to the bottom of the valley and others gave the Monastery Germans a chance to compare Fifth Army rations with their own, but any supplies at all were welcome and the Gurkhas and their Rajputana guests—not to mention the isolated New Zealand company at the Point 202 hairpin—were grateful for the ten or fifteen per cent of the total that they were able to retrieve. It wasn't quite so lonely up there now that these airdrops were to become a daily occurrence.

For the Essex it was a difficult day. That night they were to hand over Castle Hill and the lower hairpin bend to the Rajputana Rifles, and then move up to Hangman's Hill to assault the Monastery with the Gurkhas. The relief alone was going to be a major operation, because Castle Hill had become a permanent trouble centre. In addition to the fire which constantly rained down on it from above, it was now being fired on from the direction of the town. The previous night the Germans had managed to filter more men down the ravines to positions between the Castle and the town. The Essex had to carry out a difficult relief in the early hours of the morning, reorganize themselves, trudge up the mountain, and be ready at six a.m. to charge the final steep slope to, of all things, the Monastery.

Their plan was to dispatch two companies to Hangman's Hill as soon as the relief began, the other two following on as soon as it had been completed. In readiness for this the four companies of the battalion were collected in the Castle Hill area (which made it very congested as it only provided room enough for two) and late in the afternoon the New Zealand tanks were asked to deal with one of the interceptor posts on the outskirts of the town from which the Germans had started troubling them the previous night. The post was in a turreted house. The tanks obliged by directing volleys of armour-piercing shells at the building; but some of these, passing over the target, hit the Castle, collapsing one of the walls and burying a number of the Essex men. Some others, trying to disperse themselves about the crowded rock face, stumbled in the darkness and fell down a 150-foot precipice. The evening had begun in misfortune.

The relief did not start until shortly after 5 a.m. and as the lower hairpin bend changed hands the two leading companies of Essex set off for Hangman's Hill. Within five minutes the Castle would have been handed over, and the other two companies were already preparing to follow on the heels of the first two. On Hangman's Hill, the Gurkhas, who had been ordered to be ready to attack at 6 a.m., looked anxiously down the mountainside for the Essex men who should by now have joined them. In the gun-pits far across the Rapido Valley gunners made ready to discharge great concentrations of shells on every satellite strong-point that was not too close to the advancing troops. In the heart of the mountain mass, two columns of tanks prepared to pick their way along the mountain trails and defiles which, if all went well, would bring them to the back door of the Monastery by the one route from which the Germans would not expect a tank attack. Behind the fetid swampland that had once been Cassino's Botanical Gardens, the fresh Maori battalion prepared to fling themselves at the Continental Hotel, only 200 yards away, but 200 yards that had defied other battalions for four days and nights. On the new bridge carrying Highway Six over the Rapido at the eastern entrance to the town an impassive sergeant of the Military Police, anticipating events, set up a smartly painted sign-board bearing the legend: 'Go Slow—Bridge Ahead—Await Signal By Military Policeman.' That night there could be a traffic problem in Cassino.

Day was breaking on Sunday, March 19th, and the divisions of the New Zealand Corps were poised on the mountain and in the ruins of the town for the decisive stroke. It was at this moment that the Germans chose to launch their counter-attack on the Castle.

For ten minutes only they swept the area with a paralysing hailstorm of machine-gun fire which ricocheted about the rocks and the broken Castle walls without pause. Then they came racing down the mountainside from the Monastery, a battalion of them. The leading two Essex companies had just got a little way up the mountainside clear of the area: the other two, having handed over to the Rajputs were about to move off. They were taken completely by surprise. The Germans swept down from the upper hairpin, tore through the bewildered mixture of Essex and Rajputs at the lower hairpin, and came on towards the Castle walls. There was a mixed garrison of about 150 to meet them. Positions were hurriedly taken up and something approximating to a mediaeval siege battle took place. Germans trying to scale the walls were blasted off with grenades or pushed off with rifle butts. The Germans pressed their attack regardless of casualties. More and more of them kept following up. But after the first shock of surprise, the Essex machine-guns and mortars, sited behind an adjacent crest were able to get into action, and the first onrush was halted. The Germans withdrew, but only to the hairpin bend area, where there was cover, and it was clear that they were re-forming to make a second assault. They had left behind many dead, and the defenders had lost many men too. Meanwhile the other two bewildered Essex companies plodding towards Hangman's Hill watched the battle from above, wondered if any of their battalion below would survive, wondered if they should go back and join in. They were ordered by wireless to keep going. The Brigade commander was not going to be rushed out of his attack on the Monastery just yet. The Gurkhas were told that the attack on the Monastery was postponed, but only temporarily.

At eight o'clock the Germans came in again. This time the Essex had a curtain of mortar and artillery fire ready to bring down on them, and after another short, sharp battle, the attack was thrown off. Later in the morning a third attack was broken up. A wounded German paratrooper said that of 200 men who had been engaged only forty remained. But the Essex and the Rajputs had also been reduced to a handful. About the time this third battle was petering out, word came through that the two Essex companies that had started up the mountainside shortly before the German attack began had reached Hangman's Hill. More precisely, seventy men had arrived of whom thirty were wounded. They had run into trouble on the way and had had to fight their way through.

The Germans had beaten the Commonwealth men to the draw by a matter of minutes. And although the attack on the Monastery was still scheduled to take place that afternoon, it was obvious that it could not go in unless something miraculous happened elsewhere on the front. In fact no miracles took place that day.

At dawn, as scheduled, the Maoris had begun their attack on the Continental Hotel. By the middle of the day they had made little progress though they had taken prisoners. During the morning, too, the tank attack round the mountain flank had been made. For a time it went well. But when the tanks had reached the end of the road made by the sappers, and had to negotiate a rough mountain track they ran into difficulties. The track was only wide enough for them to advance in single file. As they approached Massa Albaneta—a large farm building half a mile from the Monastery—they came under heavy fire and ran on to mines. The leading tanks blew up and blocked the way. German infantry appeared on the scene with bazookas and knocked out more. Having no infantry with them to assist, the force had no alternative but to withdraw. It had been a worth-while gamble but it had not come off. The column withdrew leaving behind nine tanks. They had to be content with the negative satisfaction of learning later that intercepted German messages indicated that the first appearance of the tanks had caused considerable alarm. But alarm wasn't enough in this battle.

In the afternoon the attack on the Monastery was postponed indefinitely. The traffic notice erected by the military police-man at the Bailey bridge which now carried Highway Six, the historic Via Casilina, across the Rapido into Cassino, remained in position. But it was not going to be needed just yet.

Sunday afternoon was the turning-point, the end of the second phase of the battle. The initiative had passed to the Germans. They had correctly appreciated that Castle Hill, the gateway to Monte Cassino, was the vulnerable point on the Allied front. Close the gate and the forces up the mountainside would be cut off and helpless. They had tried to do this in the morning. They had sacrificed a battalion in the effort, and they had not succeeded. But they had virtually destroyed the Allied force holding it. They would undoubtedly be back. They would keep hammering away at the Castle.

To strengthen the Castle, now the priority weak point, Freyberg that night sent in the 6th Royal West Kents of the 78th

Division to relieve the handful of survivors of the Essex and Rajputana Rifles. The new battalion had a quick blooding. Before they moved in, and as their commander was holding his briefing conference on an adjacent viewpoint, a shell landed in the middle of the group killing two company commanders. But the relief was effected and the fresh battalion were in position to repel another strong attack on the Castle area soon after their arrival. At the same time the Maori attack on the Continental Hotel had finally failed. They had fought all day. They had taken nearly 100 prisoners. But they could not break the final resistance of a strong-point which included tanks buried hull-deep in what was once the hotel lobby, and supporting positions, above and on both sides, which could rain down a curtain of fire on the final approaches.

It was now no longer a question of new gains but consolidating and making secure what was already held. It was also a question of how long to continue. The Allied effort was expended. But the Germans had had heavy losses too. At such a stage of a continuous killing match—as this battle had been for five days and nights—a general is tempted to go on a little longer in the hope that the enemy may crack first. General Wilson was in favour of continuing but Freyberg replied in the one word: 'Passchendaele', and Alexander agreed. The 1st Parachute Division and the Monastery had won.

In the next three days the gains were thoroughly secured, the sappers completed their work on the bridges, the front was stabilized, formations were regrouped and reorganized, the isolated Gurkhas on Hangman's Hill and the New Zealand detachment below them were extricated with some difficulty. The Fifth Army then went on to the defensive, with 78th Division taking over the mountain sector from Castle Hill upwards, and the 1st Guards Brigade relieving the New Zealanders in the town.

Monte Cassino had a new set of soldiers over which to cast its spell and another five weeks in which to cast it. There had been gains. The Station, the greater part of the town, and Castle

Hill. But the cost had been crippling. In the two battles of Cassino the New Zealanders had lost 1,600 men, and 4th Indian Division over 3,000. As a fighting formation the Indian Division was for the time being non-existent. The New Zealand Division was never quite the same again.

4

THE pattern of the battle is clear enough from the narrative outline of its course. For the nature and flavour of the week's fighting it is necessary to look more closely. What was it like for the New Zealanders in the reeking, waterlogged warren of a ruined town?

It is not easy to convey. This kind of fighting has little coherence, no design that is easy to follow. For the New Zealanders it was a mosaic of grim little fights over small distances: a lethal game of hide-and-seek in ditches, cellars, craters, mounds of rubble, sewers, and fragments of buildings that resembled stumps of teeth, but each of which concealed one or more abscesses in which a man, or a gun, or even a tank could be hidden. Enough of the prepared fortifications—reinforced cellars, gun emplacements, ground floor bunkers—survived the bombing well enough to preserve a hard core of defence at the western end of the town, barring the way to the Liri Valley.

The New Zealanders had for days studied a town layout on maps and air photographs. The shambles into which they filed on the first day of the battle bore no relation to what they had so carefully memorized. The Germans on the other hand knew their way about. They were in strong positions prepared long before. They had no distances to cover. They could readily dart from one to another along covered ways that had been carefully constructed. They knew the ravines and walls and other covered approaches that led from the slopes of the mountains into the town. Night after night they could filter little parties of additional men into the ruins: and an area that was clear of Germans by nightfall had sprouted a machine-gun post or a few snipers by the following day.

It was the disposal of this kind of post, the capture, one at a time, of cellars concealed in heaps of debris, that kept the New Zealanders occupied for more than a week trying to advance and clear what was a ludicrously small ground area. Their difficulties can most readily be appreciated if one fills in a little of the detail that made up the complex whole.

From the first the sniper came into his own. Even in modern war there is, strangely, nothing more effective than the sniper in conditions that suit him. The rubble of Cassino was a sniper's paradise. Shelling, mortaring, and machine-gun fire provide a generalized hazard, a generalized death. It is easier to face them than the particular, personal, selective menace of the sniper. Men can be inspired to rise from cover and charge through the generalized kind of fire. It is much more paralysing for the soldier to know that as soon as he shows himself he may be deliberately aimed at by a single, concealed marksman. Throughout this battle snipers grew overnight like weeds in different parts of the rubble, and on the lower slopes of the mountain commanding the rubble.

Occasionally they could be disposed of by concentrations of tank shells on the area in which they were hidden, but mostly they had to be dealt with a harder way. A man had to expose himself deliberately to draw their fire, while one or more others, watching with Bren guns cocked, would try to spray the marksman during the split second he revealed his position by firing. It took cold courage to act as a decoy in this way. It was generally one of the old hands who volunteered to do it. Many irreplaceable desert veterans died that week showing themselves to snipers so that the others could make a quick dash across fifteen yards of open ground to yet another cellar, or fragment of wall, or ruined house or sewer.

The closeness of the combatants at times gave a quality of fantasy to the proceedings. A Field Ambulance of the Indian Division had established a medical aid post in the cellar of a building at the foot of the mountainside. On one occasion they were asked by a New Zealand tank troop if they would temporarily vacate it. The New Zealanders had spotted Germans entering an upper storey of the same house, and they wished to shoot at it.

On another occasion a New Zealand battalion headquarters were mystified by the sound of a tank engine turning over quietly. It appeared to be coming from the next building, yet no tank was visible. An investigation revealed that the German tank was sealed inside the house. An officer thereupon crawled through the rubble, guiding two New Zealand tanks to a point from which they could fire at it. He was spotted and heavily mortared but his shouted instructions got the tanks into position and they began firing at the house. A platoon then stormed it, and as soon as they entered, it collapsed. Inside they found the tank intact, but the crew had been killed. The engine was still running. The tank had been used as an observation post in their very midst for five days. It explained the uncanny accuracy of the fire they had had to endure. An underground passage had been constructed from the room in which the tank stood to the cellar, and thence under a courtyard and the road to an embankment on the other side. Thus the crew could be relieved regularly and safely. It would not have been detected had the commander not been compelled to run his engine for a short while to charge his radio batteries. This was the kind of thing the New Zealanders were up against. The Germans had had a long time to prepare the Cassino defences. They had prepared them well.

There was the 26th Battalion's capture of the Station. They had spent two nights and a day in the ruins. They had had their baptism of snipers' fire. They had had no hot food or drink for forty-eight hours. Their radio sets were out of action—mainly through the damp but also because their aerials had given away their position to snipers. They had to cross 600 yards of mostly open ground to storm the Station. Only 600 yards. But the ground was in full view of the strong-points 500 yards to their right, the vantage points up the mountain, and of course the whole east side of Monte Cassino.

They set off a company at a time, covering the distance in two or three scrambling charges. The first company got through without too many losses (though three tanks leading them were knocked out). But by the time the turn of the others came the Germans had got the range. One after the other the men of these companies ran the gauntlet. Some of them got through, enough to seize the Station and an adjacent strong-point at the point of the bayonet. But in that short action which took little more than an hour they lost eighty-eight men of whom the high proportion of thirty-three were killed. There was nothing particularly skilled about the operation. It was an old-fashioned 'over the top' series of charges and short dashes. It just needed courage and this was available.

Like the Indian Division, the men in the town suffered from the necessary torment of the smoke screen which was maintained throughout each day. 'There is no day,' one of them recorded, 'only two kinds of night—a yellow, smoky, choking night, and a black meteor-ridden night.' For the many the smoke was an insufferable addition to their other troubles, but for the few it was essential, and so it had to be kept up.

Despite the difficulties they did not lose their sense of humour. The company that climbed the lower slopes of the mountain to attack the Continental Hotel from behind gaily informed their Indian neighbours that they were off to 'break into the Continental Hotel by the servants' entrance', a few minutes before they lost a third of their strength failing to do so.

Some men of a reserve battalion, not committed in the early days of the battle but standing by in readiness, were quartered in the town gaol. They passed the time producing a daily newspaper, the Cassino Evening Post. It was hand-written on army message forms and relied for most of its substance on the B.B.C. news. The first issue carried a short leader which concluded: 'After only two days in the gaol the proprietors are fully convinced that crime does not pay and are quite prepared to sell their interests to anyone requiring a home.' (In addition to being infested with rats, the gaol was a favourite target of the German gunners.) The paper was distributed each night with the rations.

There was humour as well as panache in a solo effort carried out by the Regimental Sergeant Major of the Maori battalion. It was during one of the attacks on the Continental Hotel. Fire from an intermediate ruin was holding up the advance. The R.S.M. went forward to investigate; worked his way right up to the building; managed to pinpoint the source of the trouble. Flattening himself against the building and using his best parade-ground voice he succeeded in directing the fire of a New Zealand tank through various gaps in the walls. A handful of Germans at once came out and surrendered to him. The R.S.M. was not satisfied. He was certain that many more remained inside. Using what the New Zealand official historian describes as 'dire threats and novel means' he indicated to the prisoners that it would be better for one and all if they persuaded the rest of their comrades to come out.

The precise nature of the 'dire threats and novel means' is not disclosed, but R.S.M.s have a notorious talent for unconventional menace: whatever it was on this occasion, it worked. The prisoners shouted into the building. To everyone's surprise sixty more came out with their hands up.

It was incidents like these, repeated many times over, which made up the pattern of that confused nightmare week in the ruins of Cassino. Under the pitiless glare of the Monastery they fought for eight days and nights from craters filled with brown water to flooded rat-infested cellars; from an upper floor of a ruin to a lower. And many times they were grateful to take shelter for a few minutes in the stinking course of a mutilated sewer to escape a stream of bullets which was never directed haphazard, but always with specific care by well-protected eyes that could watch every inch of ground across which they could crawl or squirm or run.

In one respect the men in the town were better off than those up the mountain: most of them could look forward to a warm meal each night. After the first two nights, it was generally possible to take hot food and drink to the scattered posts in the town ruins. Tea or cocoa was poured into jerrycans which were then wrapped in straw and placed inside sandbags: tins of food were similarly wrapped. They were then taken by jeep to the outskirts of the town where carrying parties met them and rushed the loads to units and sub-units—enabling the jeeps to get away within a few minutes of arrival and so avoid the deluge of fire that would come down on them if their presence was suspected. The straw kept the food warm for two hours. It made a tolerable substitute for the insulated containers from which hot meals were normally distributed when the enemy were not so inconveniently close.

That was how the New Zealanders lived and fought for eight days and nights. For the Indian Division, a few hundred yards away up the mountain, it was an entirely different battle in a different world: and in the extraordinary ordeal of the 1st/9th Gurkhas on Hangman's Hill, it provided one of the genuine epics of the war.

Of all the races that made up the Indian Army, the Gurkhas of Nepal were always the most popular with the British soldiers. They are short, stocky men, with round flat mongoloid faces: they have a great sense of fun and laugh easily: they are great drinkers, when they get the chance: they walk with an endearing swagger. They were perhaps the Gascons of the old Indian Army. One of the most touching sights on these corpse-littered mountains was a Gurkha cemetery. The graves seemed too short for a man, and the boots at the end of each one, too small. (There was always a steel helmet at one end of the grave, boots at the other.) The rows of little boots always gave the impression that this was a burial ground of children. There was a childlike quality about their manner too. Once, during the Cassino battle, a Gurkha got lost during the night and ended up in the town. He sheltered in a ruined tank. A German sergeant approached. The Gurkha shot him in the throat. Then, at some risk, he delayed his departure long enough to dress the German's wound, and finally made his way back up the mountain—triumphantly laden with American cigarettes he had found in the wrecked tank.

For eight days and nights this battalion of Gurkhas on Hangman's Hill occupied an exposed shoulder of the mountain: an area about 200 yards square, 250 yards from the Monastery—concealed from it only by a crag. On a slope that was more of a cliff-face than a mountainside, they lived in shallow trenches scooped out of craters, or in clefts in the rock, or in the unsatisfactory stone breastworks the Indian Army called *sangars*.

To get there at all they had had to travel light. Ammunition had to come first, and that meant leaving behind greatcoats and blankets. For eight days and nights, therefore, they lived on an exposed cliff-face, in mid-winter, without even a coat to protect them against the icy winds, the frequent rainstorms, and a temperature which seldom rose above freezing point, and at night was well below.

To begin with, the only source of water they could find was a rain-filled bomb crater. When that had been used up they found a well in the courtyard of a ruined house some way down the mountain. This kept them going for a day or two, but if they visited it by day they were fired at from above, and at night they ran the risk of meeting German patrols. When the level had been reduced by four feet, and the water was developing a strange taste, they discovered that there was a dead mule in the well. Luckily the New Zealand company in equally splendid isolation at Point 202 below them had found another well, and thereafter the Gurkhas shared it with them.

Food was a much bigger problem. They had to exist entirely on American K rations. This is a small emergency pack of dried food designed to provide one meal for one man to tide him over for a day or so until normal feeding can be arranged. The best the Gurkhas ever managed was two K rations between three men—not for one meal but to last them for twenty-four hours. Most of the time it was two rations between four men. When the porter parties came up, they had to give precedence to ammunition. When the airdropping of supplies began, only a small percentage reached the battalion. This was nobody's fault. It was impossible to drop supplies on so small an area of a steep mountainside without large numbers of the canisters going astray.

It requires no feat of the imagination to realize what it must have been like for these men, half-crazy with hunger and cold—having had no hot food or drink for days, and not even more than a few mouthfuls of cold food—to watch the parachuted canisters landing just a few feet out of reach, and then bouncing down the slope. The temptation to run after them was sometimes irresistible. But the penalty was invariable—a burst of machine-gun bullets in the back from the watchful German machine-gunners.

In addition there was the uncertainty. They never knew whether porter parties would get through to them or not, and when the aeroplanes appeared and the parachutes began to drop, they never knew how many—if any—would be retrievable.

Because they were so close to the Monastery, half of them had to be awake and alert throughout the day and night. On top of everything they were constantly hit by the empty smoke shells fired by their own guns to maintain the smoke-screen in the town. At the week-end they had to watch the counter-attacks on the Castle, knowing that if it was recaptured they would be cut off: they would have endured all this for nothing.

They could not even provide proper attention for their wounded. Because there was no place for it on Hangman's Hill, the battalion medical aid post had been left at the bottom of the mountain. Three times during the eight days their medical officer brought stretcher-bearer parties up the mountain in daylight under the protection of the Red Cross flag. In the meantime the best they could do for the wounded was to place them in a culvert under a stretch of the mountain road which ran below their positions. The only comfort they could provide for them was to give them the felt packing from ammunition boxes as a meagre mattress, and such parachutes as they managed to recover as sheets.

By the week's end their company had been augmented by the handful of Rajputana Rifles who had brought them supplies, and the Essex men who had come up on the Sunday morning to assist in the attack on the Monastery that never took place.

They were glad of the additional rifles but the extra numbers to be fed made the miracle of the loaves and fishes more than ever a daily necessity.

When, on the 23rd, it was decided to call off the offensive there remained the problem of how to extricate the Gurkhas from Hangman's Hill. The Germans would know that they had to be withdrawn: they would be waiting. It was decided that the withdrawal would be carried out on the night of the 25th, and this was how it would be done. The artillery would fire a running barrage between the upper hairpin bend and the Monastery, and another along the lower slopes of Monte Cassino behind the area of the Continental Hotel and the Hotel des Roses. At the same time the Royal West Kents would simulate an attack on the hairpin bend area from the Castle. Under cover of the feint attack and between the two walls of artillery fire the Gurkhas would hurry down the mountain through Castle Hill to the valley. The New Zealand company at Point 202 would act as rearguard and then follow hard on the tail of the Gurkhas.

The point was how to convey the plan—which called for careful and exact timing—to the Gurkhas. The only link with them was by radio and it would be far too risky to transmit these orders over the air. There was only one alternative. The orders must be issued verbally. It was decided to send three officers to Hangman's Hill on the preceding night, each having memorized the orders.

They would go by different routes to make sure that one got through. Each would take a carrier pigeon, and each was given a code word. The return of the pigeon with a slip of paper bearing the code word would indicate that the orders had arrived, and which officer had delivered them.

On the night of the 24th the three officers set forth up the mountain. One got through without too much difficulty, but the suspense was not over. The pigeon proved to be allergic to darkness. As soon as it had been released with the appropriate code word it circled slowly round and came to rest on a rock just out of reach. There, watched in an agony of suspense, it defiantly waited for half an hour until daybreak. Only then would it consent to take off and complete its duty to the relief of the equally anxious men waiting for it in the valley. One of the other officers arrived shortly after this, but as he had had to crawl a good deal of the way with the pigeon in his battle-dress blouse it was no longer airworthy. The third officer failed to arrive.

At ten-fifteen that night 8 officers and 177 other ranks—out of the 400 who had been on Hangman's Hill a week before—stumbled down the mountain between two walls of artillery fire.

> . . . as in a dream they find
> Strength in their feet to bear back that strange whim
> Their body.

After they had gone by, the New Zealand detachment withdrew from Point 202 and followed on behind. These Gurkhas and New Zealanders were in that condition in which the eyes stare without seeing and fatigue seems to have become a skin disease. But those who watched them march to the trucks that would take them away to rest were struck by their cheerfulness.

It was curious that a battle that had opened with the majesty of five hundred bombers depended for its final action on just one pigeon.

5

NOTHING reflected the sombre intensity of Cassino more than the problems it raised for the medical services. The usual procedures for the handling of battle casualties had to be augmented in special ways to meet the exceptional circumstances.

Traditionally the basis of medical practice in battle is a system of rapid evacuation. The wounded are picked up by their own stretcher-bearers and taken back to the unit medical officer who, after giving them the minimum necessary attention, passes them back to an advanced dressing station where more facilities are available. From there they are taken back another stage to a casualty clearing station which is in effect an emergency hospital. It is at this stage that the first surgery is normally carried out. From that point the casualties would be sent by hospital train or ambulance (on some occasions by aeroplane) to one of the general hospitals established in the base areas far behind the battle zone. In normal conditions this system—which could be telescoped or modified to meet the circumstances of a particular battlefield —worked very well, ensuring that the forward medical stations were cleared as rapidly as possible so as to be ready for new arrivals. It could not, however, be applied at Cassino for two reasons: the length of time required for the first stage of the evacuation and the exceptionally severe nature of the wounds sustained in the mountain sector from shells and mortar bombs exploding at varying heights on the flint-hard rock.

Men wounded in the mountain salient had to be carried down the steep treacherous paths for more than two miles. The only way in which this could be done was to establish a chain of stretcher-bearer posts every two hundred yards from the top to the valley. What with the sheer physical difficulty of the descent, and delays caused by the constant harassing of this supply route by the German artillery and mortars, the long carry invariably took several hours. It was a difficult ordeal for a badly wounded and shocked man to have to endure. The stretcher was constantly tilted or suddenly put down as one of the bearers stumbled or slipped. The night temperature was generally below freezing point, and frequently the journey took place in rain or snow. On top of this the stretcher-bearers and their unfortunate burdens were frequently hit by the enemy gunners. When a badly wounded man had survived this nightmare start to his evacuation, he obviously had to be treated as quickly as possible. So the newly-created Field Surgical Units were deployed for the first time on this front, providing, under canvas extensions to specially equipped lorries, full surgical facilities, including blood transfusion. Because of the time it took to get away from this front line the hospital, in effect, had itself to be brought near to the front.

This was not all. It happened that Cassino produced a much higher percentage of head and eye injuries than usual. Thanks to the design of the human body and the conditioned reflexes of the experienced soldier in the matter of personal preservation, by far the greatest number of wounds in normal conditions are confined to the legs and arms. But in the winter battles of Cassino the frequency of head and eye wounds was such that special arrangements had to be made to handle them. The Field Surgical Units had to be supplemented by a Forward Head Injury Unit to deal solely with head cases. And the special nature of the injuries required a higher proportion of eye specialists than are normally attached to a field force.

There was a reason for this incidence of head and eye injuries. A shell bursting on ordinary ground partly buries itself (and some of its effect) and directs its blast and shrapnel forward. A shell or mortar bomb bursting on the flint-hard slope of a mountain had a much more damaging effect, and the fragments of metal flew farther and less predictably. In addition the troops were denied, as we have seen, the normal cover of trenches as these could not be dug into the rock. Their only protection was the *sangar*, a breastwork of loose stones. A concentration of shells bursting above them could strike down into the heart of these inadequate sanctuaries. In such conditions shrapnel could kill or wound at a range of a hundred yards or more, and many serious injuries were caused, not by the shells themselves, but by the sharp pieces of rock they sent flying in all directions.

It was not only in the mountain sector that eye injuries were frequent. The valley kept the ophthalmic surgeons busy too. In order to defeat the mine-detector—which performs its duty by humming when it is brought near to metal—the Germans, as we have previously noted, had that winter gone over to the extensive use of mines with wooden cases. These 'schu' mines, the casing of which was a small wooden box, were made almost without metal, but not quite. They had to carry small brass hinges and some metal parts in the firing mechanism. They exploded when trodden on, usually blowing off the foot that stepped on them and damaging the legs. In addition, the small metal parts, especially fragments of the brass hinges, flew upwards and often lodged in the face of the victim. A large proportion found the eye, and removing these particles of metal from eyes became a melancholy and difficult daily occurrence in the Forward Head Injury Unit. The loss of a foot and damage to at least one eye was a common result of stepping on the vicious little 'schu' mines which were buried in thousands along the valley and in the town.

It was one of the more tragic features of the winter battles that so many of those who survived them with their lives were blinded or disfigured. The proportion was exceptional enough for two hospitals to have to make special arrangements to deal with these injuries. The 92nd General Hospital became partly an eye hospital, the 65th was reserved for head, facial, and neurosurgical cases.

There was, however, a more humane side to the picture. The exceptional closeness of the combatants, together with the restriction

it imposed on daylight movement, led gradually and sponta-
neously to the practice of openly evacuating wounded men
in daylight under the Red Cross flag. Nothing was arranged
officially. It was done sparingly. But it was done, and both sides
respected the Red Cross. It was one of those situations in which
front-line soldiers, separated by a hundred yards or less, seem to
develop a strange kinship in extremity. In the mountains the
stretcher-bearers of both sides made these occasional daytime
excursions into the boulders and thickets of no-man's-land, and
sometimes they exchanged words with one another.

During the period in which the Gurkhas were isolated on
Hangman's Hill their medical officer made three daylight trips
up the face of Monte Cassino with a party of orderlies to bring
down wounded men to his aid post in the valley. Each time he
was stopped by a German post, taken to the nearest headquarters
and then given permission to continue. The second time he was
told not to do it any more. But he risked a third journey and was
merely told that this must be positively the last.

On Snakeshead Ridge the Royal Sussex, who had to man this
exposed and dangerous salient for a month after the crippling
February attacks they had unsuccessfully launched from it,
rescued many of their wounded under the Red Cross flags: they
also began a systematic clearance of the large number of corpses
which by that time littered the area—sending a few down each
night on the backs of the mules that brought up their food, water,
ammunition, and letters. In the town, where the contestants were
sometimes separated by only the width of a building, the Red
Cross was also on occasion used—and respected.

When the third battle ended and the Gurkhas had to be
extricated from Hangman's Hill, the New Zealand company that
had been their neighbours down the hillside at Point 202 acted
as rearguard. This position half-way down the mountain had in
the course of the week become a collecting post for stragglers
from many other units, especially wounded. As there was a
likelihood of this depleted detachment—the last to leave—having
to fight its way down to the valley in the wake of the Gurkhas,

the commander had the difficult duty of telling the wounded that he would have to leave them behind. He left them a keg of rum and a large Red Cross made out of the silk of the parachutes that had dropped the rum and other supplies that afternoon, and promised to return for them the next morning.

He was not in the event allowed to return himself, but a party of volunteers under a New Zealand medical officer went off next day. They could not, however, find the wounded in the area where they had been left. After a long and somewhat hazardous search they found that—fortified by the rum and also perhaps by the uncertainty of their future—they had decided to struggle down under their own steam. They had managed to reach the road and were slowly making their way along it. As the rescue party reached them a German soldier also appeared on the scene. He said that they could not continue without first obtaining permission from the local commander. A delegation duly presented itself and the German officer then handed them a written note addressed to 'The English Commander' stating that this was the last party that would be allowed to pass through. A German orderly then conducted them towards Castle Hill by a devious route so that they could not see the layout of the German posts. When they were clear he shook hands with them and wished them luck.

That was Cassino. A battlefield on which for weeks the dead could not be moved or buried: which occasioned such a high proportion of head and eye injuries that special steps had to be taken to cope with them: which made survival, even at an animal level, an achievement in itself: yet on which the medical orderlies of both sides fell into the habit of wandering, almost at will, in a mute kinship that in its spontaneous charity was perhaps the most ironic witness of all to the folly that made it necessary.

It may be wondered what it was like for the defenders of Cassino who had three times repulsed the Fifth Army's attacks. How did they feel about it all? The diaries and letters of men killed in action or captured give some indication.

The German soldier, subject to an iron discipline more rigorous than that of the British and American armies, seems to have found a compensating outlet for his feelings in his letters and the thoughts he communicated to his diary. Once beyond the immediate control of that discipline he would express himself volubly and emotionally. This tendency even extended to his conduct after capture. It was a source of worry to the German High Command—reflected in orders on the subject—that their men talked more freely when they had been taken prisoner than the British or American soldier. These extracts from diaries and letters can therefore be accepted as a fair indication of the true feelings of their authors.

These were the impressions of a machine-gunner who moved into the Cassino sector in time for the battle which began with the bombing of the Monastery on February 15th:

Feb. 13. I've been in the line for several days now. We have taken up new positions close to Tommy. I'm sure I can maintain that the Somme battlefield did not look worse. It is fearful, and horror overcomes you as you wonder when this misery will stop. The air vibrates with shells and death.

And this was how he saw the third battle which began on March 15th:

Mar. 15. Today hell is let loose at Cassino. Cassino is a few kilometres away to our left. We have a good view of everything. Almost 1,000 aircraft bomb our positions at Cassino and in the hills. We can see nothing but dust and smoke. The boys who are lying up there must be going mad. In addition the artillery puts down a concentration of fire throughout the whole day. The ground is shaking as if there was an earthquake.

Mar. 17. In spite of all the bombs and shells we still hold Cassino. Today we were relieved quite unexpectedly. It does not appear to be a good thing, for it comes too suddenly, but the main thing is that we get out of these hills.

Mar. 18. At B Echelon we remove our beards and above all are deloused.

Mar. 20. Yes, it came too quickly. Tonight we go into the line at the most stinking bit.

Mar. 22. We are back in the hills behind Cassino. What we are going through here is beyond description. I never experienced anything like this in Russia, not even a second's peace, only the dreadful thunder of guns and mortars and there are planes over and above. Everything is in the hands of fate, and many of the boys have met theirs already. Our strong-point is built round with stones. If one is dropped among them then we'll have had it.

It will be noted that the last two entries cover the period of the battle when the Allied attacks were on the wane and the initiative had passed to the Germans. On March 25th, by which time both sides were back on the defensive this machine-gunner made the following entry:

Mar. 25. There has been a heavy fall of snow. It is whirling into our post. You would think you were in Russia. Just when you think you are going to have a few hours' rest to get a sleep, the fleas and bugs torment you. Rats and mice are our companions too.

It was the last entry he made.

A soldier whose family seem to have kept up a voluminous correspondence was captured shortly after the second battle. The letters found on him give not only another impression of Cassino, but a comprehensive idea of what a typical German family was enduring at this time. There was an unposted letter from himself to his father serving in Russia:

Dear Father,

For two weeks we have been in action. The few days were enough to make me sick and tired of it. In all that time we've had nothing to sleep in but foxholes, and the artillery fire kept us with our noses in the dirt all day long. During the first few days I felt very odd, and didn't eat anything at all. I lost my appetite when I saw all that. . . . Ernst was wounded. The two fellows from home did not get leave because all leave was cancelled, and now both have been captured. I hope that I'll get my leave soon . . . not a single man of my original squad is left. It seems to be the same in the entire company.

The other letters were from different members of the family and had been received by him while he was at Cassino.

From his father in Russia:

Dear Son,

We are on the retreat and we have retreated quite a bit. . . . Everybody is sick and tired of the war, but it does not look as if the nonsense will come to an end. . . . Enemy planes are coming over Germany night after night and even during the day. . . . Before our last retreat the Russians certainly gave us hell . . . we were loading ships on the Dnieper when we got a direct hit and ten of my comrades were killed.

From a cousin on another front in Italy:

Dear Kurt,

Just a few lines. I'm sitting in my foxhole. Tommy is firing all the time with his awful mortars. It is impossible even to lift your head. I wish this idiotic war would end. My leave was a sad one. Just as I arrived home I learned that Helmut had been killed. A few days later the news arrived that Else's husband had been killed. Then we heard that Karlchen had been killed. Just before I left the news came that Fritz was killed in the Crimea. The worst has happened to our family.

From a brother in France:

Dear Kurt,

I'm fine and hope that you're all right too. We are serving as a flak unit near the Gulf of Biscay. The British come regularly and we have to be on the alert day and night because we are completely on our own here. . . .

From his mother in Germany:

Dear Son,

I'm waiting and waiting and always worried about my sons . . . to have you in this great danger is hard for a mother. Be careful, for my sake. Here at home we have an alert each night. Today of course just as usual. We have to spend at least three hours in the cellar every night. The night before last they were here between 2 and 5 in the morning, last night they came at the same time. We go to bed at 7 in order to get enough sleep before 2 a.m. when we have to get up. Sometimes they fool us and come at 8 in the evening and force us out of bed. . . .

The air raids on Germany were a dominant theme of the letters the soldiers were receiving from home. A private in a tank regiment had this one from his young cousin two days before he died in action:

Dear Helmut,

Thank you for your dear letter. We are all well though on Jan. 30 we almost lost our lives . . . fortunately we had gone to the shelter half an hour before they even sounded the alert, otherwise maybe we would not be alive. Aunt Trudie was killed . . . she couldn't make it down to her cellar. The alarm came much too late . . . I tell you this war is something horrible. . . . All that is left now is ruins. . . . Every evening we ride down to the air raid shelter because it must be terrible to be buried alive in your own house. That's about all I can think of today, except that I have seen more good movies lately. That's just about the only thing that affords you a little distraction. I hope we shall see you soon on your leave. Till then, with best regards,

Your little Cousin Susie.

That is how some of the German soldiers felt that winter. Those were the letters they were receiving from home. Yet they hung on. The ground they defended was naturally strong. The fortifications of the Gustav line had made it infinitely stronger. But it still required first-class soldiers to man those defences to the death. These soldiers were willing to do that and their defence of Cassino that winter was a great feat of arms.

The 15th and 90th Panzer Grenadier Divisions, the 5th Mountain, and the 71st Infantry all took their turn, but it was the 1st Parachute—who were there in time for the third battle—who left the most lasting impression on the Allies who fought them.

The Parachute divisions were Nazi formations under the direction of the Luftwaffe. They considered themselves a race apart from the ordinary army divisions, and were therefore not too

popular with the orthodox army men under whose command
they came. Like the SS Divisions they could by-pass army
channels and deal direct with the party leaders—Goering in the
case of the Parachute formations. This message, sent by Kesselring
to the Tenth Army Commander after one of the successful
German counter-attacks, is indicative: 'Convey my heartfelt
gratitude to 211 Regt., and 1 Para Regt. not quite so strongly . . .'
Nevertheless they were fine soldiers.

On March 15th the Allied Command had psychiatrists standing
by to examine the first prisoners that came in to see what effect
the bombing had had on them. It was assumed that there would
be many cases of nervous collapse. The paratroops, mostly boys
in their teens or early twenties, seemed to know what was
expected of them. When they were asked about the bombing
they forced a smile, shrugged their shoulders and said that it was
nothing. Their attitude was that of a schoolboy who, emerging
from the Headmaster's study rubbing his behind, defiantly in-
forms his friends: 'It didn't hurt.' Of the first three hundred
prisoners to come in, only one was found in a nervous condition
directly attributable to the bombing.

There was an indication of their mentality during the German
counter-attack on Castle Hill which turned the tide of the battle.
After the first ferocious assault down the mountainside had been
held, a sergeant-major and half a dozen lightly wounded paratroopers surrendered to the Castle garrison. When the second
German attack came in all except one, the sergeant-major, volunteered for duty as stretcher-bearers. They worked very hard and
constantly exposed themselves to danger. One even saved the life
of a British officer by jerking him out of the line of fire of a
sniper. While the battle was raging—the attackers were getting
right up to the walls of the besieged castle courtyard—the
sergeant-major watched the proceedings with a dispassionate
professional eye, almost as though he were an umpire. When it
was all over (and it was a particularly unpleasant close-quarter
fight) he approached the senior surviving British officer, con-
gratulated him in formal terms on his handling of the situation,

and asked him to accept his Paratrooper gauntlets as a token of his admiration.

It is difficult to explain this attitude, except as the product of an indoctrination and discipline so complete, that once capture is an accomplished fact—and, through injury, unavoidable and therefore honourable—a man instinctively welcomes the nearest available discipline because he cannot get along without it.

These were the men who moved General Alexander to remark to General Kippenberger some weeks later: 'If you had not been faced by the best division in the German Army you would have succeeded.'

Military critics have been inclined to dismiss the third battle of Cassino as a failure on the part of the Allies to anticipate the effects of the bombing. This is an over-simplification.

It was already well known from previous experience—especially in Sicily—that the preliminary bombing of a town always turned it into an obstacle and created a major problem of clearance. It was therefore imperative that infantry should follow up the bombing swiftly and in large enough numbers not only to make up for the likely inability of tanks to join them at once, but to provide a screen behind which the sappers could immediately tackle the work of clearance. Bulldozers would be more important than tanks in the first hour or two of such a battle.

At Cassino the bombardment was the only possible means of inflicting real damage on the exceptionally strong fortifications created by the Germans in the town. But only one infantry battalion followed up the bombing on that first vital afternoon, and when the supporting tanks were held up by the bomb damage, no additional infantry other than a single company were sent in. This was the fundamental error in the directing of the battle on the first day. Ground which could have been overrun immediately after the bombardment had later to be fought for painfully, yard by yard, after the Germans had had time to recover.

The other lesson was that first-class troops cannot be defeated by sheer weight of metal alone. Aeroplanes cannot win land battles single-handed. After the destruction phase of a battle, the ground troops have to come to grips with one another to settle the issue. Even in the nuclear age it may be thought that where armies and nations are equally matched this principle must still apply. Destruction alone is not enough. Men must eventually settle the issue with men.

The intervention of rain on the first night—a stroke of luck to the Germans, a bitter blow to the Allies—merely underlined these two lessons: it did not teach them for the first time. Nor can it be too strongly emphasized that the performance of the German Parachute Division was altogether exceptional. Indeed an impartial umpire might be inclined to view this occasion, not as a battle the Allies lost—for which excuses must be found—but one which the Germans won.

Two days before the end of the battle Mr. Churchill sent General Alexander a signal which reflected the discouragement, tinged with impatience, of those who followed the course of Cassino from afar.

I wish you would explain to me why this passage by Cassino, Monastery Hill, etc., all on a front of two or three miles, is the only place which you must keep butting at. About five or six divisions have been worn out going into these jaws. Of course I do not know the ground or the battle conditions, but, looking at it from afar, it is puzzling why, if the enemy can be held and dominated at this point, no attacks can be made on the flanks. It seems very hard to understand why this most strongly defended point is the only passage forward, or why, when it is saturated (in a military sense), ground cannot be gained on one side or the other. I have the greatest confidence in you and will back you up through thick and thin, but do try to explain to me why no flanking movements can be made.

Alexander replied by pointing out that outflanking movements had been repeatedly attempted—from the north through the mountains, and from the south when the Americans tried to force a crossing of the Rapido. He explained how geography and the winter weather had contributed to the failure of these operations. Freyberg's frontal attack—designed to achieve a quick result by surprise and overwhelming fire-power—had been thwarted by the devastation of the bombing and the tenacity of the Paratroopers. He ended:

> The Eighth Army's plan for entering the Liri Valley in force will be undertaken when regrouping is completed. The plan must envisage an attack on a wider front and with greater forces than Freyberg has been able to have for this operation. A little later, when the snow goes off the mountains, the rivers drop, and the ground hardens, movement will be possible over terrain which at present is impassable.

It was a long, detailed, and lucid recapitulation of all the factors which had influenced the course of operations since mid-January. But General Alexander would not have been very wide of the mark if he had replied, more shortly, that the winter battles of Cassino had been lost on the underestimated playing-fields of Anzio.

V

THE FOURTH BATTLE

'Only numbers can annihilate.'   NELSON

I

THE fourth and last battle of Cassino was General Alexander's masterpiece: an operation in C major with full orchestra.

For the first time in this campaign he was able to mount an offensive at a time and place of his own choosing instead of being precipitated into action by events and pressures elsewhere. For the first time summer weather would make it possible to deploy large formations: the new offensive would be fought, not by companies and battalions, but by massed divisions. There would be a greater superiority in guns and machines than ever, but this time there would also be a preponderance of infantry. As Alexander himself remarked, quoting Nelson: 'Only numbers can annihilate.' This time there would be numbers. It was to be the vindication of Churchill's Mediterranean strategy: the justification for the long winter agony: the triumphant salute of the Mediterranean veterans to those new armies poised to strike across the English Channel and open the final chapter of the war. In the grand design of the war as a whole, the summer offensive in Italy was the prelude to the finale. But it was also a climax in its own right.

As long ago as February 22nd, shortly after the second Cassino battle, Alexander had redefined the strategy of the campaign—'to force the enemy to commit the maximum number of divisions in Italy at the time the cross-channel invasion is launched'. This could not be done merely by pushing him back another few miles: the Germans had to be drawn into a major battle and destroyed. Alexander's plan for achieving this had a classic simplicity.

He would pack the front that led to Rome, not with one army

but two. The Fifth and Eighth Armies, operating side by side on the twenty-mile front between Cassino and the sea would smash the Gustav Line and advance on Rome together. When the pursuit of the beaten German Tenth Army was in full cry, the Fifth Army's Anzio force, now reinforced to a strength of six divisions, and an army in its own right, would drive out of the beachhead and move across at right angles to the main advance to cut off the retreating Germans in the Alban Hills, the last ground on which they could make a stand before Rome. If all went according to plan large numbers of those recoiling from the Cassino front would be trapped.

The essence of the plan was that it would permit Alexander to attack with the necessary superiority of three-to-one at the point of main effort: the problem was to carry out the extensive re-grouping and movement of divisions entailed without the Germans getting wind of what was afoot. To cover this re-grouping, which took nearly two months, Alexander devised an ingenious and elaborate deception plan.

The basis of this plan was to persuade Kesselring that the Allies accepted the impossibility of breaking through the Gustav Line and that the summer offensive would take the form of a new sea-borne landing north of Rome at Civitavecchia. This would cause him to keep his mobile reserves north of Rome in readiness, and too far away from the area where the attack was really going to be delivered, to be of any use until it was too late.

To encourage this belief a fictitious landing operation was elaborately put in hand. The 36th U.S. division, not required in the early phases of the offensive, was sent to the Salerno-Naples area to carry out intensive training in combined operations. Assembly and embarkation areas were marked out as they would be for a genuine operation. Roads leading to these were prom-inently signposted with the maple-leaf badge of the Canadian Corps. Signals exercises were devised to give the German radio monitors the impression that the two divisions of the Canadian corps and the U.S. 36th Division were the force destined to make the landing. In Naples harbour the Royal Navy carried out fictitious exercises of the kind that precede assault landings. Concentrations of landing craft were formed up, or simulated by skilful camouflage. The air forces carried out repeated reconnaissance of the beaches of Civitavecchia. And while the bogus assembly areas at Salerno made a great display of the Canadian Corps sign, the two divisions of that corps who were to play a prominent part in the real battle moved secretly up to the front, with signs and flashes removed or concealed.

That was the first part of the deception plan. The second part of it was to maintain absolute secrecy about the switch of the Eighth Army to the Cassino front, and to cover the vast amount of movement and preparation necessary to the offensive.

To achieve this all movement in forward areas was confined to the hours of darkness. Formations holding the front line positions were moved as little as possible. If an armoured formation moved, it left behind dummy tanks and vehicles so that the area appeared exactly the same. A strict control was maintained over all artillery activity so that the total volume of fire each day never varied, and the enemy could have no suspicion that many new batteries were being moved into position. These new guns were always moved into sites that had previously been camouflaged.

When the Polish Corps relieved the 78th Division in the mountains behind the Monastery a strict wireless silence was imposed on them so that their language would not give away the fact that they had now come into the line. If they had to use wireless they used English signallers attached to them for the purpose. Where a total ban on daylight movement of transport was impossible, elaborate camouflage was arranged. For instance, in the case of a Polish divisional headquarters in view of the Monastery a vertical camouflage screen was erected along a mile of roadway, and trucks daily drove to and from the headquarters without being spotted.

To assist the projected crossing of the Rapido many tracks had to be repaired, or improved, and many new ones made. The work was done at night, and before the area was vacated at first light the new tracks would be carefully covered with brushwood and other camouflage material.

While the two divisions that were to carry out the river crossing were lying in their final assembly positions, the 78th Division, a crack formation which the Germans would expect to be in the vanguard of the coming offensive, were ostentatiously practising river crossings fifty miles behind the line.

In those six weeks of spring and early summer between the end of the third battle on March 24th and May 11th, D-Day for the new offensive, the whole of the Allied front presented a daily picture of desultory defence. There were sporadic exchanges of a few shells: an occasional round or two of mortar. But there was no noticeable change in the landscape: no new roads or discernible gun positions: no troop movement. There was nothing to indicate that the approaches to the Rapido could now handle considerable volumes of traffic, that some of the mountain tracks could now bear tanks, that the number of artillery pieces between Cassino and the sea had swollen to 1600. Only in the fictitious embarkation area of Salerno was there any noticeable activity and in Naples harbour where the navies seemed exceptionally busy.

The cover plan was entirely successful. Kesselring was completely deceived as to the time, the place, and the strength of the attack.

When the offensive opened on May 11th, General von Senger, commander of Fourteenth Panzer Corps, was on leave in Germany, having left behind a special order of the day ordering his formation to expect the Allied attack any time from May 24th. General von Vietinghoff, commander of the Tenth Army, was less fortunate: he had planned to go on leave that day, May 11th.

The fictitious landing operation was swallowed. Two German divisions (one armoured) were tied up near Civitavecchia: two armoured divisions were in reserve to the Anzio front with orders to be ready to switch to meet a new seaborne landing. These forces could have done great damage had they been available to come into the main battle in its early stages.

Finally, the build-up of Allied strength had been totally concealed. Hardly a shell fell on the new gun positions before May 11th, indicating that they had moved into place without being spotted. The French Expeditionary Corps, built up to four divisions packed into the small Garigliano bridgehead from which they were to attack, had moved in so skilfully that the Germans credited them with having one division in the line instead of four. The concealment of the two Canadian divisions succeeded completely. The presence of these divisions in the Liri Valley, when they were supposed to be 'messing about with boats' at Salerno, was one of the major surprises that discomfited the Germans as the offensive developed. As late as the second day of the battle Kesselring estimated that the Allies had six divisions against the four with which he was defending the Cassino front, and he considered these forces sufficient to take care of the immediate situation. In fact there were thirteen.

Alexander had achieved the vital three-to-one local superiority accepted as essential to a major break-through against modern prepared defences. He had achieved total surprise as to the time, place, and strength of the attack. The inventors of the blitzkrieg were to experience a classic demonstration of it.

It was one of the best pieces of planning and staff work of the war: it ensured that this battle was half won before the first shot had been fired.

The German plan for the summer was a continuation of their winter policy. The Tenth Army under von Vietinghoff would continue to block the main front: the Fourteenth Army of von Mackensen had the task of containing the Anzio beachhead and dealing with any new landings. The disposition of these armies supplies the final confirmation of the success of Alexander's deception plan. Kesselring rightly guessed that Alexander would not attack on the Adriatic front and he thinned out his holding forces to the bare minimum necessary to contain the equally thin Allied screen strung out between the Adriatic and the central mountains. This was his only good guess.

On the left half of the mountainous centre he had three divisions, with the 1st Parachute remaining in charge of Cassino and Monte Cassino. Between there and the sea (about twenty miles) he had four divisions. That was the layout of the Tenth Army. On the other hand five divisions of the Fourteenth, with a Panzer Division in reserve, were massed to prevent the Anzio forces from breaking out of the beachhead, and more divisions, as we have seen, were uselessly tied up north of Rome in readiness for a new landing.

The basis of Kesselring's summer defence of the way to Rome was three lines. First there was the redoubtable Gustav, along the river line of the Rapido and anchored to Cassino. It had been dented in the winter battles but it had not been penetrated. It had withstood the impact of three battles. There had been every opportunity to make it even stronger as the winter weeks went by and the three Allied attacks on it showed where improvement and repair were necessary. During the two months' lull before the final offensive there had been ample time to develop it to a new pitch of strength.

Six miles behind the Gustav, the Germans had since Christmas been constructing a second line, the Adolf Hitler. Built to a depth of half a mile, it consisted of the usual minefields, anti-tank ditches, barbed wire, and pillboxes—many of these being tank turrets sunk into the ground and mounting the devastating 88-millimetre gun. This line, stretching from the mountain massif through Piedmonte across the Liri Valley, was intended to take care of any force that succeeded in breaking through the Gustav. The relationship between these two lines created the effect of a swinging gate, with Monte Cassino as the gatepost. Should the gate be forced it could swing back across the penetrated valley to the Hitler position—with Monte Cassino providing the hinge and the firm fixture. Then it would be unhooked and lifted back a mile or two to its new gatepost at Piedimonte: and Piedimonte, an old fortress town crowning a rocky hill, would become the new Monte Cassino.

It was felt that between them these two prepared lines could effectively deal with anything the Allies could do along the Liri Valley–Highway Six route to Rome. The only snag from Kesselring's point of view was the presence of a large Allied force at Anzio. If that force succeeded in breaking out and covering the few miles necessary to cut Highway Six, the Hitler Line would be useless. In March, therefore, the Germans—who are nothing if not thorough—had been working on a third line, the Caesar, in the Alban Hills or Colli Laziali.

The Albans—the last hill mass before Rome—were about twenty miles from the capital. They straddled not only the two main highways, Routes Six and Seven, but also the road astride which the beachhead force would have to advance. They provided, therefore, a hill area about eight miles wide and four deep where both German armies could be coordinated in a last ditch stand south of Rome.

In addition to these three prepared defence lines there was another factor to be considered in appraising the German approach to the summer. For them, as for the Allies, Cassino had developed an emotional, almost mystical, significance. Throughout the winter they had been dying there in scores. They had resisted three offensives. They had endured the devastating bombardments of the Allied guns and aeroplanes.

Hitler was fascinated by Cassino. He had remarked to von Senger that it was the only battlefield of the second war that reminded him of Ypres and the Somme. He had issued repeated orders that it must be held, and his soldiers had done as they were asked. In the course of time the defenders of Cassino had developed a mystique of their own. Prolonged defence, because it is negative, can develop a defence neurosis and eventually sap the determination of an army. At Cassino, where the Germans only employed their best troops, this was not so. Defending Cassino to the death had become a dedicated mission on its own, outside the general context of the war. Ever since Thermopylae *ils ne passeront pas* has for the best soldiers (but only the best) always been as inspiring as any bugled exhortation to the attack. To its German defenders Cassino had become what in the earlier war Ypres was to the British, Verdun to the French. It was a cause in its own right, a cause to die for.

It was the same for the Allies. In turn the Americans, the British, the New Zealanders, and the Indians had taken it on. Three times they had tried and failed and suffered appalling losses doing so. They knew that they had got to beat it in the end: that it was a climactic test of strength. To the divisions flexing their muscles for the summer offensive Rome was incidental. Retrospectively this would be known for convenience as the battle for Rome. The mere mention of the word Rome gave the occasion romance and glamour. Rome would be a wonderful prize to show for what had been endured and what lay ahead. But to the powerful forces secretly moving into position it was Cassino that mattered. No one doubted that once Cassino—an idea and an obsession, as well as a sombre reality of rock and steel—had been disposed of, nothing would matter very much. What followed would be easy. They would chase the beaten enemy the length of Italy and, in passing, Rome would make a handsome addition to the leave centres.

So Cassino at this hour of final decision was no longer just a disputed piece of ground: it was a crucible. To the Germans, against whom the general tide of the war had turned, it was an emotional anchorage to which a waning belief in their invincibility could still cling—could still sustain itself in a final defiance of the Götterdämmerung. For the Allies it had become an ultimate test of personal worth. The victories of the previous year no longer mattered. It was at Cassino, the seemingly impregnable, that they must reaffirm their skill, their strength, their maturity in combat, their right to victory.

To those taking part, therefore, eleven o'clock on the night of May 11th, 1944, was the moment of truth. And the theatrical splendour, as well as the devastation, of the setting added a sombre elegiac grandeur that made it seem also a moment of destiny. Whichever way it went this would have to be a long and costly battle to the death, for both sides had something to prove.

2

IN its broad outline Alexander's plan was a model of simplicity. On the right the Eighth Army would break into the Liri Valley, dispose finally of Cassino, and advance towards Rome along the axis of Route Six. On the left the Fifth Army would drive towards Rome astride the other main road, Route Seven,

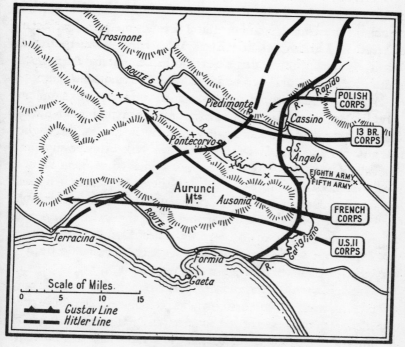

FOURTH BATTLE

Fifth and Eighth Armies break through and begin successful advance on Rome and through the mountains that provide the left wall of the Liri Valley. When he judged the moment had come for the *coup de grâce*, Alexander would order the Anzio divisions to storm out of their beachhead and cut off the Germans retreating before the main advance.

It is important, in view of what was to happen later, to note that from the start Alexander defined his intention as 'to destroy the right wing of the German Tenth Army; to drive what remains of it and the German Fourteenth Army north of Rome; and to pursue the enemy to the Rimini–Pisa line, inflicting the maximum losses on him in the process'. From the first he stressed that the capture of Rome was incidental. Morally and psychologically it would be fine to capture Rome. To the weary combatants of the Italian campaign it would be a precise and splendid prize, something heartening to show for what they had endured since the previous September. But it was not the primary military objective. The important thing was to engage and destroy as many as possible of the large German forces that had been drawn into Italy and would soon be sorely missed in France.

Although both armies were to strike massively and simultaneously along the main part of the front, the heavier burden during the first stage of the offensive would be borne by the Eighth Army. For the Eighth were allotted the task of disposing once for all of Cassino. No matter how widely the offensive was spread, success or failure depended in the end on what happened at Cassino. Until Cassino had fallen successes elsewhere would be academic. Not that its fall would mean the end of the battle. There would still have to be many more days, even weeks, of hard fighting. Rome would still be seventy miles away. But the day that Cassino fell, victory would be certain, for the Germans had staked everything there. It would remain only to be seen whether it was total victory, or whether appreciable numbers of the defeated army succeeded in extricating themselves, and by skilful rearguards survived to set up a new defence line two hundred miles to the north.

The Eighth's plan was a combination and elaboration of the

unsuccessful efforts of the Americans and the Indian Division in January and February. The Polish Corps, operating from the mountain salient north of Monte Cassino, would tackle the heights that had defeated the Indians in February; try to isolate the Monastery feature by seizing the adjacent heights and pushing on down the slopes to cut Route Six. In the valley, where the Rapido is stretched like a cord across the entrance to the Liri Valley, a powerful British Corps (the Thirteenth) would force a crossing of the river, and while one half pushed on towards the Hitler Line, the other would wheel round to the right to join up with the Poles on Route Six about two miles west of Cassino. Cassino and Monte Cassino would thus be pinched out and the bastion would become a death trap.

But whereas in January the Americans had attempted the Rapido crossing with one division, the Eighth would use two divisions for the crossing, with two more to pass through them as soon as they had secured the bridgeheads. In addition two armoured divisions would be supporting the crossings and the follow-up. Whereas in February the 4th Indian Division had had to fight alone from Snakeshead Ridge across the ravines and boulder-strewn slopes to Point 593 and Monastery Hill, the Poles would employ two divisions and in addition would be able to use tanks. But the Polish divisions, it must be added, consisted of only two brigades.

The task of the Fifth Army, advancing on the left of the Eighth, was lighter for two reasons. The defences they had to overcome were less formidable than those which the Germans had so diligently developed in the Cassino sector. Secondly, they had the advantage of starting on the enemy side of the river.

It will be remembered that as a preliminary to the first battle of Cassino, the British Tenth Corps of Fifth Army had forced a crossing of the Garigliano (a continuation of the Rapido) and attempted to turn the German flank. They had failed to turn the flank, but they had succeeded in consolidating a bridgehead across the river. At the time it had seemed a limited reward for a

costly operation. But now it was to pay dividends. Into that
bridgehead crowded the four divisions of the French Expeditionary Corps. But if the Fifth Army's task was easier than that
of the Eighth, it did not mean that it was a walkover. On their
front as on the other there was an enemy willing to die rather
than yield ground: an enemy on defendable ground of his own
choosing.

In addition to being the most powerful force yet mustered for
an offensive in Italy, Alexander's army group was also the most
international. The four main thrusts of the initial attack were
to be (reading from left to right) American, French, British, and
Polish. Fifth Army had two American divisions on the left to
drive up the coast: four French divisions and 12,000 Moroccan
goumiers to cut through the mountains on the left of the Liri
Valley and Eighth Army. The Eighth had six British and
Commonwealth divisions (including two armoured) for the
main battle in the Liri Valley and the encirclement of Cassino
from the left: two Polish divisions and the Polish Armoured
Brigade to cut it off from the right through the mountain tops.
The Eighth also had a South African armoured division in
reserve, and the mountainous right flank was to be protected by a
mixed force consisting mainly of the New Zealand Division with
a number of small groups under command—including an Italian
force.

The presence of the French and the Poles gave an added bite to
the offensive. To the British and the Americans, fighting had
become a trade. They had had an awful lot of it. In the course
of time they had learned to be good at it. Each new battle
was another job to be done, a dirty job, but a job nevertheless. The Hitler evil had to be dealt with in the same way as an
armed criminal must be captured. It would be foolish to imagine
that the average British or American soldier went into battle
thinking he was helping to save democracy. It is safe to say that
he never gave democracy a thought. He went into battle because
battle had become the whole of his life, his job. In the meantime

he could still make the best of his situation. He still made jokes and laughed and scrounged: he played football or baseball when he got the chance: he minimized the difficulties: he proudly insisted that his particular lot always seemed to land the unpleasant tasks: he made no attempt to disguise his pleasure when his unit or division happened to be in reserve. By all means let someone else have a go. His turn would soon come round again. For the time being he might as well make a cup of tea or get some sleep while he had the chance. To the outsider this attitude could be deceptive. Surely such soldiers were not to be taken seriously? In fact it was not a weakness but a strength, for it embraced a resilient philosophy of soldiering. It was why, in the end, men who instinctively disliked soldiering, and knew themselves to be temperamentally unsuited to it, still managed to overcome German opponents who in an odd way seemed always to be more professional and efficient.

With the French and the Poles it was quite different. The Free French Expeditionary Corps (to give it its full name) under General Juin was the first French land force to have the chance to hit back after the humiliation of 1940. The first two divisions had come into the line the previous Christmas and had made a spectacular début during the advance to Cassino. Now there were four divisions and the 12,000 *goumiers*, 100,000 men in all. Mostly these divisions were North African Colonial troops, but their officers were Frenchmen who knew that the liberation of France was at hand, and that they were to take part in a preliminary to that liberation. These Frenchmen represented the resurgent military pride of France, and the Liri Valley was for them not only the road to Rome but the road back to Paris. In their eagerness they were sometimes a little intolerant of their British and American allies, considering that they placed too much reliance on logistics. 'Show us where you want us to go and we'll go there,' was their attitude. 'Never mind about transport. Give us a few mules and send the rest of the stuff on later.' This panache and impatience to make France a power in the field again—coupled with the fact that these were mostly first-class regular troops of the old Colonial army—provided General Alexander with one of the trump cards of his offensive.

The situation of the Poles was akin to that of the French but more so. Every Pole who had reached the Polish Corps of General Anders had endured a personal epic to get there. They had escaped from their ravaged country and hitch-hiked to the Middle East: or escaped from German or Russian prisoner-of-war camps. Most of them had lost their families. The French could at least look forward with certainty to the liberation of their country. For the Poles the situation was not the same. Their country had been occupied from one side by the Germans, from the other by the Russians. Poland did not exist any more. Poland was these men in Italy, their comrades in the Royal Air Force, and a resistance movement that before the war was finished would have to contend with its 'ally' Russia as strenuously as with its German enemy. These men had lost everything and even at this stage it was clear to them that the end of the war would not mean the end of their troubles but the beginning of new ones. For the Poles it was a crusade. There was a cold, contained fury in their demeanour. More than any soldiers on the Allied side they had good reason to hate. They had come a long way and endured a great deal to fight the men who had ravaged their country in 1939, and there would be no half-measures about the manner in which they went into the attack. At times their seriousness seemed to contrast noticeably with the apparent casualness of their British comrades in the Eighth Army. Could they, the Eighth men sometimes wondered, understand it? Or did they think that the British treated war as a sort of game? The British, for their part, wondered whether the intensity of the Poles might not sometimes be their undoing and cost them many lives. For modern war is a skill as well as a test of courage, and bravery is not enough. Assault had to be cunning as well as fanatical.

What was certain was that these men would give everything. They had willingly taken on the unpleasantest of the many unpleasant tasks that this offensive entailed—the scramble across those vicious ridges that now were strewn with nearly as many corpses as boulders.

To support the offensive a prodigality of fire power was available. Behind the Eighth Army there were 1,000 guns, behind the Fifth, 600. Some 2,000 tanks were at hand. The entire Mediterranean air forces—now built up to a strength of more than 3,000 aircraft—would be on call in the opening stages of the attack. Army-air cooperation, which had not always been too successful on previous occasions, had been overhauled. One result of this was the 'cab rank'. During the opening stages of the offensive the battlefield would be continuously patrolled by relays of fighter-bombers with a radio link to the Forward Army H.Q. Just as the advancing infantry could call for artillery fire on any given point, and receive it within a few minutes, they would now be able to do the same with the air. A call for an air strike on a map reference would be received by an air force officer watching the battle, and he would immediately detach the necessary numbers of aircraft from the 'cab rank' in the sky and order them to attack the required place. In practice this meant that close air support would now be available in a matter of minutes instead of hours.

But in spite of this plethora of guns, aeroplanes and tanks, no one was under any illusions. This battle would have to be fought out by infantry. The Germans had been ordered to stay and they would fight for every yard. They were in well-protected positions. They had abundant supplies for a month's fighting despite the optimistic claims of the Allied air forces that they had 'isolated the battlefield'. 'Only numbers can annihilate.' It would be heartening to have so many tanks and aeroplanes and guns. But in the end it would be men against men, as in the end it always had to be. It would not be over until the enemy had had such crippling losses that he had to give up, and to inflict these losses the attackers would have to endure similar casualties themselves. This battle could not begin to be won until the beautiful fertile Liri Valley—which the early Benedictines had called

Campania Felix—had a glimpse of Armageddon: until the fields had been scarred with the blackened steel of many burnt-out tanks: till wooden crosses, as well as poppies, sprouted in the wild, untended corn.

H-hour was fixed for 2300 on the night of May 11th. This was half an hour before moonrise. Those in the first assaults would thus have half an hour of total darkness in which to make their preliminary moves to their jump-off points: then, for the main business of the night, they would have moonlight.

3

IT had been sunny for many days. Spring had turned into
early summer and even the desolation of a winter of war
could not prevent the countryside from looking beautiful.
Trees as well as men had died in hundreds that winter, and the
slopes of Monte Cassino bristled with lacerated stumps where
they should have been cushioned with acacia, olive, orange,
vine, and oak. But the valley was soft and green again. No
artillery on earth could stop the wild corn growing, or the
poppies. And even in destruction Monte Cassino had a towering
nobility that was deeply moving. Especially in the early summer
morning when the rising sun, bursting through the dawn haze,
bathed the blue-grey mountain and the honey-coloured ruin of
the Abbey in a glow of gold and pink. But on the morning of
May 11th it was unusually cloudy. It remained dull all day,
a little rain fell, and by afternoon there was a haze over the
valley.

To the watchful Germans it was just another day. The Allied
front was exactly as it had been for weeks. Nothing was happening. Static warfare was monotonous, but it had its advantages.
It was just another day in the front line when all is quiet. It had
been like this for weeks now. And 'they' did not expect it to be
any different for a while. May 24th, the Corps Commander
General von Senger had said, hadn't he? Be ready for the balloon
to go up any time after that. Oh well, the 24th was a long time
ahead. In any case the officers seemed to think that when the
attack did come it would be at Anzio or perhaps another landing
north of Rome. That made sense. With all those aeroplanes of

theirs and control of the sea. After all they have had three tries here, and we have beaten them off every time. . . .

In the Allied lines it was a day of disguised tension. Maps and orders were studied for the tenth time. Stores and equipment were checked and re-checked. Fitters and drivers spent the day under their vehicles. Officers and N.C.O.s attended last-minute conferences. Men with nothing to do tried to sleep: it might be some time before they slept again. The new men who would be going into action for the first time wondered how they would stand it and tried not to show that this was what they were wondering. The ones who had survived many actions wondered how long their luck could hold, and these concealed their feelings behind a jocularity that was often forced. The best unit commanders went out of their way to wander informally among their men that day, and to talk with most of them. The more anxious ones took refuge in aloofness. In a score of battalions they demanded to know why it was always they who had the dirtiest job to do. All day long men asked other men 'Are you quite clear about that? Have I forgotten anything?' Most of them wrote a letter. The one which begins 'Don't worry if you do not hear from me for a while . . .'. All day long they busied themselves with these last-minute routine matters, and if they had none to attend to, and they were not minded to rest, they invented things for themselves to do. But by the afternoon everything had been done, everything was ready. There was nothing left now but to wait for it to begin. That was when the tension began to be felt because there was now nothing to do but wait, and eleven o'clock was a long time off. And it was then, in the late afternoon, that something happened to increase that tension.

Cassino could always be relied upon to produce some strange touch of theatre. Once again it rose to the occasion. It was part of the Allied plan that artillery fire on the Cassino sector should cease before nightfall. During the day it would not be heavy, but in the afternoon it was to peter out altogether to heighten the sense of disinterest and calm before the cataclysm broke one hour before midnight.

By chance it happened that the Germans ceased firing about the same time. A strange, unnatural silence descended on Monte Cassino and the valley: a silence as pregnant in this situation as the effect when ship's engines stop. But, because of the circumstances, it was uncanny and oppressive. Only once since Christmas had the guns of Cassino been silent for more than a few minutes. That was on Easter Morning when a spontaneous firing truce was observed by both sides. The British units then in the line had been told not to fire any weapon before noon unless the enemy did so. The enemy had not fired, and the morning had passed in silence. But this was different.

Though of course it could not be known at the time, the Germans had a good reason for silencing their guns. They intended to carry out extensive reliefs that night. They wanted a quiet night and had called off their guns so as not to provoke the hostility of the Allied artillery.

But to the Allied troops, now fretfully ticking off the minutes to H-hour, the silence was unreal, oppressive, even sinister. It added considerably to the suspense. And after an hour or two, the army commander, afraid it might begin to make the Germans wonder what was happening, ordered the gunners to fire a few bursts of harassing fire at intervals during the rest of the evening just to restore an atmosphere of normality. In the front line silence is something sinister and barely tolerable.

The sun set at a quarter past eight, and soon after this, commanders, staring upwards, were relieved to see a bright starry sky and to know that they would not be deprived of the services of the late moon when it rose half an hour before midnight. They would need that moon.

At eleven o'clock 1,600 guns tore the night into shreds, and began a forty-minute bombardment of every known German headquarters, battery, and defensive position. Behind, as far as the front-line eye could see, was a flickering horizon of dancing hills: ahead, as the valleys and ravines echoed and re-echoed the crash of the shells, there developed a single continuous reverberation of thunder, counter-pointed only by the high chromatic soughing of the shells as they streamed over in hundreds.

Fifty miles behind the line, where a reserve division lay in readiness to move up to the battle, an officer was finding it difficult to sleep because of the numerous nightingales. That night, through the song of the nightingales, he sensed, rather than heard, another sound: a sound that was little more than a faint vibrant shimmering of the atmosphere. He looked at his watch. It was eleven o'clock. It had started.

4

AS the first salvoes crashed overhead at eleven, the two American divisions (the 85th and 88th) on the left of Fifth Army moved straight into the attack on the nameless ridge to the front of them; a piece of anonymous high ground that had never been important before and would never be again; but ground which for two days and nights would provide these Americans with a private universe to remember all their lives.

Forty minutes later, the skilled mountain fighters of two French divisions (2nd Moroccan and 4th Mountain) on the right of the Americans drove into the heart of the Aurunci mountains towards an objective 3000 feet high.

Five minutes after that, the first of the assault boats of the 8th Indian and 4th British divisions of Eighth Army, operating on the right of the French, splashed into the fast-flowing current of the Rapido river and also into a tempest of German machine-gun fire.

Exactly an hour and a quarter later, at one o'clock, both divisions of the Polish Corps swept across the slopes and ridges against the defences of Monte Cassino.

Two hours after the Allied guns had opened fire the two armies were locked in a clinch more than twenty miles wide. An offensive had been arranged and now it had to take its course. There was nothing the army commanders could do now except wait and hear what happened. Once it had started, it was no longer prongs and thrusts, pincers and penetrations, movements of divisions and corps. It was men. The compact design on paper was now a sprawling pattern of separate human ordeals. There is no difference between the great offensive and the small battle except of degree. All battles are small groups of men fighting other small groups until one or the other can fight no more. The large offensive simply means there are more of these groups operating over a greater extent of ground. A small group takes a small objective and reports that it has done so to its company headquarters. The company tells Battalion, Battalion tells Brigade, Brigade tells Division, Division tells Corps, Corps tells Army. And when a number of these reports have filtered through and begin to bear a relationship to each other, then the Army commander can report that the offensive is making good progress or proceeding according to plan. Then he can say that the Fifth Army or the Eighth Army has made important local gains or improved its position or effected preliminary penetrations, or whatever term appeals to him. But when he says that the Fifth Army is pushing ahead or that the Eighth Army has driven a salient into the enemy positions he is really saying that fragmentary messages have filtered back indicating that a number of small groups of men have outlasted a number of other small groups of men on a hillside or among some farm buildings.

It takes time for these actions to resolve themselves and more time for reliable news of their results to be collected and passed back and so it is some time before a coherent picture can be built up, and results can be condensed into convenient little arrows on the maps that accompany the newspaper reports.

This was the position at two o'clock in the morning when the Polish Corps delivered the last of the four main attacks that together made up the offensive. At the higher headquarters there was nothing to do but wait for reports of the night's doings to begin to come through. Everything possible had been arranged in advance. The concept was huge, the preparation had overlooked nothing. But now it was neither a theory nor a plan. It was men. And it would be several hours before it could be known how those men were faring in a hundred and one little fights. Not until the black night gave up its secrets could the sum of its many smallnesses become a totality with meaning.

Before going into what actually happened, it may be worth

recapitulating the pattern of intention behind that evening's work.

The key to the whole operation was the pinching out of Cassino by the British and Poles of the Eighth Army. Success on the Fifth Army front would be helpful but it could not be conclusive. It would be fine if the Americans scored a swift success against the German right wing. It would be excellent if the French achieved surprise (as they were intended to do) by advancing across trackless mountains which the enemy would consider impracticable for a large-scale attack. Success at any one point of this co-ordinated attack would be helpful to those elsewhere along the front. But the vital news for which the High Command would be waiting the next morning would be that one or both of the Eighth Army thrusts to pinch out Cassino had made a decisive start. For it was along the Rapido and in the mountains behind Cassino that the greatest strength of the Germans was still concentrated. It was desirable that the Poles should break through the mountain strong-points near Monte Cassino that night. But it was absolutely essential that the British divisions should be firmly across the Rapido by daylight. For failure there would give the Germans a whole day in which to recover from the first shock of surprise and the following night the river crossing would be more difficult than ever. It was therefore on the performance of the Eighth Army that this opening phase of the offensive depended.

In the event both armies had to report one failure and one success. In the Fifth Army attack the Americans made no progress that first night and by daylight they had taken none of their objectives. They had little more success when they renewed their attacks throughout the day. On their right the French were more successful. Both divisions made a rapid initial advance, and both had captured their preliminary objectives four hours after the start of the battle. That completed their progress for the night but they had advanced sufficiently for General Juin to feel confident enough to send his motorized division into action soon after dawn to fan out to the right in the direction of the Eighth Army, rolling up German positions between the two armies.

In the Eighth Army sector the 4th (British) Division on the right and the 8th Indian on the left had both crossed the Rapido by soon after midnight, but they were strongly opposed. It was touch and go whether the Indian Division (which had made better progress) could win the battle with the short night and get the all-important bridges over by daylight. It was touch and go whether the British division could keep itself across the river at all, as it was pinned down in a very small bridgehead and was from the first heavily counter-attacked.

Among the measures taken by the Germans during the night to hamper the crossings was to blind the river banks with smoke on a very large and concentrated scale. This had the effect of nullifying the moonlight and adding considerably to the confusion and difficulty which in any case attends a river-crossing operation. At times the smoke was so thick that a man could not see a yard in front of him, and columns had to edge their way down to the boats with each man holding on to the bayonet scabbard of the man in front. Into the midst of this choking, blinding smoke there rained a constant stream of machine-gun and mortar fire. But when dawn came the pall of smoke, now thickened by a river mist, proved an advantage, for it prolonged the night long enough for the Indian Division to complete its bridging. By eight o'clock the first bridge was completed and within a matter of minutes a squadron of tanks was across to fortify the bridgehead. Shortly after this an ingenious and unorthodox piece of work by Canadian tank men and engineers made a second bridge available.

To the astonishment of the waiting infantry, a tank moved slowly towards the river carrying on its hull a completed Bailey bridge. It was followed by a second tank with its front coupled to the end of the bridge to keep it level. The first tank dipped slowly into the river, drove towards the middle and sank with dignity—the crew abandoning ship. The second tank then gently pushed the bridge across to the far bank where it was quickly secured.

The 4th Division had no bridge to show for their night's work, but they held to their tenuous bridgehead and succeeded in ferrying across enough ammunition and necessary stores to ensure that they could consolidate their small gains. As an indication of what they were up against, one brigade of this division had thirty-five out of their forty boats knocked out by eight that morning, and by afternoon they had lost the other five. They would be on their own until darkness made it possible for the sappers to resume bridging.

While the battle for the river was at its height, the Poles made their drive against the mountain strongholds clustered about Monte Cassino. As we have seen, this mountain salient, which the Americans had captured in January and from which the 4th Indian Division had unsuccessfully attacked Monte Cassino a month later, was based on the two long parallel mountain features Maiola and Castellone. Facing the forward extremities of both heights was a chain of German defences designed to prevent a break through the mountains to Route Six down below. Facing the end of Maiola were Monte Cassino itself, Points 593 and 569: protecting the end of Castellone were Phantom Ridge and Colle S. Angelo. Guarding the exit from the gorge between Maiola and Castellone was the fortified Albaneta Farm which was also on the main German approach track to the Monastery.

The Indians had tackled Monte Cassino by the shortest route, i.e. from Snakeshead at the forward end of Maiola, intending to take Point 593 first and then wheel leftwards along the ridge to the Monastery. What had defeated them had been, not only the strength of Point 593, but the fire support it could receive from the Monastery and from all the other hill positions. Being only one division strong, the Indians could do nothing about the German positions opposite Castellone–Phantom Ridge, Colle S. Angelo, Albaneta Farm. It was crossfire from these places that had always made 593 impossible to hold when they had got on to it in their various attacks.

The Polish Corps Commander, General Anders, planned to overcome this difficulty by attacking all these German positions simultaneously so that they would be too engrossed with their own troubles to be able to support each other. With one division he would attack Point 593 from Snakeshead, as the Indians had done. But at the same time he would send another division from the lower slopes of Castellone to attack Phantom Ridge and Colle S. Angelo. He made a further change from the Indian plan. Instead of turning from Point 593 to Monte Cassino, the division on the left would carry straight on down the slope and capture Albaneta Farm.

The effect of this plan, if it worked, would be that the entire chain of defences would be saturated by a two-divisional blow and Monte Cassino itself would be cut off, and could be mopped up later.

The Polish Corps had certain advantages denied to those who had preceded them. The problem of supply in the mountains—which the Indian Division had had to improvise from scratch—had by this time been developed to a fine art. The Poles would have the benefit of summer weather. For many weeks tracks and paths had been improved out of all recognition. There had been time to build up huge dumps of ammunition and other stores near the forward positions. Finally, whereas in February the Indian Division had fought the Monastery with only the support of a New Zealand battalion attack on the railway station, the Poles would be taking part in a concerted attack along the whole front.

Nevertheless, there was no doubt at all that the task of the Polish Corps was the least enviable of the lot. The basic difficulties still remained the same: the appalling nature of the ground itself, the natural strength of the German positions plus the extent to which they had additionally been fortified, and the exposed jump-off positions which reduced preliminary reconnaissance to almost nil. The Poles could not even patrol in advance as the loss of a single man would have revealed the fact that the Polish Corps was in this sector—and it had been an important part of the main deception plan that their presence should be concealed.

At the high climax of that night of May 11th the two Polish

divisions (each deploying a brigade) began to pick their way through the boulders and thickets, across the gullies, and above the ravines which unpredictably cut across these mountains: through the thorn and gorse: through the extensive and gruesome debris of the previous battles: through the corpses that still littered the entire area: and soon the ubiquitous machine-guns, that had been there so long they seemed almost to have grown into the rock, began to mow them down as they had mown down the Americans, the Indians, and the British. But the Poles pushed on and for the rest of that night they fought hand to hand as successive waves of them flung themselves at Point 593 and Phantom Ridge. Both divisions had reached their preliminary objectives, and both spent the night fighting to keep them, but men were falling all the time and communications with their rear headquarters broke down. They were on their own. When daylight came a handful of survivors of the Carpathian Division had a foothold on 593, small groups of the Kresowa Division clung hazardously to Phantom Ridge half a mile to the right. But no attacker could survive long on these exposed slopes by day. As the sun came up, the Germans began to pick them off. They could not be reinforced, nor could they be supplied. They were on their own and they continued to fight as best they could from whatever precarious cover they could find until a merciful order to withdraw reached them in the early afternoon. In a few hours half of both divisions had been crippled. No ground had been gained. But the Germans had been badly mauled. By their sacrifice in the mountain tops the Poles had eased the burden of the British divisions operating in the valley.

The position on the afternoon of the 12th, therefore, was that the Poles on the extreme right were back on their start-line: the Americans on the extreme left were still battling for their first objectives. But the French were continuing to push ahead, and the confident General Juin was sending in more and more troops to exploit their success. Most important of all, the 8th Indian and 4th British were slowly but surely increasing their bridgeheads across the Rapido and beating off the furious counter-attacks that

were smashing into them all day. The river crossing, the key to
the encirclement of Cassino, had succeeded.

It was clear now that there must be a day or two of attrition.
In plain words this meant that the numerically superior Allied
forces had to keep on attacking day and night, accepting casualties
heavier than those of the Germans, until there just weren't enough
Germans left to hold on any longer. Such a battle of attrition is
the quintessential ordeal of infantry fighting and it is unavoidable
when a well-positioned and determined enemy is willing to defend
to the death the ground he holds. The Germans were willing.

So the fighting continued throughout that first day and all
through the night. During the night more bridges were thrown
across the river and the bridgehead divisions pushed out a little
farther. By the following morning, the 13th, the pressure was
beginning to tell. Outflanked by the surprise advance of the
French, weakened by their battle of attrition on the coast, the
German right wing began to give way to the Americans. The
French, with four divisions now in the line, captured Monte
Maio, the 3,000-foot peak that was the key to their part of the
battlefield. With Maio in their hands, they now controlled the
defile which cuts through the Aurunci mountains to the southern
side of the Liri Valley. The French were now in a position to give
material flank assistance to the slower advance of the Eighth
Army—slower because it was against the Eighth that Kesselring
was now throwing in every reserve unit he could lay hands on,
to delay the demise of Cassino and give himself time to switch
to his second prepared line, the one named after Adolf Hitler.

The Poles, whose heavy losses on the first night had necessitated
extensive reorganization, were told that they would not be called
upon to attack again until the complementary encirclement of
Cassino through the valley had made more decisive progress.
The 8th Indian and 4th British, now heavily supported by tanks,
were ordered to try to achieve this decisive progress. The
reserve divisions of the Eighth Army—the 1st (Infantry) and 5th
(Armoured) Divisions of the Canadian Corps and the 78th
(British) Division, prepared to exploit a break-through or make

one. They moved up in readiness to do so. Throughout the next day, May 14, the 8th Indian and 4th British Divisions kept up the pressure, and the French scored a new success on their left: they captured the key point of Ausonia—in the defile which cuts at right angles into the Liri Valley thus providing a side-door into it. General Juin chose this moment to unleash his *goumiers*.

The *goumiers* are hawk-faced Moroccan troops whose speciality is mountain fighting. They wear the Arab *burnous*, and though they will consent to carry rifles, they prefer their knives. They are not organized in normal military formations but in *goums*, groups of about seventy, officered by Frenchmen. Their especial value is their uncanny gift for moving silently through trackless mountain country. Their method of working is similar to the action of an incoming tide on a series of sand-castles. These waves of *goums* could be unloosed on a shapeless mass of mountain country that orthodox troops would find impassable. They would move up silently on any opposition that presented itself, dispose of it and push on regardless of what was happening to those on their right or left. They had a habit of bringing back evidence of the number of victims they had killed, which made them an unpleasant enemy to face. They provided an additional surprise factor in this battle. For now General Juin proposed to unloose 12,000 of them against the trackless waste of mountains ahead of him on the left of the Eighth Army. While an orthodox advance was set in motion by the American and French divisions on the left, this horde of *goumiers* was sent off through the mountains on a parallel axis to the Eighth Army down below them in the valley. The Germans had assumed that no one would attempt to traverse this mountain route, so the *goumiers* not only advanced rapidly but met practically no opposition. Their swift advance soon outflanked the Germans fighting in the valley and this had a material effect on the Eighth Army's progress down there.

On the 15th the 78th ("Battle-Axe") Division were ordered to cross the river, pass through the bridgehead divisions and execute the turning movement that would dispose of Cassino from the valley. The 78th were perhaps the most sophisticated division in the two armies. They had fought continuously through North Africa, Sicily, and Italy. They had never known defeat. They had developed a tremendous *esprit de corps* and there was, to an exceptional degree, a complete understanding between their staff and the fighting units. This Division, if little known to the general public, was much respected by the rest of the British Army.

It had been hoped that the 78th would be able to bring its experience to bear on the exploiting of a break-through. But resistance was still stiff. There was no break-through yet. The Division had to enter the battle with a set-piece attack on the morning of the 16th. At the same time the 1st Canadian Division were to attack on their left.

The 78th, supported by the 6th Armoured Division, carried out a classic formal attack which swept them through the Liri defences towards Highway Six, and by nightfall it was evident that if they could keep it up on the following day—and at the same time the Poles delivered a new attack through the mountains —the *coup de grâce* would be near. Everything went according to plan. On the 17th, the Poles duly attacked the mountain positions, and the 78th continued their wheeling advance. They had made it all seem easy but in thirty-six hours they had taken 400 prisoners, killed or wounded 400 others, destroyed forty tanks and self-propelled guns, and won their third V.C. of the war. By evening the Polish right had captured S. Angelo Hill and their left was on Point 593 : the 78th were contemplating the seemingly innocuous Highway Six, and fretting because they were forbidden to cross it. The reason for this was that it was the boundary between the Division and the Polish Corps and at that time the positions of the Poles were not exactly known. It was not until the early hours of the 18th that the 78th Division were ordered to send a patrol to make contact with the Poles across Highway Six, two miles west of Cassino. By this time the junction between the two wings of Eighth Army was not a military operation but a formal ceremony. Rising to the occasion, the commanding officer of the battalion concerned nominated three corporals, all holders of the Military Medal, to make the journey and convey the compliments of the 78th to the

Poles. At 10.30 that morning, May 18th, a Polish detachment completed another formal ceremony. It marched across the slope from Point 593 and occupied the Abbey of Monte Cassino from which the last of the garrison had escaped during the night. The Poles had again fought magnificently to seize and hold the mountain strong-points. But in the end the necessity to storm the Monastery never arose. When they marched into it in broad daylight there were only a few wounded men left behind to surrender to them.

All of a sudden it did not matter any more. Cassino was again just a name on the map. The entire might of the Eighth Army was now streaming across the Rapido bridges into the Liri Valley or along the main road, Highway Six, to pour through the town. There was a constant stream of traffic that would last for days. A victorious army was on the move. The ruins of the town, the pock-marked slopes of Monte Cassino, the vast hideous ubiquitous wreckage immediately belonged to the past. Cassino was no more than a passing curiosity for the endless stream of troops that could now move through this town as easily as any other. Highway Six was the main artery of advance again, and the iron corpuscles of war, pounding ceaselessly up the bloodstream of a victory advance, would for days and nights pass through Cassino. The soldiers would gaze at it in wonder for a few moments, and then pass on to new battles. Cassino was no longer important.

But perhaps a few, just a few, of those who passed by, and looked up in awe at the terrifying splendour of the desolated abbey on the mountain top, might pause and think that this had been St. Benedict's battle too.

5

THE fall of Monte Cassino on May 18th might at first sight seem to be the end of the story. But, as was pointed out earlier, a modern battle does not exist in a vacuum. It is part of a continuous process. It is related to what has gone before and to what follows. The first battle of Cassino had begun as a hurried resumption of a tired advance, undertaken in support of the Anzio landing. The last was the opening phase of a summer offensive designed to destroy substantial enemy forces and capture Rome. But as Cassino was where the Germans had chosen to establish their main defence of Rome, the battle of Cassino was also the battle for Rome. For the Allies, this battle would not be over until the objects of the offensive as a whole had been achieved—or abandoned. Only on the banks of the Tiber could Cassino end in victory. This story would therefore be incomplete without some account of the fifteen days which followed the slaying, as it were, of the giant, signified by the hoisting of the Polish flag above the ruins of the Monastery.

Within a very few hours, the advance guards of the Eighth Army were pushing up the Liri Valley to try to rush the Adolf Hitler Line, six miles beyond the Gustav, before the retreating Germans could re-establish themselves in these new prepared defences and convert them into the 'long stop' position they were intended to provide. The gamble nearly came off, but these early attacks did not carry enough weight. The mobile forces which made them soon ran into extensive minefields, chains of pillboxes. and areas heavily fortified to a depth of up to 1,000 yards. It became clear that the Adolf Hitler Line would require the full treatment. In the meantime the main body of the Army was temporarily delayed by reorganization necessary after the heavy fighting of the previous week, and also by traffic congestion. With 2,000 tanks and 20,000 vehicles surging through the broken Gustav, traffic control was for the time being more important than any other military consideration. The congestion was almost awe-inspiring and it was proud evidence of the total mastery of the skies by the Allied Air Forces that mile upon mile of vehicles could move nose to tail in perfect safety. Some of the older hands, who remembered Africa when the sky belonged to the Luftwaffe, could scarcely repress an occasional shudder of apprehension when they surveyed this prodigious mass of transport, choking every road, track, or traversable piece of ground. In open country a deadly pursuit of the enemy could have been launched at once, but in Italy the close country excites the tank man only to frustrate him a mile or two farther on with ground that forces him back on to the few available roads. The most important soldier in the army at this time was the Military Policeman, struggling to keep the flood of transport moving.

In due course General Leese informed General Alexander that the Eighth Army would be ready to make a set-piece attack on the Adolf Hitler Line on the 23rd, twelve days after the opening of the offensive. General Alexander decided that that would be the time for the Anzio force of Fifth Army to launch their attack out of the beachhead. So the offensive approached its high climax. On the morning of May 23rd the Eighth would smash at the Adolf Hitler Line, and American divisions of the Fifth Army beachhead force would break through the perimeter that had imprisoned them since the landing at Anzio in January.

The timing turned out to be excellent. Kesselring, deceived by the original Allied design and now desperately trying to make up for lost time, was sending his armoured reserves south to the Tenth Army one after the other to try to delay the Eighth Army. This left his Fourteenth Army, facing the Anzio beachhead, without a single armoured division. There was only a handful of

Tiger and Panther tanks there to support the five weakened infantry divisions which General Truscott would be attacking on May 23rd. As a final blow, his last reserve, the 26th Panzer Division, which had been uselessly tied up north of Rome waiting for the fictitious landing at Civitavecchia, left for the south on the 22nd. On the 23rd, therefore, the crucial day when it was most badly needed, it was in transit between the two fronts and of no use to either: thus completing the success of the original Allied deception plan.

On the eve of the new attack there was an unexpected and eloquent indication of how the German High Command were feeling about their prospects. The Adolf Hitler Line underwent a sudden and discreet change of name. They began to call it the Dora Line.

The morning of May 23rd was the beginning of the end. At dawn the 1st Canadian Division made the main attack on the Dora (neé Adolf Hitler) Line while the Poles attacked Piedimonte on the right. One hour later General Truscott launched his attack from the beachhead with the 3rd U.S. Infantry and 1st U.S. Armoured Divisions, and a Special Service Force. By the 24th the Canadians had breached the former Hitler Line, and the 5th Canadian Armoured Division were pouring through the gap. On the following day, the 25th, the Poles completed the destruction of the Hitler Line by taking Piedimonte. In a fortnight these two under-strength Polish divisions and their Armoured Brigade had lost 281 officers and 3,503 other ranks—of whom one-third were killed, and only 102 missing. These terrible figures speak for themselves. The gallantry of the Poles was beyond praise and there is a particular poignancy in the inscription on the Memorial in their war cemetery which now stands on the slopes of the hill known as Point 593.

> We Polish soldiers
> For our freedom and yours
> Have given our souls to God
> Our bodies to the soil of Italy
> And our hearts to Poland.

By their selfless immolation the Poles converted that grim mountainside into a memorial to soldiers everywhere.

On that same day, the 25th, Truscott's men captured Cisterna, their first objective, and made contact with the rest of Fifth Army advancing up the coast on the main front. For the first time since Christmas Fifth Army was one again.

For General Alexander it was a great day. A fortnight after the opening of the offensive everything was working out exactly as he had planned. The Eighth Army, supported by the Fifth, had smashed through the Gustav and Adolf Hitler lines and turned the German Tenth Army into full retreat. The beachhead force of Fifth Army had stormed out of its containment and was driving across to cut off the Germans retreating from the main front. Every major Allied move had achieved complete surprise. Kesselring had been out-generalled at each important stage of the battle. All of his reserves had been committed, but too late and piecemeal: piecemeal they had been mauled or destroyed. The Tenth Army was in very bad shape, and the Fourteenth was in the process of being reduced to the same condition by Truscott's advancing American divisions. The kill was at hand. The fall of Rome was merely a matter of time. The only question now was how many of the remnants fleeing from the main front could be cut off by Truscott before they could escape to the north. It seemed likely to be very few, for the main battle had drawn in every available German formation and the break-out from the beachhead had been perfectly timed and was making rapid progress.

By May 25th Truscott's spearheads were within striking distance of Valmontone. On the following day they would be astride the main German line of withdrawal. It was only twenty-four hours since the Adolf Hitler Line, fifty miles to the east, had been breached. The road back to Valmontone was choked with the large retreating forces that had been sucked into the battle of attrition by the Eighth Army and put to flight. The trap was closing. . . .

But now came an astonishing change of plan. On this crucial day, May 25th, General Clark ordered General Truscott to change the direction of his main thrust from Valmontone to the north-west and head straight for Rome. Truscott has described how he felt about this new development:

> Late that afternoon I returned to the command post feeling rather jubilant—but not for long. Don Brann, the Army G–3, was waiting for me. Brann said: 'The boss wants you to leave the 3rd Infantry Division and the Special Force to block Highway Six and mount that assault you discussed with him to the north-west as soon as you can.' I was dumbfounded. . . . This was no time to drive to the north-west where the enemy was still strong; we should pour our maximum power into the Valmontone Gap to insure the destruction of the retreating German Army. I would not comply with the order without first talking to General Clark in person. Brann informed me that he was not in the beachhead and could not be reached even by radio . . . such was the order that turned the main effort of the beachhead forces from the Valmontone Gap and prevented the destruction of the German Tenth Army. On the 26th the order was put into effect.

At the climax of a battle of this size operations inevitably become fluid and confused. An army commander is justified in adapting existing plans to meet the changing situation. Even so, it is difficult to understand why Clark ordered this change of direction when the original plan was going so well and was so near to fulfilment.

Possibly he had good reasons, but part of the explanation does seem to lie in a curious obsession he had about being first into Rome. A meeting between the two generals three weeks before prompted Truscott to note in his memoirs that Clark 'was fearful that the British were laying devious plans to be the first into Rome'. While Clark himself has written:

> On the other hand, as I have pointed out, I was determined that the Fifth Army was going to capture Rome, and I was probably over-sensitive to indications that practically everybody else was trying to get into the act.

The curious part of all this is that there was never any question of anybody other than Fifth Army capturing Rome. The inter-

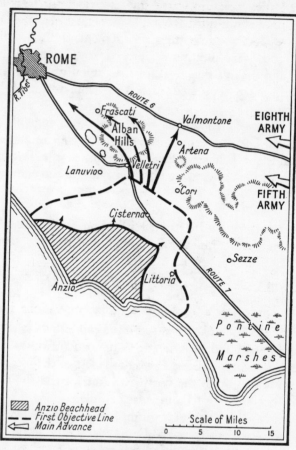

ANZIO BREAKOUT

Showing switch of main beachhead force from Valmontone cut-off line to Rome

army boundary had been clearly laid down by General Alexander before the battle began. Rome was allocated to the Fifth Army sector from the beginning. Furthermore, it was constantly impressed on the Eighth Army men as the battle progressed that they had no immediate concern with Rome: their job was to draw the Tenth Army into battle and destroy as much of it as possible. When the time came they would by-pass Rome and continue the pursuit northwards.

This was war, not a sporting engagement, and the notion that British forces were plotting secretly to trespass on Fifth Army territory and make a race of it for the capital was a figment that could only have suggested itself to a romantic and harassed imagination.

The decision of General Clark to make this change of direction must remain one of the mysteries of the Italian campaign. There are grounds for believing that it diminished the extent of the defeat which the Allies were able to inflict on the enemy at that time.

The break through the Adolf Hitler Line and the break out of Anzio were the beginning of the end, and the last days of the battle are of no particular interest. The covering of the last twenty miles to Rome was simply a matter of overcoming the rearguards behind which the Germans were striving to organize a withdrawal of their two beaten armies.

By June 2nd the final advance on the capital was launched. By the morning of Sunday, June 4th, American armoured cars were in the city outskirts. During the day the last of the German rearguards passed through the northern limits of the city. By midnight the occupation of Rome was complete.

In twenty-four days of fighting, impregnable Cassino had fallen, two German armies had been thoroughly defeated, 20,000 prisoners had been taken, three defence lines had been smashed, vast quantities of tanks and guns had been destroyed, and the two Allied armies had advanced eighty miles. It was not quite the victory it might have been, for the plain truth is that a substantial remnant of the Tenth Army did manage to extricate itself from the Allied trap. But by any standards it was still a considerable one.

On the following morning, June 5th, while the Fifth Army

mopped up and the Eighth, by-passing the city, continued its pursuit of the Germans—a pursuit that was to last all summer and drive them another hundred miles to the north—General Clark celebrated the Roman triumph that meant so much to him by holding a press conference on the Capitoline Hill. The morning after that, June 6th, the Allies landed in Normandy and Italy was no longer front page news.

It can be left to the official historians to decide to what extent the Allied failure to annihilate the beaten Tenth Army was due to General Clark's change of direction when the beachhead force was preparing to close the Valmontone trap: to what extent it reflects the skill and stubbornness of Kesselring's men in extricating themselves from a desperate predicament. One authority, at any rate, has little doubt about this. It is, of course, possible that all the facts of the situation have not yet been brought to light, but in his recorded afterthoughts on the campaign, Mark Clark's compatriot and close associate General Truscott has written:

There has never been any doubt in my mind that had General Clark held loyally to General Alexander's instructions, had he not changed the direction of my attack to the north-west on May 26th, the strategic objective of Anzio would have been accomplished in full. To be first in Rome was poor compensation for this lost opportunity.

So ended the series of battles which had come into being at Cassino nearly five months before. It had opened in the cold, wet fury of the Abruzzi winter: it had ended in the scorching noon of the Roman summer. It had passed through many changes of fortune and cost many nations many lives. It had inspired both sides to a high order of courage and endurance that often seemed sacrificially useless. But when, two days after the fall of Rome, a new army crossed the English Channel to invade France, it owed more than it knew to General Sir Harold Alexander and his Allied Armies in Italy who, by their combined and unrewarding efforts, had helped to prepare the way.

And now the Fifth and Eighth Armies, flushed with success and sweeping forward on an irresistible flood tide of victory, were poised to finish the job—to complete the rout of the enemy and compel abandonment of the Italian front altogether, or at least heavy reinforcement from a central reserve that could no longer spare it.

But this was not to be. A crowning act of strategic folly was at hand. As a final irony, the Allied Armies in Italy were to be deprived of total victory at precisely the moment when it seemed at last to be within their grasp.

Alexander had 28 divisions chasing 21 German, of which more than a third had been reduced to impotence. The chase was in full cry and there was no reason why the broken armies of Kesselring should not be driven back to the Alps. With the Normandy landing now well established it was the perfect moment for a knock-out blow in Italy that could have taken the Allies to the frontiers of central Europe, the end to which Winston Churchill's far-sighted strategy had been aimed from the very beginning of the Mediterranean campaigns. But at Teheran the previous year it had been decided that an invasion of Southern France should follow the Normandy landing. Generals Eisenhower and Marshall now insisted that this decision be rigidly adhered to. The invasion of Southern France must be put in hand at once. Alexander must provide the force.

The Allied commanders in Italy might from time to time have had their clashes of temperament and their differences of opinion in matters of tactical detail. But now, as never before, there was passionate unanimity. With one voice the American and British commanders protested against the folly of weakening their armies at the very moment when total victory was at last within their reach. Desperately Alexander pleaded for the retention of the forces that he had brought to the brink of a final triumph that would make up for all the disappointment and sacrifice that had gone before:

> I cannot over-emphasize my conviction that if my tried and ex-
> perienced commanders and troops are taken away for operations

elsewhere we shall certainly miss a golden opportunity of scoring a really decisive victory and we shall never be able to reap the full benefits of the efforts and gains we have made during the past few weeks. I feel strongly that it is of the greatest importance not to let go the chance that has been so hardly won.

Alexander was supported up to the hilt by Churchill in this urgent plea to be allowed to retain his full strength to finish the task so auspiciously begun. But the American Chiefs of Staff were adamant. The invasion of Southern France must go through. And so at the height of its victorious pursuit, the Fifth Army had to withdraw seven of its best divisions—three American, four French —for the new operation.

At first the Germans were incredulous, suspecting some new and subtle deception. Then, grateful for this unexpected stroke of luck, they put new heart into the delaying tactics at which they had become so expert. By the summer's end they had established themselves on yet another mountain barrier, the Gothic Line, south of the Po. For the Allies it seemed a poor reward for the long winter heartbreak of Cassino and the great offensive with which Alexander had brought it to an end.

The pattern of the Italian campaign was now complete. It had started, owing to the disinterest of Washington, as a secondary campaign. This had led, with the inevitability of Greek tragedy, to the climactic deadlock of Cassino. Anzio, designed to break that deadlock, had aggravated it. In spite of everything, Alexander's spring offensive had brought the campaign to the verge of total victory. Washington chose this moment to draw the teeth of the pursuit. Italy was once more a secondary campaign.

Cassino, so costly in human life and suffering, and thus deprived at the last of the full victory that would have made it worth while, was in the end little more than a victory of the human spirit: an elegy for the common soldier: a memorial to the definitive horror of war and the curiously perverse paradoxical nobility of battle.

BIBLIOGRAPHY

In addition to many personal, regimental, and formation records, official and unofficial, I have consulted the following main sources:

Official Despatch by Field-Marshal The Viscount Alexander of Tunis, K.G., G.C.B., G.C.M.G., C.S.I., D.S.O., M.C., in his capacity as former C-in-C 15th Army Group later known as Allied Armies in Italy.

The Second World War, Vol. V: 'Closing The Ring', Winston S. Churchill (*Cassell*).

History of the Second World War, Vol. V: 'Grand Strategy', John Ehrman (*H.M.S.O*).

History of the Army Air Forces in World War II (*University of Chicago Press*).

The Struggle For Europe, Chester Wilmot (*Collins*).

A History of the Fifth Army, Lt.-Col. Chester G. Starr (*Infantry Journal Press, U.S.A.*).

The Campaign In Italy, Eric Linklater (*H.M.S.O.*).

Italy In the Second World War, Marshal Badoglio (*Oxford*).

Calculated Risk, General Mark Clark (*Harrap*).

Command Missions, Lt.-Gen. L. K. Truscott, Jnr. (*Dutton*).

Infantry Brigadier, Maj.-Gen. Sir Howard Kippenberger, K.B.E., C.B., D.S.O. (*Oxford*).

The Road To Trieste, Geoffrey Cox (*Heinemann*).

Inside Rome With The Germans, Jane Scrivener (*Macmillan*).

Monte Cassino: La Vita L'Irradiazione, Tommaso Leccisotti (*Vallecchi*).

L'Epopée Française D'Italie, René Chambre (*Flammarion*).

An Army In Exile, Lt.-Gen. W. Anders, C.B. (*Macmillan*).

Road to Rome, Christopher Buckley (*Hodder & Stoughton*).

The History of 78 Division, Cyril Ray (*Eyre & Spottiswoode*).

Fourth Indian Division, Lt.-Col. G. R. Stevens (*McLaren & Son*).

Monte Cassino, General Frydd von Senger und Etterlin (*New English Review*).

The Defence of Britain, Liddell Hart (*Faber & Faber*).
Official History of New Zealand in the Second World War.

Documents Vol. II. ⎫
History of the 19th Battalion ⎪
    ,,   ,,   21st   ,,   ⎬ War History Branch of the
    ,,   ,,   24th   ,,   New Zealand Government
    ,,   ,,   26th   ,,   ⎪
The Campaign In Italy, N. C. Phillips ⎭

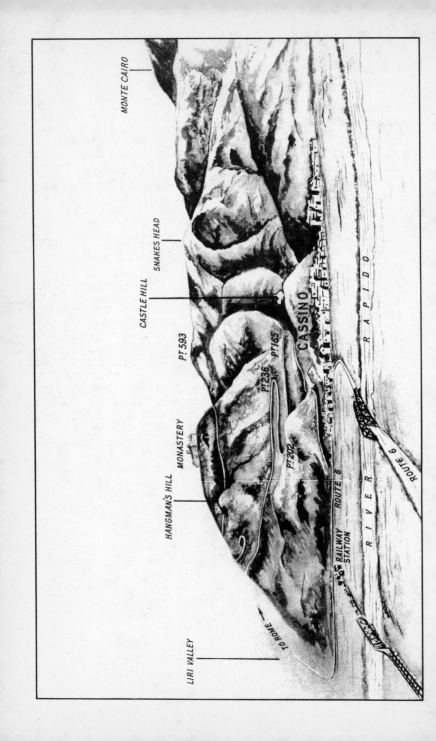

INDEX